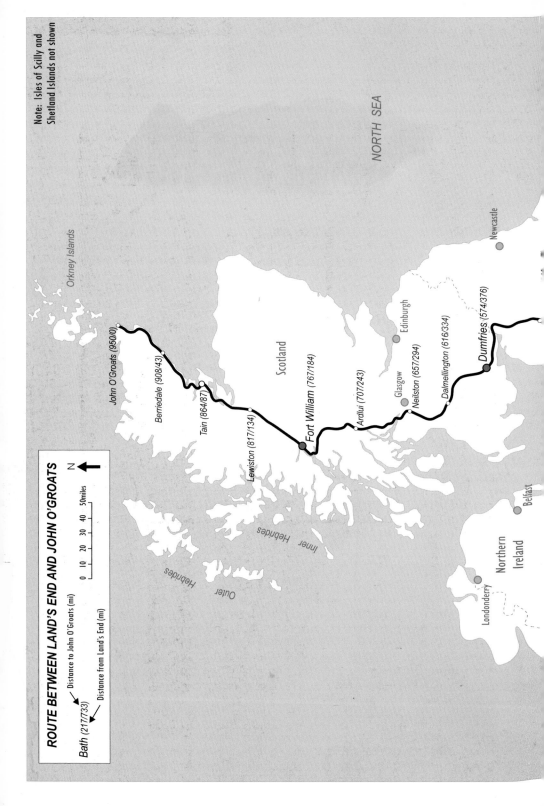

ROUTE BETWEEN LAND'S END AND JOHN O'GROATS

N

0 10 20 30 40 50miles

Bath (217/733)

← Distance to John O'Groats (mi)

← Distance from Land's End (mi)

Note: Isles of Scilly and
Shetland Islands not shown

NORTH SEA

Scotland

Orkney Islands

Outer Hebrides

Inner Hebrides

John O'Groats (950/0)

Berriedale (908/43)

Tain (864/87)

Lewiston (817/134)

Fort William (767/184)

Ardlui (707/243)

Neilston (657/294)

Glasgow

Edinburgh

Dalmellington (616/334)

Dumfries (574/376)

Newcastle

Belfast

Northern
Ireland

Londonderry

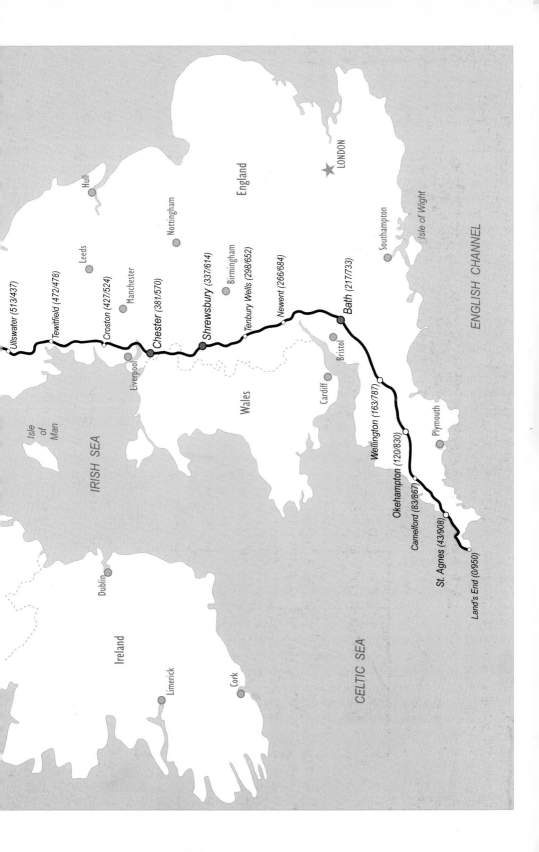

For Athol & Julie

BIKE BRITAIN

CYCLING FROM LAND'S END TO JOHN O'GROATS

Paul Salter

AN
EPIC
GUIDE

Epic Guides
PO Box 31053
Milford
New Zealand

www.epicguides.co.nz

1st Edition Published 2002
Copyright © Epic New Zealand Ltd, 2002
ISBN 0-9582256-1-3

Disclaimer and Safety Note:
The author and publisher accept no responsibility for the safety or enjoyment of any person using this book or for any errors or omissions. No guide can identify the limitations of every reader, or all the potential hazards on a journey; check conditions before setting out and use common sense on your trip.

INTRODUCTION

Britain is the perfect place to explore by bike - a compact island with a vast network of quiet roads linking charming villages and historic sites. These features make it a great destination for cyclists looking to do their first extended tour, and for experienced tourists there are countless interesting options.

This guide focuses on the classic British long distance tour of Land's End to John O' Groats. Since the end of the 19th century this trip has been the tour of choice for those wanting to cycle mainland Britain from one end of the road to the other. There are plenty of ways to go "End to End", from speedy dashes following main roads, to more sinuous routes sticking to minor roads and scenic areas. The tour described in this guide is a relatively direct route that follows quieter minor and "B" roads where possible - taking in Cornwall's dramatic coastline, the historic cities of Bath and Chester, Lake District National Park, and the rugged lochs of the Great Glen, among other things. The quickest routes from Land's End to John O' Groats are about 840 miles and have been ridden in less than two days! This route is about 950 miles and can easily be done in around three weeks (an average of 45 miles a day) - taking more or less time as suits.

The guide is designed to provide cyclists with detailed directions for navigating the route, information on conditions and facilities along the way, as well as some of the history on places the tour passes. A unique feature are the photographs taken every 25 miles along the route; these snap-shots give an idea of countryside and road conditions the tour covers.

The book is split into two parts; "Preparations" and "The Journey". The initial sections of Part I are mainly for cyclists coming from overseas, with details on getting to Britain with a bike and familiarising oneself with British culture. Later sections deal with when to tour, what to take, and what to expect cycle touring in Britain. Background information for beginner bicycle tourers is included, as well as details on getting to Land's End and getting back from John O' Groats.

Part II describes the journey from Land's End to John O' Groats. The tour is split into 21 manageable stages ranging in length from 32 to 61 miles. Each stage is laid out over 4 pages, as described on pages 34 and 35. Details on possible intermediate stops are listed so these stages can be lengthened or shortened depending on individual fitness and riding conditions. The option of camping or sleeping in a bed under a roof is available on most stages and the guide has listings for a selection of campground, hostel, bed and breakfast, and hotel accommodation. Details on information centres and bike shops are also included.

A strip map and elevation profile is included for each stage, along with a table listing turn by turn directions for the route. The accompanying text has a description of the stage including notes on the general cycling terrain, however individual hills are typically not listed. Even at this level of detail, British back roads can become a tangled spider web in places, so be prepared for a few unintended detours - all part of exploring by bike.

If Land's End to John O' Groats is not quite far enough, appendices have additional information on the Isles of Scilly to the south, and the Orkney and Shetland Islands to the north.

Biking Britain End to End - one day at a time and at your own pace - is within the reach of most reasonably fit cyclists, and is a cycling experience you'll never forget.

Good luck and enjoy cycling Britain.

TABLE OF CONTENTS

PART II – THE JOURNEY

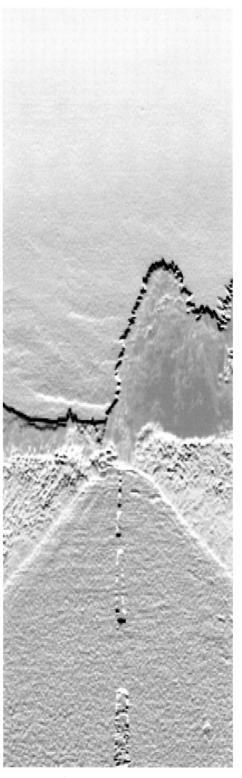

PART I
PREPARATIONS

Airlines and Bringing a Bike

Britain is the entry-point for most tourists visiting Europe and all the major airlines fly to London. Choosing the airline you fly will depend on your departure point, any desired stopovers, and price. Britain is a competitive route for airlines, so shop around for a good fare and always search the fine print for additional charges. A British departure tax of £20 (economy) or £40 (business class) is automatically included in your ticket price. Many airlines fly non-stop to Britain, which can be a good way to avoid the hassle of collecting and re-checking your bike gear for connecting flights.

Bicycles can be brought on your flight as personal luggage, although your total baggage must still be within the airlines weight allowance. Check the costs for bringing your bicycle - some airlines charge nothing, others charge £50 or more (each way). Most carriers require a bicycle to be bagged or boxed, with the tyres deflated. Some airlines will allow your bike to be loaded unboxed with the pedals removed or turned inwards, the handlebars turned sideways, and the chain covered. Cardboard bike boxes can usually be obtained free of charge from bicycle shops, which normally throw them away after new bikes have been delivered. Pack your touring gear in plastic bags around your bike to protect it in the box.

Europeans also have the option of getting to Britain by boat, train, or car ferry.

Entry Requirements

Normally, to enter Britain you need a passport and a visa. Although if you are a citizen of the European Union (EU) you may not need either, or if you are a citizen of one of the countries that is visa-waived - USA, Canada, Australia, and New Zealand for example - you may only need a passport (check with a travel agent or British Consulate before leaving home).

Passports are issued in your home country and can take a while to process, so don't plan on getting one a few days before your flight. Keep your passport with you at all times, it's your most important travel document and losing it could mean an extended stay in Britain until your Embassy, Consulate or High Commission can re-issue a new one. It pays to carry a separate photocopy of your passport, and leave another copy at home. The passport should be valid for the length of your stay in Britain and at least two months beyond.

A visa gives you permission to enter the country for a certain period. Depending on your citizenship, obtaining a visa can be a formality or an involved process whereby an application must be submitted, along with your passport, to a British diplomatic office in your home country.

A typical tourist visa will let you stay in Britain for six months. You can apply for a longer stay, either before you leave home, or in Britain before your current visa expires. Obviously, working is not permitted on a tourist visa.

Immigration officials are screening incoming visitors very carefully these days. You may be asked to provide proof you have sufficient funds for your stay and onward travel plans. A credit card, traveller's cheques, and a return ticket can help here.

Entry regulations change from time to time so double check the visa requirements before leaving home.

Customs

Her Majesty's Customs and Excise are being particularly vigilant following the recent Foot and Mouth Disease outbreak, so ensure your shoes, camping equipment, and bicycle tyres are free of dirt. Like other western countries, Britain has strict regulations on the importation of firearms, weapons, explosive or flammable goods, narcotics, live animals, products made from endangered species, organic goods and food items. Keep in mind your home country's duty regulations when returning with purchases made in Britain. Before travelling you can have Customs at your departure point stamp a list of high priced items you are taking with you, if you think your purchases in Britain will put the total value of your goods over your home country's duty limit when returning.

Health
No special health precautions are needed before going to Britain. However, people who have recently visited countries where yellow fever is known, may need an international certificate of vaccination to enter the country.

The quality of tap water in Britain is good, although river, stream and certain campground water supplies may be affected by giardia and should be treated before use.

Britain's weather is best described as variable. In hot conditions be aware of the possibility of heat exhaustion, and in the cold - hypothermia. Also see the Hazards section on p.31.

Insurance
Travel insurance is worth having when travelling overseas. Comprehensive policies cover medical expenses, airline cancellations, and loss of luggage. Some credit card companies offer free insurance if you use their card to book travel - check with yours. Almost all policies exclude pre-existing medical conditions, and many have exclusions for activities classified as "dangerous" like skiing and motorcycling, so check the policy covers bicycle touring. Citizens of EU countries, and some Commonwealth countries, can complete a form available at post offices, and apply for partial coverage under Britain's National Health Service (NHS).

Discounts
Britain has a peak-season (centred around July and August) when some accommodation and travel costs are more expensive. The off-season (from about October through to April) is cheaper but some attractions may be closed.

Discounts on local travel and entrance fees are often available for students, families, and seniors (over 60). A student ID or ISIC card will often be requested to get a student discount. Some places offer a youth discount instead, for under 26-year olds.

An Automobile Association card from you home country may get you discounts on car rentals and accommodation. Rail passes and rail/drive passes for tourists from outside Europe (see Train, p.18) offer good discounts over regular fares, although these must be purchased prior to coming to Britain. Bargaining over items with a price tag is typically not done in Britain.

Arriving in London
Most international flights to Britain land at Heathrow or Gatwick airports. Heathrow, the world's busiest airport, is about 15 miles west of central London. Gatwick is about 25 miles south of central London. There are rail and bus connections to central London from both airports. Taxi fares are upwards of £40 (Britain's old-style taxis are generally big enough to fit a couple of boxed bikes and passengers - at a push). From Heathrow, the Heathrow Express train (£11) runs to Paddington Station every 15 minutes (trains for Penzance, near Land's End, leave from Paddington). These trains

are level with the platform and have enough luggage space to accommodate a boxed bike, although it can be a squeeze during peak periods.

With a rental car you can load up and drive directly into London, or on towards Land's End (see p.19 for rental cars). Land's End is about 320 miles from London.

To cycle fully loaded from the airport into London would be daunting, but possible. Get a detailed map, avoid main roads, and be prepared for a lot of traffic. The London Cycle Network (Guildhall 2, Kingston upon Thames, Surrey KT1 1EU, Ph 02085 475907) has details on cycle paths and routes in the city.

For details on getting to Penzance and Land's End from London see p.33.

IN BRITAIN

AN ABBREVIATED HISTORY OF BRITAIN

It is impossible to give a brief history of Britain - so much of the world's history is associated with this small island state. More history is included in Part II of this guide, but here is a brief overview:

Britain, or more correctly Great Britain, refers to the three nations of England, Scotland, and Wales (The "United Kingdom" is Britain plus Northern Ireland, several small islands, and a few overseas possessions).

Many of Britain's history texts start around the time of Christ, when the Romans started showing an interest in this island, then expanded their Empire to include it as the province of Britannia. Before this time is considered "pre-history" even though bands of fishermen and hunters had arrived from Europe thousands of years earlier, building complex monuments that in many cases endured longer than Roman structures. The Celts had arrived by the second millennium BC and had a well-established society by the time Julius Caesar landed with his first exploratory force, in 55BC. Caesar came back briefly the next year, but for the following 97 years the Celts had to live with the knowledge that the Romans were across the Channel and probably coming back en-masse. When they did, central England was quickly conquered, London was founded, and road building commenced to extend their control (more details on the Romans in Britain are on p.84).

The Romans neglected Britain from the early 400's, and by 402 had stopped sending coins to the province. By 409 the Legions had departed and Romanised citizens were left in their villas alongside their Celtic neighbours, at the start of the Dark Ages.

By the mid 400's Saxons were arriving, firstly invited as mercenaries by rival Celtic leaders, then on their own accord as invaders. The Celts held them back with a major victory at Mons Badonicus around 500 (possibly lead by the legendary King Arthur). But by the 600's independent Anglo-Saxon kings had gained control over much of England and were fighting amongst themselves. The smaller kingdoms were slowly merged or defeated, and in 825 Egbert of Wessex effectively became king over England. Unfortunately for the Wessex's, by the late 700's the Danes had started making raids on remote monasteries. These were soon followed by full-on invasions, including the plundering of London. Saxon warring against Danes and Norsemen continued back and forth into the 11th century, when Ethelred ordered all the Danes in England to be massacred. Several massacres did take place, prompting the Danish King, Sweyn, to arrive personally and plunder Norwich before leaving. More invasions, retreats, and battles followed - Sweyn's son, Canute, gaining control and marrying Ethelred's widow Emma in his attempt to consolidate. He had Ethelred's

0BC   The population of Britain is about 5 million

eldest son killed, but the other sons escaped to Normandy and eventually returned. By 1066 Harold, a Saxon and the last of the Wessex dynasty, had risen to the throne. He was challenged almost immediately on two fronts. In September 1066 he marched his army to York and fought off a Norwegian invasion, then headed back south to face a disastrous defeat 2½ weeks later at Hastings, to William of Normandy.

The Norman reign started with a detailed accounting of Britain's available resources - recorded in the Domesday Book. The 1066 invasion was the last in British history, and resulted in French becoming the language of the nobles for the next 300 years. Soon the Normans and Saxons were intermingling - Henry I, the third Norman king even marrying the Saxon Princess Matilda. Several usurpers tried to claim the throne on Henry's death but eventually his grandson Henry II became the first king from the House of Anjou, a lineage that produced the next fourteen kings.

The 1200's were a period of warring all around; rebellion and civil war in England - which resulted in the Magna Carta, a document extolling liberties for common folk - as well as wars in France, Wales, Scotland, and involvement in the on-going crusades.

By the end of 13th century England had gained control of Wales and Scotland and was enjoying a measure of peace, although in the 14th century the tide turned again; Robert the Bruce defeated Edward II, who was eventually murdered on his wife's orders, the Hundred Years' War with France started, and the flea-borne Plague arrived, killing about 40% of the population.

As the fighting overseas ended, war at home started with the Duke of York battling Henry VI in the War of the Roses (red for the Lancastrians and white for the Yorkists). After 30 years of toing-and-froing the Yorkist Edward IV had Henry killed in the Tower of London. The same fate then befell his own sons, including the 12-year old king Edward V, possibly on the orders of their uncle who became the next king - Richard III. Richard did not last long. He was killed at Bosworth Field, in 1485, by the first of the Tudor kings - Henry VII (a Lancastrian) - who took the monarchy and quelled much of the turmoil surrounding succession by marrying a prominent Yorkist. His son, Henry VIII, was less successful in marriage. His efforts to get a divorce from Catherine of Aragon resulted in the separation of the Church of England from Rome and the Pope, effectively endorsing the Protestant Reformation.

Elizabeth was Henry's third child (her mother was Anne Boleyn) and the third of his children to reign (after Edward VI and Mary Queen of Scots). Her long reign, into the 17th century, saw England and English culture prosper. When Elizabeth, the Virgin Queen, died James VI of Scotland became James I, uniting that country with England and becoming the first Stuart king.

During the reign of James's successor, Charles, relations with Parliament worsened to the point of civil war, with Oliver Cromwell, then his son, replacing the monarchy and leading a period of Republic. However, England was not without a king for long. In 1660 the Restoration returned Charles II. During this period Britain's international interests expanded to include America and India.

At the end of the 17th century a "Glorious Revolution" took place with Queen Mary and her husband William signing an Act of Settlement that limited the monarch's absolute power. When Mary's sister, Anne, died childless the crown went to distant German relatives from the House of Hanover - a dynasty that lasted until Queen Victoria's death in 1901.

The 18th and 19th centuries saw huge technological and cultural changes in Britain. During the Industrial Revolution steam and iron effectively became king, and the Empire continued to grow with the addition of Australia, more land in the Americas, and other foreign territories. At home, a Prime Minister - Sir Robert Walpole - was installed to run the country for the first time. When Victoria started her 64-year reign, Britain's colonial power was enormous, despite having lost America. International tensions had increased by the time the Edwardian era arrived with Victoria's heir Edward VII. Germany's naval expansion was seen as a considerable threat, and when Anglo-German discussions on the subject failed, things looked ominous. The spark came in June 1914 when Archduke Ferdinand was assassinated in Sarajevo, and within 2 months Britain was drawn into a 4 year "war to end all wars".

Even when WWI ended, peace did not fully come to Britain. From 1919 to 1921 war continued with the IRA, until the Catholic majority in Ireland's south eventually gained independence.

The 1920's saw an initial optimism in post-war Britain, then pessimism among the working classes as unemployment rose and living conditions worsened. The result was a General Strike for 9 days in May 1926. The latter part of the 1920's saw some improvement, however economic conditions started deteriorating again at the end of the decade when the American stock market crashed in October 1929. By 1932 unemployment had reached 3 million in a land of 45 million.

1936 was a year of three kings; George V died, Edward VIII abdicated, and George VI started his 16-year reign. During the late 1930's a gradual rearmament programme started, partly in response to Hitler's own rearmament that had started in the early Thirties. When Hitler annexed Austria and threatened Czechoslovakia in 1938 Prime Minister Neville Chamberlain's approach was to accept this in return for a promise of future non-aggression. The Prime Minister's promise that this would bring "peace in our time" evaporated a year later when Hitler invaded Poland. Churchill, the leading critic of the Appeasement policy, was installed to lead the country through WWII.

Six years later Britain and her allies were victorious, but the toll on the economy had been heavy. Churchill was voted out after the war and for six years a Labour Government set about fulfilling the aspirations of many of the returning soldiers for a fairer and better life in a welfare state. In 1951 Churchill was elected Prime Minister again, and the following year Elizabeth II became Queen on her father's death.

The late 1940's into the early 1960's saw most of Britain's colonies gain independence. In 1963 Britain tried to enter the European Common Market but was blocked by France (it did not join until 1973).

In the 1970's Britain struggled to maintain her economic advantages. The oil crisis spurred development of the North Sea oil and gas fields, but also inflation. The oil shortage, combined with demands for higher wages and rising unemployment, sent inflation to 20% at the start of the 1980's. Enter, Margaret Thatcher. Her tough economic policies saw many people consigned to life on welfare until the economy started turning in the mid-80's. In 1990 "Thatcherism" ended when she was dumped for John Major. The Conservatives grip on power ended in 1997 when Tony Blair led a "New Labour" to victory.

The 1990's also saw a willingness from Westminster to entertain the concept of more autonomy for the other home nations. In 1996 the Stone of Scone, which symbolises Scottish royalty and had resided in Westminster Abbey since 1296 (apart from a few months in 1950 when Scottish nationalists stole it), was returned and in 1999 a Scottish Parliament was reconvened for the first time since 1707.

Still one the world's leading industrialised nations and a member of the G8, Britain celebrated the new millennium by building the teflon-coated Millennium Dome, the world's largest, along the Prime Meridian at Greenwich.

139   Construction of the Antonine Wall, from the Firth of Forth to the River Clyde starts. However by 163 the Romans have retreated to Hadrian's Wall

ACCOMMODATION

Tourist accommodation in Britain is generally of a high standard, despite the jibes the country's plumbing gets. Accommodation costs may vary with season (peak season being anywhere from April to September, but centred on July and August). Britain's National Parks and popular tourist towns can get busy during peak season holidays and last-minute accommodation may be harder to find.

Local tourist offices have accommodation listings, although they may only recommend "approved" listings, and other non-approved accommodation can be present nearby (campgrounds are a typical example). Some tourist offices put a list of accommodation on their doors, for late-arrivers. Local storeowners may be able to point you in the direction of lodging if everything else seems closed.

This guide lists a selection of accommodation along the route, although the author has not stayed at all these places, so inclusion is not necessarily a recommendation and if alternates are available this is usually stated.

Accommodation costs are always changing and prices often vary with the season, so check when booking. Prices in this guide are ballpark only. Also, establishments in smaller villages are particularly susceptible to economic pressures and some have been impacted by the recent Foot & Mouth Disease outbreak - you may want to check lodging is still offered in areas where there are limited options.

Camping

There are public and private campsites in Britain. Public sites are included on the maps and listings provided by tourist offices (most of the campground listings in this guide are public sites). To stay at private campgrounds you may need to become a member of The Camping and Caravanning Club (£27.50 to join). This club has several thousand sites across the country that range from farmers' paddocks to campgrounds with full amenities. Be aware that some "Caravan Parks" do not allow tent camping, while others do.

At a minimum Britain's campgrounds typically have tent sites, toilet and shower facilities, and water available. In addition, some offer cabin-style accommodation and laundry facilities. Campgrounds generally do not have cooking facilities.

The opportunities to free camp in Britain are somewhat limited, there are designated areas in National Parks and you may be able to camp on farmland if you can get the farmer's permission. Some hostels also offer camping.

If you plan to camp have a good quality lightweight tent that doesn't leak (see p.28 for other suggested camping gear).

Hostels

There are hundreds of hostels throughout Britain. The Youth Hostel Association (YHA) and Scottish Youth Hostel Association (SYHA) run about 300 hostels throughout Britain, and there are many excellent independent hostels - some are in historic buildings, even castles.

Hostels provide dormitory and sometimes private rooms, shared bathroom facilities, and cooking facilities (some also provide cheap meals). Dormitory rooms are generally single sex. Many hostels have in-house tourist information services and they are a good place to network with budget travellers. Age is not a factor for staying in hostels.

Bed and Breakfasts (B&B's)

B&B's are a British institution. Basically private homes that take in a few travellers at a time, B&B's are a great way to connect with the locals. Most B&B's have signs that can be seen as you ride past. A bed and linen is provided in a room that may or may not have en-suite facilities (there will be a shared bathroom if there is no en-suite). Towels are almost always provided. Breakfast is typically a starter of cereal, toast, and juice, followed by a fried ensemble of bacon, sausages, eggs, and tomato, and a cup of tea. B&B owners get up early to make breakfast, but cyclists who like to leave at the crack of dawn should double check what time breakfast is served from. Also check that the B&B has a place to park bikes - often it will be some place in the back yard.

Most establishments do not take credit cards and some, in popular tourist areas, do not take single night bookings during peak season. If you book a B&B then can't make it be sure to let the owners know. Typically, hosts are genuinely interested in their guests' travels and will sit down over a cupper to find out your plans and have a chat. These folks are a great source of local information. B&B's are found throughout Britain and are generally cheaper than hotels.

Hotels

British hotels vary from bottom-of-the-barrel budget, to top-notch luxury. Most hotel rooms have tea- and coffee making facilities and an en-suite including a washbasin, toilet, and shower or bath (although some historic hotels may have the bathroom down the hallway). Room rates often include a continental breakfast. Brand name hotel chains are present throughout the UK (their regional offices can supply location lists) and there are plenty of independent hotels.

Other Accommodation

In small towns and villages traditional inns, and some pubs, offer lodging. Furnished houses, apartments, cottages, and caravans are available for rent, typically by the week. The National Trust (Britain's cultural caretaker) has listings of historic buildings that you can stay in. Some farmhouses take in guests and the YHA has lists of camping barns - converted farm buildings that offer cheap accommodation. Universities sometimes make their dormitories available during holiday periods (their main holidays cover July, August, and September). In canal areas, marinas sometimes have moored canal boats they rent out as accommodation. Some YMCA's and YWCA's have accommodation. Motels (offering private rooms with cooking facilities, a refrigerator, and a private bathroom) exist, but are not very common. The British Tourist Authority (BTA) and their local tourist information centres (TIC's) have details and listings for many of these options.

TRANSPORT IN BRITAIN

Train

Britain still has an excellent rail system, despite privatisation in 1995. Trains link most of mainland Britain's major cities and large towns, and the network also extends to many small towns. Route information is available from National Rail Inquires (Ph 08457 484950), Railtrack (*www.railtrack.co.uk*), or *www.rail.co.uk*.

On most trains you can wheel your bike straight into the guard wagon, then find a seat for the journey. However, on long-distance trains popular with cyclists (for example the southbound trains from Wick and Thurso) a paying reservation system for bicycles in enforced, and if the guard wagon is fully booked you will not be able to get your bike on the train.

The cheapest fare from A to B is not always a standard one-way ticket (called a "single"). Check for the best available fares when purchasing. Generally, advance purchase tickets are cheaper, as are tickets for travel after 9:30am. Discount cards for young people (16 to 25's) and seniors (over 60's) can be purchased. Tickets for the popular travel days of Friday and Saturday may be more expensive.

A Britrail Pass, which is purchased before coming to Britain by visitors from outside Europe, may be a good option if you plan on some sightseeing before or after cycling. Flexipasses allow a certain number of travel days within a two-month period, and could be used to get to Land's End and back from John O' Groats, as well as some additional sightseeing.

Coach

Coach travel is slower than rail but cheaper (the term coach refers to a long-distance bus). Coach services link major cities and large towns across Britain, and in some instances go to places rail doesn't reach. The primary national service provider is National Express, which has its hub at Victoria Coach Station in London (Ph 08705 808080 or see *www.nationalexpress.co.uk*). They also have branches at Heathrow and Gatwick airports. Scottish Citylink (Ph 0990 505050) is a National Express subsidiary. Coaches are air-conditioned and most have on-board toilets. Explorer or Rover passes offer unlimited travel for certain periods. Bikes will be carried but they need to be boxed and there is a small surcharge. In addition, some companies run "hop-on hop-off" bus services on routes popular with backpackers.

Plane

Flying is a relatively expensive way to travel domestically, and with a bike it can be a hassle. British Airways and various discount airlines fly internally to the large cities and have connecting flights to many smaller centres. Bikes can usually be taken as personal luggage provided you are within your weight allowance (normally 20kg (44lbs)), but check with the airline before booking. There is often an additional charge. Carriers may require bicycle tyres to be deflated, handle bars turned sideways, pedals removed or turned inwards, and the chain wrapped, and some require bikes to be boxed. Discounted fares are available by booking in advance, or, if you have flexibility in your travel arrangements, flying standby.

Rental Car

Renting a car is also expensive, although discounts can be obtained by booking before coming to Britain. If you want to carry a bike you'll need to hire a car big enough to fit your dismantled bike in, or get a carry rack. Renting a car and dropping it off in Penzance is one way to get to the start of this tour, although this is a pricey option (likewise, a one-way rental from Wick or Thurso could be used to return south).

The major rental companies include Alamo, Avis, Budget, Hertz, and InterRent. There are also smaller rental companies that offer competitive rates. Check the insurance, deductible, and damage waiver details (your personal auto insurance or credit card company may cover some of these costs). Rates for automatics are higher. The minimum driver age for most rental companies is 25 (Alamo is 21 with compulsory additional insurance). Petrol costs about 75p a litre. See p.30 for details on driving in Britain.

Other Transport

Renting a campervan (also called caravans) is one option conducive to travelling with a bicycle. You can drive to interesting areas then explore them by bike. Cruising by houseboat on Britain's extensive web of canals and inland waterways is an interesting option. Bikes can be used to explore towpaths and nearby areas. The ferries that link Britain's mainland ports and outer islands are another option.

BANKS, ATMS, AND EXCHANGE RATES

Banks are open weekdays from 9:30am to 4:30pm (some open later on Thursdays, and on Saturday mornings). Most banks cash travellers cheques and change foreign currency (except coins) on the spot.

ATMs (called cashpoints in Britain) are common in cities and large towns. Certain cashpoints give cash advances on major credit cards - the logos on the machines tell you which ones (Visa is widely accepted). Depending on your home bank, you may also be able to get account balances and cash directly from your account at home (the balances will show in pounds, of course). PIN numbers need to be four digits to do this. The exchange rates from cashpoints are often better than the rates and commissions charged by banks and bureaux de change's for cashing travellers cheques, although, check the fees associated with using a particular cashpoint, and know the fees your own credit card company charges for cash advances. When using a debit card, cash can be obtained from many stores as "cashback".

Britain uses pence (p) and pounds (£) in the following denominations; 1p and 2p copper coins, 5p, 10p, 20p, and 50p silver coins, £1 and £2 gold coins, and £5, £10, £20, and £50 notes. Pounds are also referred to as pounds sterling (a sterling was a Saxon silver coin and large sums of money were measured in "pounds of sterlings" - later shortened to pounds sterling). In addition to accepting pounds sterling, Scotland also issues its own pound notes. The Scottish notes are equivalent in value to English notes, and are technically legal tender in England although they are accepted less enthusiastically the further you get from the border (banks inter-change these notes at no cost). Britain has not joined the movement to the single European currency, yet.

Exchange rates at the time of printing mean one pound sterling buys the following;

Country/Currency	£ sterling will purchase
American dollar	1.42
Australian dollar	2.73
Canada dollar	2.26
Euro	1.64
Japanese yen	189.3
New Zealand dollar	3.35

SHOPPING

Normal trading hours are Monday to Saturday 9:00am to 5:30pm. Some stores open Sunday. Late night shopping is usually on a Thursday or Friday till 8:00pm. Supermarkets, pubs, restaurants, service stations, and corner stores have extended hours. In small towns and villages some shops close for lunch, and close up early one day a week.

The cheapest food prices are normally in supermarkets, rather than smaller stores and service stations (which often sell a limited range of food items). Some ballpark prices are listed below;

Loaf of bread	40p	Milk (1 litre)	50p
Bananas (1 kg)	£1.15	Cheese (500 g)	£1.85
Marmite (125 g)	£1.10	Beef Mince (500 g)	£1.20
Small chocolate bar	30p	Fish & Chips	£2
Big Mac	£1.90	Cup of Tea	40p
Sandwich	90p	Pint of Guiness	£2.10
35mm film 36 exp.	£5	Petrol (1 litre regular)	75p
Diesel (1 litre)	75p	Local phone call	10p
Internal letter rate	26p	30 min at Internet Café	£2.50
Movie ticket	£6	Compact disc	£12
Dorm bed at hostel	£10	Hotel room (outside city)	£30
Hotel room (in a city)	£50	Bicycle inner tube	£3
Day Pass London Tube	£4	Bicycle tyre	£12

Major credit cards are widely accepted. Tipping is not prevalent in Britain (many restaurants already add a service charge to the bill). One exception are taxi drivers, who expect a tip of around 10%.

A Value-added tax (VAT) of 17.5% is included on most price tags (food is exempt). Many shops participate in a VAT refund programme that enables tourists from outside the EU to claim back their VAT on leaving the country. Not all purchases are eligible and some shops have their own minimum-purchase amounts (usually around £50). To claim VAT back you need to show the shop your passport and ask for an "ETS Refund Form" (also called a shopping cheque) or a "407 Form". To get your refund, have Customs at the airport stamp the form - then go to the ETS Counter (if you have an ETS Refund Form) for your money. If you have a 407 Form you will have to send the form back to the shop and they will send you the refund. Another way to avoid this tax is to have the shop ship the goods directly to your home and not charge you VAT at all.

COMMUNICATIONS

Telephone
A local call from a public phone box costs 10p. The line starts beeping when you need to pay more, and if you have time left at the end of your call you can push the FC button for a follow on call. Phone boxes take either coins (from 10p to £1) or phone cards (widely available from newsagents and other outlets).

For local calls you do not need to dial the area code. For the operator dial 000, for directory assistance (calling information) dial 192. Numbers starting with 0500 or 0800 are toll-free. Calling a cellular phone is more expensive than a normal call.

International calls can be made from any phone using an International Direct Dial number or through the operator. For international call assistance dial 155.

Check on the costs for operator-assisted calls and calls from hotels, and also the cheapest time of day to make international calls (generally after 5:00pm). Calling cards (you dial a toll-free number, make the call, and it's charged to your home phone bill) or prepaid phone cards are the cheapest ways to call home from Britain.

When calling Britain from overseas; dial your international access code, 44 (the

991 Ethelred II, suffering under Viking attacks, signs a treaty with the Duke of Normandy agreeing not to provide assistance to each other's enemies

21

country code for the United Kingdom), leave the 0 off the area code, then dial the phone number.

Emergency calls to 999 are free.

Mail

Post offices are open Monday to Friday 9:00am to 5:30pm, and Saturday 9:00am to 12:30pm. The internal letter rate is 26p for first class (quicker delivery) and 19p for postcards and second class letters. Postcards to Europe cost 30p, and to most other countries 38p. Airmail letters up to 20g to Europe cost 30p. Airmail letters up to 10g to most other places cost 44p. Check these rates are still current when posting your mail (you can also check on-line at *www.royalmail.co.uk*).

Post Offices offer a Post Restante service that will receive and hold packages for three months, free of charge (letters posted internally, or from overseas, will be held for two weeks, and one month, respectively). Items should be marked "Post Restante" or "To Be Called For" on the address and you will need your passport, or similar proof of identity, to pick these up. This service can be a good way to rid yourself of excess weight as you cycle the country (used maps and tourist stuff can be sent to a Post Office near your departure point for pick-up later). American Express also offers a similar service to cardholders.

The central post office in London is at 24-28 William IV St, Trafalgar Square, WC2N 4DL, London, Ph 02074 849307.

The Internet and E-mail

Access to the Internet is quite good in Britain. All major cities and most large towns have cyber cafés or Internet service shops. Most public libraries have Internet access, and more and more hotels and hostels are starting to provide net services and hook-ups.

TV, Radio, and The Press

Free-to-air TV channels include the British Broadcasting Corporation's BBC1 (news bulletins at 1pm, 6pm, and 9pm) and BBC2 (entertainment programming). These channels are government funded and add-free. ITV is an independent channel that broadcasts news and regional programmes. Channels 4 and 5 are the other free-to-air TV channels. Satellite TV (the main one is Sky), and cable channels are also available.

The BBC run Radio 1 through 5 (Radio 4, at FM 93.5, has news and current affairs including the world renowned World Service). There are plenty of independent regional stations.

Major newspapers include the more serious broadsheets, such as *The Times* and *The Independent*, and the Tabloids (smaller in size but larger in circulation) such as *The Sun* and *The Daily Mail*. There are numerous monthly magazines with news, arts, and entertainment information.

EMERGENCY CONTACTS

Dial 999 for Police, Ambulance, and Fire services. In an emergency (e.g. loss of passport, arrest, serious injury) your Embassy, High Commission, or Consulate in Britain can help with contacting relatives at home, and if you get into serious trouble may provide a temporary loan which will have to repaid. Your Embassy can also assist with repatriation in emergencies. Most Embassies are in London, listings can be found in the phone book.

HOLIDAYS

Public Holidays

Banks, Government offices, schools and most businesses are closed on public holidays. As a result there is generally an increase of traffic on the roads at these times. Public holidays are listed below. Some British towns add their own holidays to this list.

Holiday	Date
New Years Day	January 1
Day after New Years Day	January 2 (Scotland only)
Good Friday	Late March or April
Easter Monday	Late March or April
May Day	First Monday in May
Spring Bank Holiday	Last Monday in May
Summer Bank Holiday	First Monday in August (Scotland only)
Summer Bank Holiday	Last Monday in August (Not Scotland)
Christmas Day	December 25
Boxing Day	December 26

Note: 2002 had two additional public holidays (June 3 & 4) marking the Queen's Golden Jubilee.

School Holidays

The summer school holidays are traditionally mid-July through to the beginning of September. There are also two-week long breaks around Christmas and Easter, and shorter (week-long) mid-term breaks in early-February, late-May, and late-October. Domestic travel and accommodation in tourist areas can be more difficult to book around these times.

TIME

Since 1884 Britain has run on Greenwich Mean Time (GMT), to which all other time zones are referenced (the prime meridian ($0°$ longitude) passes through the principal transit instrument at Greenwich Observatory, a few miles east of central London).

Britain goes into daylight saving time from the end of March to the end of October (clocks move forward 1 hour from GMT). If you are visiting from the US remember Britain, Europe, and most of the rest of the world lists dates by day/month/year (not month/day/year).

WEIGHTS AND MEASURES

Britain went metric in the 1980's, however many people have been reluctant to adopt the system (A "British Weights & Measures Association" actively campaigns against metric use). As a result both imperial and metric units are found in everyday usage. In general, temperatures are reported in Celsius, distances in miles and feet, weights are pounds and ounces or kilograms and grams, and volumes are either litres or pints.

Air compressors at service stations use pounds per square inch (psi) to measure tyre pressure. See Appendix G for conversions between metric and imperial units, and visa versa.

1017 King Canute divides England into 4 earldoms; 2 run by Danes and 2 run by Britons (Leofric, and his famous wife, Lady Godiva, rule Mercia)

23

ON THE ROAD

WHEN TO CYCLE TOUR

Late spring, summer, and early autumn are the best times to do this tour. The days are longer, the weather is typically more favourable, and most attractions and facilities are open. For the British, summer is centred on July and August, when people take their annual holidays (as a result these are also the busiest tourist times). June, July, or August, on a whole, are typically the driest, warmest, months and have fewer days of very strong winds compared to other months (although this is based on historic averages and cold, wet, and windy conditions can also occur during these times). Late autumn, winter, and early spring are not recommended times to undertake this journey, due to the increased likelihood of persistent poor weather and low visibility, although a few, well prepared, people do tour during the colder months.

Being an island nation, ocean temperatures play a major role in the weather across Britain, with the Atlantic being slightly warmer than the North Sea. Along this tour the southwest of England is generally warmer and drier, with the Lake District and the Highlands of Scotland being cooler and wetter. Topography also plays a major role in this - with temperatures normally dropping about $0.5°C$ for every 100m gain in elevation. The Met Office has a good rule of thumb to keep in mind; it typically rains on about one day in three in England (somewhat more often in winter) with occasional long, dry spells. In the Scottish Highlands it rains, on average, 250 days a year (on average every $1\frac{1}{2}$ days). Appendix D has more data on temperatures and rainfall for various locations in Britain.

Fortunately for this tour, winds are most common from the southwest in Britain (another average statistic that will mean little to a cyclist faced with several days of headwinds). Watch for stronger winds going over mountain passes, such as Kirkstone Pass in Cumbria, and at higher elevations - as in the Scottish Highlands.

A benefit of doing the tour towards the end of summer is that the days get longer, giving cyclists more available riding time. This trend also gets more pronounced the further north you travel (The Shetlands for example, get 4 more daylight hours than the south of England in mid-summer).

In summary, think about doing this tour during summer, or a month or so on either side of summer, but be prepared for all types of weather no matter when you go - then if you strike a spell of settled good weather, consider it a bonus.

CYCLING END TO END

Land's End to John O' Groats is a great ride for those looking to do a their first extended cycle tour. It starts in the mild, more populated, counties of Cornwall and Devon before heading into the rugged, less populated, Scottish Highlands (although Cornwall and Devon are quite hilly). In fact the 950 or so miles of this tour are do-able for almost anyone who is reasonably fit and has some basic cycle touring experience. [For first time tourers, a little additional research is recommended (there are plenty of instructive books that deal with touring and touring equipment) along with a couple of shorter shakedown tours - to find out if cycling End to End is something that really interests you].

You may not be alone at the start of this journey either - during summer a lot of people do the End to End trip, many for charity. However, Britain's vast network of roads means you may rarely bump into other End to Enders, except near the start and

1042 The throne lapses to a Briton; Ethelred's son Edward (The Confessor), after King Hardicanute dies of a "horrible convulsion" at a wedding

finish. The route described in this guide is a fairly direct route between Land's End and John O' Groats, following the Cornish coast before heading inland, through Devon, to Bath and The Cotswolds. The tour briefly crosses into and out of Wales then passes between Liverpool and Manchester before entering The Lake District - a beautiful area that includes a tough climb over Kirkstone Pass.   The route enters Scotland near Carlisle and soon after enters some of the quietest and prettiest rural scenery of the trip, in the Southern Uplands between Dumfries and Glasgow. Between Loch Lomond and Loch Linnhe the tour crosses Rannoch Moor a dramatic but exposed stretch that can be radiantly sunny or wildly wet, windy, and cold (weather conditions that can occur anywhere along the tour actually). From Fort William, at the foot of Ben Nevis, the route follows the Great Glen northeast past Loch Ness - a busy tourist area in summer. The last part of the ride crosses the Black Isle between Beauly Firth and Cromarty Firth, then follows the windswept and largely unspoilt Caithness coastline to John O' Groats.

The tour travels mostly on quieter "B" and minor roads, where practical, and is sealed all the way (a few miles are unsealed if you decide to take the Caledonian Canal option on p.118). Traffic is heaviest where the route joins A roads, and nearer large towns and cities - often more so in the mornings and evenings as people travel to work (p.29 has more info on the types of roads in Britain).

The route has been divided into convenient stages ranging from 32 to 61 miles in length, but these can be shortened or extended depending on riding conditions and individual capabilities. Food and accommodation are available at the end of each stage, and camping facilities are available at the end of most stages. Bicycle shops are found in all the major towns en-route, but are less frequent in rural areas and the north of Scotland.

The maps section *(p.31)* has details on how to stay on track but be prepared for a few unintended detours on Britain's spider-web of rural roads - all part of the fun of exploring. The 25-mile photographs in this guide will give you an idea of the type of countryside that you will be travelling through.

The topography along the route is discussed in general terms in the text and is summarised on the stage profiles. Not every climb is mentioned. The terrain is described (in increasing steepness) as flat, gently rolling, rolling, or hilly. Flat terrain may include a few climbs and descents, but where these are present they are generally gentle.   Terrain described as gently rolling includes gentle rises and falls with occasional moderate climbs, but rarely any steep climbs. Rolling countryside includes moderate and some steep climbs, and hilly terrain is just that; hilly and hard going. Of course the wind direction, weather conditions and individual fitness are strong influences, and a tough head wind can make even flat terrain hard going.

WHAT TO TAKE

Experienced tourers tend to have their own ideas on equipment and touring technique, based on what has worked best for them in the past. The following sections include some gear suggestions relevant to this tour and tips that those new to extended cycle touring may find useful.

Deciding on the accommodation that you plan to use on this tour will make a big difference to the load you carry. Carrying camping gear gives you the flexibility of choosing to camp, or not, depending on circumstances, and is the cheapest touring option. Deciding to stay in B&B's, hotels, and hostels that supply linen (sometimes called credit card touring) means you can leave behind sleeping bags and camping gear

1066 William, Duke of Normandy, lands in Sussex. King
Harold is killed at The Battle of Hastings and William
advances to London to become King

25

and travel lighter - although this is obviously a more expensive option and restricts your options somewhat. Regardless of the type of accommodation you choose, aim to minimise the amount of gear you carry. Travelling as light as possible allows you to cycle a decent distance in a day and avoids over-stressing you and your bike. A good rule is to take the minimum gear needed to cover the worst anticipated conditions, then add just enough to be able to live from day to day. A suggested packing list and more details on gear are given below.

A Bike

Cyclists have ridden End to End on all sorts of bikes. The three most common types you'll see on this tour are touring bikes, mountain bikes, and hybrids.

Touring bikes are a variant of road (racing) bikes, that have a wider range of gears (21 or more), sturdier components, and a frame geometry tweaked to be more comfortable for long periods in the saddle. These bikes have 700c wheels and have historically been the preferred bike of long distance tourers for rides on sealed roads.

Mountain bikes are solid work horses with good load carrying capabilities and a wide range of gearing. The smaller frame geometry of these bikes results in a different riding position compared to road bikes, which some riders do not find suitable for long rides. Others like the lower centre of gravity and stability of mountain bikes. Mountain bikes have smaller diameter wheels compared to road bikes and fatter tyres that cannot be pumped to the same pressures (making them slightly less efficient). Cyclists that use mountain bikes for road touring often replace the knobbly off-road tyres with slick tyres, or tyres with a smooth central strip. The suspension forks and rear-end suspension systems found on many mountain bikes do not have any significant advantages for road touring. Since this route is sealed the whole way, the off-road benefits of these bikes are negated, although with a mountain bike you do have the option of taking days off along the way, unloading, and exploring the backcountry.

Hybrid bikes are a cross between road bikes and mountain bikes, with 700c wheels and a reasonably large frame akin to road bikes, but handlebars and componentry similar to mountain bikes. Some riders find this riding position works well for them.

Whatever type of bike you take, it should be a good fit, have suitable load carrying capacity, and have a reasonably lightweight frame with high quality components.

Small adjustments to the height and position of the handlebars and saddle make big differences to the mechanics of cycling. With a well fitting bike, and some fine-tuning of these components, you should be able to find a comfortable touring position. Toe clips, or clipless pedals and touring shoes, greatly increase cycling efficiency. [A note on technique here; aim to cycle with a steady rhythm, avoiding bouts of extreme exertion, and using lower gears at higher rpm rather than grinding away slowly in a high gear].

Good quality aluminium or chrome-moly touring racks, made by companies such as Blackburn® or Tubus®, are recommended. Panniers (saddlebags) should attach securely to the racks and not lean out from the bike excessively when the bike is cornering. Use plastic bags to line the panniers and keep your gear dry, unless you are 100% confident they are waterproof.

Carrying two frame-mounted water bottles works well, although on most stages of this tour there are plenty of opportunities to refill a single large drink bottle.

Mudguards (fenders) are great on rainy days, and it is likely to rain on this tour, however, with a good set of rain gear many tourers save weight and do without them.

A cycle computer that includes trip and total distance functions is almost indispensable, especially on this tour where distances to the numerous intersections and minor roads are listed next to the strip maps. The computer should be set for the exact tyre circumference of your loaded bike with you on it (this can be done with the help of someone measuring the distance for one revolution of the wheel which has the computer sensor on).

Some tourers find a handheld Global Positioning System (GPS) unit a useful tool in navigating, although you can easily get by without one.

In Britain bikes are legally required to have front and rear lights and a red rear reflector for night riding. Touring after dark is not recommended. A small red-flashing LCD light, mounted facing the rear, is good even if it is not dark, so drivers can see you clearly in gloomy or low light conditions.

Clothing and Equipment

Britain's climate is famously changeable so be prepared for all types of weather. A good quality raincoat and lightweight rain pants are the most important items of clothing, for fighting windy and wet conditions. They should be waterproof, seam-sealed, and made of a breathable fabric. A mid-weight fleece top is your second most important piece of clothing. With a good raincoat and a warm top you should be able to survive a cold wet night stuck in most places.

Polypropylene underwear - longs and a top - are also important items that allow you to dress in layers and control your temperature (be particularly aware of getting chilled when you stop riding on cold days). You may also want a lightweight pair of fleece pants for very cold days. For warm weather riding, bike shorts and a bike shirt (or T-shirt) are generally sufficient. Bright coloured clothing is recommended to increase your visibility to other road users. A reflectorised sash, even for day use, is a good idea. Cycle helmets are not compulsory in Britain but are widely used and recommended.

Cycling gloves protect your hands by spreading the pressure on nerves and help somewhat in a fall. Wrap-around sunglasses provide protection from wind and dust - some include interchangeable lenses for use on overcast days.

Lightweight, waterproof, overgloves and shoe covers are worth having for the rain, but some tourers do without them.

If you plan on camping, take a lightweight, good quality tent (you could also consider taking a tent fly, poles, and a light plastic ground sheet rather than a full tent, in order to save weight). [Note: never cook inside a sealed tent as this has resulted in numerous deaths from carbon monoxide poisoning]. A small down sleeping bag, and an Ultralight ¾ Thermarest® pad to provide insulation from the ground, are ideal.

The following is a suggested gear list that should pack into rear panniers, on the top of a rear rack, and in a handlebar bag.

BIKE
Bike with racks..☐
Panniers and handlebar bag..☐
Water bottles and cages...☐
Cycle computer...☐
Small flashing LCD rear light...☐

CLOTHING
Raincoat...☐
Rain pants (with elastic cuffs or clip for right leg)...........................☐
Mid-weight fleece top..☐

1068 Exeter revolts against Norman rule and other parts of the country follow. This resistance is brutally surpressed over the next 2 years

27

Polypropylene underwear (longs and top), hat, and gloves........................☐
2 T-shirts or cycle tops........................☐
1 Pair of lightweight shorts........................☐
1 or 2 Pairs of cotton socks........................☐
1 or 2 Pairs of underwear........................☐
1 Pair of lightweight longs........................☐
1 or 2 Pairs of cycle shorts........................☐
Cycle gloves........................☐
1 Pair of shoes........................☐
Sunglasses........................☐
Reflector sash........................☐
Bicycle helmet........................☐

TOOLS
Pump, puncture repair kit, tyre levers........................☐
Spare inner tube........................☐
Tyre patch or spare tyre........................☐
Spare spokes (including spokes for the rear cluster side) and spoke wrench......☐
Cluster removing tool........................☐
Chain breaker and spare chain links........................☐
Spare brake and gear cables........................☐
Spare nuts and bolts (including rack bolts)........................☐
Appropriate Allen keys........................☐
Wrenches, pliers, screw driver........................☐
Zip ties, some duct tape, grease & lube, small rag........................☐

MISCELLANEOUS
Bike lock........................☐
Pocket knife with can opener........................☐
Small First-Aid and sewing kit........................☐
Plastic bags to wrap gear in wet weather........................☐
Camera and film........................☐
Toiletries and medications (including sunscreen and insect repellent)...........☐
Maps, small compass, personal documents........................☐
Water purification tablets or filter........................☐

CAMPING
Tent (or tent fly, poles, and ground sheet)........................☐
Sleeping bag and mat........................☐
Small towel........................☐
Small torch (flashlight) ....☐
Plate and spoon........................☐

OPTIONAL EXTRAS
Waterproof overgloves and shoe covers........................☐
Matches and candle........................☐
Stove, fuel, pot........................☐
Rear view mirror........................☐
Bottom bracket removal tools and parts........................☐
Light plastic sheet with tent pegs to cover bike while camping...................☐
Handheld GPS........................☐

1154 Adrian IV, born in Hertfordshire, becomes the first and only English Pope

Fluids and Food

Drink plenty of fluid before, during, and after riding. Water thins the blood making it easier for the heart to pump, and water losses of only a few % of body weight can drastically reduce performance. Britain's tap water is fine for drinking. Water from streams, rivers or other suspect sources (some campground taps for example) should be filtered or purified for giardia. Some long-distance tourers ride with one bottle of water and another with a sports drink like Gatorade® or Powerade®.

For most people the volume of food they eat increases significantly while touring due to the rapid rate they are burning off energy. Stopping every now and again for snacks (fruit or museli bars for example) and a drink, will help maintain energy levels throughout the day. For cyclists visiting the UK this is a good chance to try Britain's pub fare - Ploughman's lunches, steak & kidney pies, and curries among others. You may want to avoid the sugar rush and subsequent lethargy that results from foods rich in simple sugars, such as candy and soft drinks (sodas).

The alternative to buying lunches and dinners is to buy groceries and carry the food to make your own meals - cooking on a camping stove, at hostels, or in self-catering accommodation. This can be a cheap option, but involves carrying more weight. Either way, carry sufficient water and snacks for the day's ride.

Repairs

On a well-tuned good quality bike, carrying an appropriate load, you should have few mechanical malfunctions and some people ride End to End without a single puncture. However, be prepared and familiar enough with your bike to fix everyday breakdowns, and if you have a major malfunction, to be able to make sufficient repairs to get to a bike shop. Basic breakdowns include fixing a flat tyre, rejoining the chain, and replacing a broken spoke. The spare parts and tools you should carry, and know how to use, are in the suggested gear list opposite.

Try to get lightweight multi-function tools to cut down on weight. If you are riding in a group you can split some of the tools between you (assuming the tools are compatible between bikes), but carry the basics - including a pump and puncture repair kit - yourself. Make sure spare spokes are the correct length for your bike and include spokes for the cluster side of the rear wheel, which are usually a different length. Know how to correctly tension the spokes to true the wheel. Tools and parts for bottom bracket repairs may be useful if you know how to use them and can make such a major roadside repair, although this breakdown is unlikely to occur on a well serviced bike.

It pays to check over your bike each morning on the tour, in particular check tyre pressures, the bolts holding the racks on, and the brakes. Of course, make sure your bike is in 100% working order before setting out and test ride it fully loaded before getting to Land's End.

ROADS AND THE HIGHWAY CODE

Roads

British roads include motorways (freeways), A roads, B roads, and unclassified minor roads. Motorways link major cities and towns across Britain, are marked by blue road signs, and are usually blue on touring maps. Bicycles are prohibited on motorways. Roads labelled A102(M), for example, are also motorways.

Bikes are allowed on A roads, although some of these carry a lot of fast travelling traffic and are not great for cycling. A roads can be primary routes (green signs and green on road maps) or, slightly less busy, single or dual carriageways (with white road signs and marked red on maps). On the strip maps in this guide, primary route A roads are thicker lines with circled labels, non-primary A roads are thinner with a boxed label.

Britain's B roads are classed as secondary roads, and are great for cycling - generally less traffic and passing through small towns and villages. B roads often have traditional signposts (in some cases old stone markers) and many are hedge lined or stone walled. These roads are normally yellow on road maps.

Unclassified minor roads (called minor roads in this guide) are similar to B roads but generally do not directly link towns or villages, and are not always well signposted. Like B roads, minor roads are mostly quiet and great for cycling - many are just narrow country lanes.

All these roads are sealed. For cyclists, the shoulders on British roads vary from a wide strip to the left of a painted line on A roads, to little or no shoulder on some B- and minor roads. There is normally enough room to ride comfortably in traffic. Exceptionally steep or long hills are sometimes signposted with a red triangle indicating the %-grade. Road signs also mark upcoming cycle routes (a red triangle with a bicycle inside for local routes, or a blue circle with a white bicycle for longer distance routes).

The Highway Code
Britain's road rules are contained in The Highway Code, produced by the Department for Transport, Local Government and the Regions (DTLR). Copies are available from bookshops (for about £2) or the DTLR's web site (*www.dtlr.gov.uk*), and it's worth reviewing if you are unfamiliar with the rules of the road in Britain.

Basically, cyclists must obey all the same road signs and traffic lights as other vehicles. The British drive on the **left**, so remember to **look right first** when coming to intersections or stepping out onto the road. At intersections **give way to the right** means every vehicle on your right has priority. At **Stop** and **Give Way** signs you give way to everyone. All speed and distance signs are in miles.

Britain has plenty of roundabouts and traffic islands, these are normally signed, but where they are not give way to the right applies, as well as giving way to all traffic already in the roundabout or island. Speed limits for cars are typically 30 mph in towns, 60 mph on open roads (the open road sign is a white circle with a black slash across), and 70 mph on motorways. Wearing seatbelts in automobiles is compulsory in the front and, if installed, in the rear.

For cycling at night (not recommended for touring) bikes must have front and rear lights, and a red rear reflector. As mentioned previously, helmets are not compulsory but are recommended. You are not allowed to cycle on the footpath (sidewalk). For more information on cycling in traffic see the following section on hazards.

Traffic accidents involving damage or injury must be reported to the Police as soon as possible, and within 24 hours. The law requires you to give your name and address to the other party (if you are driving you must also give the vehicle owner's name, address, and the vehicle registration number). You are not obliged to make a statement at the accident scene. Police strictly enforce Britain's drink-driving laws (the legal drinking age is 18).

In Britain, the two big motoring organisations are the AA (the British Automobile Association) and the RAC (the Royal Automobile Club). If you are a member of a similar group at home check if it has links with one of these groups, as they provide good maps and touring information.

1170's Windmills become common in England

HAZARDS

Other road users and the weather are probably the two biggest hazards for cycle touring this route.

In city traffic, watch for car doors opening and drivers not anticipating bicycles. When approaching intersections watch for vehicles turning in front of you into, or out of, side roads and do not ride on the inside of vehicles about to turn left (pay particular attention to long vehicles with wide turning circles and poor visibility). When turning right, check it is safe to move to the centre of the road. If it is, move over, and wait for a gap in the oncoming traffic to make the turn. Making eye contact with drivers helps, and using hand signals can make your intentions clearer. At busy intersections it may be safer to dismount and use a pedestrian crossing if you feel unsafe. Be especially careful at roundabouts where drivers are often intent on entering or exiting the roundabout and are not expecting cyclists. On busy main roads trucks and buses passing at speed create a draft that requires a firm grip of the handlebars to resist.

Narrow country lanes, especially hedged or stone-walled lanes, are often only wide enough for one car and have blind corners. Pull off to the side if you hear traffic and don't think the driver knows you are on the road. Most British drivers are courteous towards cyclists, a tiny fraction, for whatever reason, are not - these are the ones who yell, honk, or drive dangerously near cyclists. The best policy is to ignore these people, or report them to the Police if they behave dangerously.

In terms of the weather, be prepared for anything from hot and sunny to cold, wet, and windy conditions. In hot weather wear loose light clothing, apply sunscreen, eat and drink water frequently to avoid dehydration (starting early in the day and before you feel thirsty), and avoid extreme exertion. When it's cold, wet, or windy be aware of the potential for hypothermia (a drop in the body's core temperature). Initial symptoms include shivering, slurred speech, irrational or lethargic behaviour, and a loss of dexterity. To avoid this, dress in layers to stay warm and dry, eat and drink regularly, and don't ride till you are completely tired out. Cyclists can be particularly susceptible to hypothermia when they stop for a rest, or breakdown, as the body can cool quickly. If you get very cold or soaked through, get out of the wind and rain, into warm dry clothes, and have hot drinks - stopping early for the day can be a pleasant break sometimes. Know the symptoms and treatment for heat exhaustion and hypothermia before setting out.

Other hazards include biters and stingers such as bees, wasps, mosquitoes, ticks, and midges. Midges are particularly bothersome in the Scottish highlands during summer - wear insect repellent and light coloured clothing. The bushes lining country lanes sometimes include stinging nettles, so watch where you stand when letting cars pass on these narrow roads.

As anywhere, be conscious of your personal security around others. A money belt is the best place for valuables and always lock your bike up when leaving it unattended. Leaving panniers unattended is not recommended.

MAPS

The dense network of numbered and minor roads throughout Britain can be daunting when trying to navigate a route. Ordnance Survey is Britain's national mapping agency. They provide topographic maps covering Britain at various scales from 1:25,000 upward. The Landranger series at a scale of 1:50,000 covers the country in 40km by 40km squares, and provide an excellent amount of detail (1km=2cm), however too many would need to be carried for cycling End to End, and on a windy day these maps can become frustrating. Ordnance Survey and motoring organisations do have good touring maps, at slightly larger scales, which are a good way to track your route. Another option is to get a road atlas at a suitable scale and, if you can bear to, cut the relevant pages out. If you do this write the order of the pages on the tops and bottoms of the pages for ease of reference.

The strip maps in this guide attempt to show the tour route in relation to the other roads in the area (including minor roads, although these are only shown extending a few hundred yards off the route). With some detailed touring maps, and the maps and directions in this guide you should be able to navigate this route without too many detours. If you do get horribly lost you can always ask the locals.

Maps can be purchased directly from Ordnance Survey (Romsey Rd, Southampton SO16 4GU, Ph 08456 050505, *www.ordsvy.gov.uk*) or the numerous agents they have throughout the country. Posting used maps home will save weight as you tour.

BICYCLE ORGANISATIONS AND CLUBS

The Cyclists Touring Club (CTC) is a national organisation that promotes cycling. Formed in 1878 the club has over 50,000 members and publishes a monthly magazine called "Cycle Touring and Campaigning". Local CTC branches also organise cycling events. Membership is £25 (£15 for seniors and students). The club has mapped out three End to End routes and can provide details on these tours. Contact: CTC, Cotterell House, 69 Meadrow, Godalming, Surrey GU7 3HS, Ph 01483 417217.

Sustrans is a large charity organisation (including 40,000 supporters) that promotes sustainable transport programmes, such as cycling, to reduce motorised traffic in Britain. Currently, their biggest project is creating a 10,000-mile National Cycle Network that can be used for touring, family rides, and commuting to school or work. To date about 6,000 miles of this network has been developed, incorporating dedicated cycle paths, quiet rural roads, and cycle lanes on busier streets. Blue and white signs, with a bike and a number, mark some of the Network's longer routes. Sustrans aims to have this project completed by 2005. This tour passes several pieces of the Network - The Camel Trail in Cornwall and The Glasgow-Loch Lomond Cycleway in Scotland, for example. More details of the National Cycle Network are available on the Internet, at *www.sustrans.org.uk* or from Sustrans Head Office, 35 King St, Bristol BS1 4DX, Ph 01179 268893.

AudaxUK is a branch of a world wide cycling movement named from the Latin for "audacious". They run timed non-stop tours, generally over very long distances (i.e. many hundred's of miles). See the Internet at *www.audax.uk.net*.

Most major towns and some small towns have local bicycle clubs focused on road racing and/or mountain biking. You could enquire at local libraries or tourist information centres if you want to get connected with these groups.

TRAINING

If you don't cycle regularly, do some training before setting off - to get your body reacquainted with riding, build your fitness, and fine tune your riding position (although some fit folks just set off, suffer for the first few days, and still enjoy themselves). In addition, if you are new to cycle touring, going on several shorter tours, overnight and fully loaded, will avoid you wobbling off from Land's End dangerously unfamiliar with the feel of your bike. These rides will also let you judge

1191 King Richard reaches the outskirts of Jerusalem during the Third Crusade

the amount of weight you are carrying and allow you to discard any unnecessary gear.

The amount of pre-tour conditioning you should do depends, obviously, on your base fitness. Train within your limitations, but plan to build up to a level where you feel comfortable spending a good number of hours in the saddle (with rest stops, of course) and have a total weekly mileage in the order of 100 miles, or more. You should also include at least a couple of rides to the maximum distance you plan to ride in a day on this tour.

GETTING TO LAND'S END

Trains for Penzance leave from London's Waterloo and Paddington stations. Penzance is the end of the South West main trunk line, which has connections from Plymouth, Bristol, Exeter, and the Midlands among others. If you are coming from afar, one option is to get a sleeper train that gets you into Penzance early in the morning to start the tour.

If coming by road, the M3 leaves London heading southwest and connects with the A303, then the A30 to Land's End. The M5 comes down from the Midlands and connects to the A30, and the A35 comes along the coast from Southampton.

There are taxis in Penzance that will ferry you and your bike right to Land's End (although it's really not far enough to justify the expense). Contact the Penzance TIC for taxi details.

From Penzance it's a 9 mile ride to Land's End along the A30, or a slightly longer ride via the quieter B3315 or B3283 routes. To get to the A30 from Penzance's Market Jew St, head southeast to Alverton Rd. Follow Alverton Rd until it joins the A30 then continue on to Land's End - literally the end of the road.

The B3315 route from Penzance to Land's End, via Newlyn and Porthcurno, is about 12 miles. About half way along this route, off to the left of the road, are the ancient standing stones known as The Merry Maidens, and on the coast near Porthcurno is the Minack Open Air Theatre - perched dramatically on the cliffs.

The B3283 route via St Buryan is about 10½ miles. Follow the A30 from Penzance for 3 miles to the B3283 turnoff at Catchall. St Buryan is a small village with a 15th century church, including a 90ft tower. About 1½ miles past St Buryan the road joins B3315 and continues through Porthcurno to Land's End.

GETTING BACK FROM JOHN O' GROATS

The nearest train and coach stations to John O' Groats are at Wick (16½ miles) and Thurso (19 miles). If you do not want to ride to these towns there are local taxi services that will take you and your bike (contact the seasonal John O' Groats tourist information centre for details - see p.133).

Note: the spaces for bikes on southbound transport from Wick and Thurso is limited, and is allocated on a pre-booked basis. Make reservations for bicycles as early as possible.

A one-way car rental from Wick or Thurso may be a good way to travel south if you want to continue exploring Britain by a means other than bicycle.

Wick also has an airport that has flights to Edinburgh, Aberdeen, and Inverness, where you can get connections to most British cities.

To continue your journey northward, ferries from John O' Groats and Scrabster (near Thurso) can take you to the Orkney Islands *(p.140)* and then onto the Shetland Islands *(p.142)*.

1200's The army starts using the English longbow, becoming
a formidable force with thousands of archers, each
able to fire 10 to 12 arrows a minute up to 400 yards

33

LAYOUT OF THIS GUIDE

Distance from the start of the stage to a particular town or village, including the facilities at that location:

c = campground
h = hostel
b&b = bed and breakfast
h = hotel
i = information centre
bike shop = bicycle shop

For GPS users, co-ordinates to the right are approximate British National Grid (BNG) references (easting and northings in metres).

A description of the stage.
This section often includes general comments on the hilliness of the stage; ranging from flat through gently rolling, rolling, and hilly (see p.25 for details).

This section includes more in-depth information on British history or culture, and generally relates to something on that particular stage.

A timeline of various dates in British history.

---

3 CAMELFORD TO OKEHAMPTON

Camelford to;

Launceston	17.1mi c, b&b, hotel, i, bike shop	233100 84700
Lifton	20.7mi hotel	238600 85100
Okehampton	37.1mi c, h, b&b, hotel, i, bike shop	258600 95200

Follow the busy A39 north from Camelford for about 3 miles, then take the A395 past the tiny villages of Davidstow and Hallworthy (there is a campground at Davidstow). About 2 miles past Hallworthy the route diverts onto minor roads through pretty countryside. About 13 miles from Camelford is Egloskerry - another diminutive rural village. Egloskerry has pretty cottages and a 15th century church, although a 19th century "restoration" has obscured much of the original building. A 2½ mile detour northeast from here is North Petherwin, and the Tamar Otter Sanctuary. Many English school children are familiar with these loveable creatures thanks to Tarka the Otter, in Henry Williamson's classic book by the same name. The sanctuary cares for injured otters (unfortunately, many are run over) and has a breeding programme that re-introduces Eurasian otters into the wild. Otter numbers are on the increase in Britain, after a decline in the 1950's and 60's that some link to the increased use of pesticides.

Launceston is dominated by the ruins of its 11th century castle, perched on a conical hill overlooking the town. The town was the ancient capital of Cornwall and hill-top fortifications were first built by the Celts. The existing structure was started by the Saxons and used by King Harold, before being added to considerably by Brian de Bretagne - the first Norman Earl of Cornwall. It then passed into the hands of Robert de Mortain, William the Conqueror's half brother and Duke of Cornwall (the castle is technically still owned by the Duchy of Cornwall). You can enter the castle walls through the north or south gates, and look at the ruins of the kitchen and administration building for free. There is a small charge to cross the moat and climb the old keep - which was never breached.

Other notable buildings in Launceston include the churches of St Mary Magdalene and St Thomas the Apostle. St Mary's is built on a site chosen by the Black Prince, and has retained its 14th century tower. The chapel walls are 16th century carved granite (stones originally destined for the church benefactor's new manor, until a death in the family made him reconsider). St Thomas's is located next to the ruins of a priory that were discovered in 1886 during railway construction (the priory was founded in 1126, but destroyed in the 16th century when Henry VIII dissolved all monasteries). The church has an impressive stone font (reportedly from the priory), a porch with a "leper squint" where the unclean could watch from, and a graveyard where the castle's deceased prisoners were buried. Slate plaques mark other interesting sites around town and the TIC has a town tour map (No. 5 Southgate St, for example, was home to Philip King, 3rd Governor of NSW, Australia). Leave town through Southgate Arch - the one remaining arch from 3 originals - and cross the River Tamar into Devon.

The road climbs in fits and spurts before dropping into Okehampton, another southern English town that changed character after the Normans invaded. This was a small Saxon settlement till the new Norman Sheriff of Devon arrived, built a castle, and moved the town next to it to establish a market. The town grew nicely until the local landlord crossed purposes with Henry VIII, resulting in the castle being wrecked. Okehampton is on the edge of Dartmoor National Park, the largest undeveloped area in southern England. There is good walking up on the moor, including the remains of an Iron Age fort near East Hill - although check routes with the tourist

48

1605 Guy Fawkes is caught with 36 barrels of gunpowder under the House of Lords in a conspiracy to blow up James I and Parliament

---

centre, as there is also an airforce bombing range nearby. The name Dartmoor is inextricably linked with Dartmoor Prison, a bleak establishment holding about 650 inmates at Princetown in the middle of the moor. Built in 1809 to hold French prisoners during the Napoleonic wars, by 1812 it was also housing American prisoners from their War of Independence. Appalling treatment and poor conditions at Dartmoor led to the deaths of 1,500 inmates in just 4 years from 1812 to 1816. An inquiry was eventually held and the prison closed, before being reopened in 1850 as a civilian prison. It currently holds about 700 prisoners.

Britain's Geology

In broad terms, Britain's rocks tend to be younger and softer in the southeast, and older and harder in the northwest (e.g. the extensive 115 million-year-old chalks of southern England vs. the 2,000 million-year-old gneisses of the Outer Hebrides). This is a result of the more recent, vigorous, geologic events along England's southern edge.

Cornwall's oldest rocks are relatively young geologically speaking - predominantly slates, grits, and limestones from the Devonian period (400 million years ago). The origins of these rocks are linked to events millions of years earlier, when, according to the Theory of Plate Tectonics, pieces of Britain were deep in the Southern Hemisphere, moving imperceptibly northward as if on a giant conveyor belt. According to Plate Tectonics, pieces of continental and oceanic crust jostle and scrape against each other as they slowly slide over the molten mantle. The oceanic plates, which are made up of basalt, are continually being added to at spreading centres along the world's mid-ocean ridges. New crust is generated at submarine volcanoes along the crests of these ridges and spreads out on either side. The continental crust is made up mostly of granite and is thicker (about 25 miles vs. 5 miles for oceanic crust) but lighter, so these pieces effectively float higher in the mantle. Most of the Earth's tectonic activity occurs along the edges of these plates as they slip past, or get squashed into, each other.

540 million years ago England and Wales were on the Northern European Plate, while Scotland was truly independent on the Canadian Plate - a completely different landmass. An ancient sea known as the Iapetus Ocean separated the two pieces. Volcanoes around the edges of this ocean resulted in the igneous highlands of the Lake District and Snowdonia. 500 million years ago the Iapetus started shrinking, and 80 million years later, as the ocean closed, Scotland and England collided and were welded together - the collision pushing up Scotland's Central Highlands. As parts of Scotland went up, much of England - Cornwall included - went down, under another sea that acted as a bathtub for the deposition of sediment and vegetation, materials that eventually formed limestones, slates, and coal measures.

Back at the mid-ocean ridges, new plate material was still being generated and with nowhere to go the Canadian Plate began bulldozing Northern Europe, with the latter, for the most part, heading underground (a portion of ocean floor did get scraped off before disappearing; these are the unusual and beautiful grey-green serpentines of the Lizard Peninsula - rocks streaked with hornblende, and the green mineral olivine). As this plate got pushed into the Earth's mantle it melted, with some of the molten rock rising. This material formed the Cornubian Batholith; molten magma squeezed upward into the existing rocks below Cornwall and Devon about 280 Million years ago - left to slowly cool in an insulated environment just below the surface. This slow cooling allowed the characteristically large crystals of granite time to grow - clear quartz, pink and white alkali feldspars with distinctive cracks along their cleavage planes, plagioclase feldspars, and the platy mica crystals of biotite (black) and muscovite (white). The intrusion gave Cornwall its backbone of granitic highlands, including Wendron Moor (near Redruth), the St Austell granite, and Bodmin Moor.

50

1613 William Shakespeare retires from play writing and returns to Stratford

---

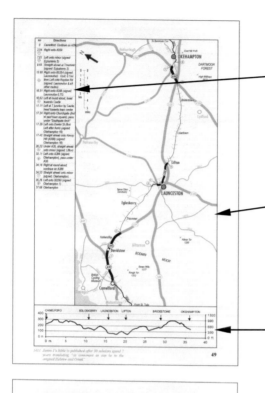

Turn by turn directions for the tour. The distance from the start of the stage is on the left. Circled markers help keep track of some of the major route changes.

A strip map for the stage. The route is shown as a black line.

A and B roads are labelled. Minor roads are dashed lines (Note: only the first ½ mile or so of minor roads off the main route are shown).

Villages, small towns and large towns are shown by progressively larger circles. City areas are shaded. Spot heights are in feet.

A profile for the stage. The y-axis scale is the same throughout the guide, the x-axis scale varies.

49

There were economic benefits from this slow-baking igneous intrusion. Contact metamorphism resulted in soft rocks around the edges being heated into slates, and, hot, metal bearing, fluids being pushed upwards from the magma and depositing dissolved metals in fissures. These veins contain combinations of tin, copper, lead, and zinc, which are still mined today. The most important mineral for Cornwall has been Cassiterite, an oxide of tin, which has been mined here for thousands of years.

By the time Cornwall's granites had formed, Britain was in the middle of the supercontinent Pangaea, a landmass consisting of all the land and covering half the globe. 200 million years before present, Britain was still land-locked, and close enough to the equator for a sandy desert dotted with salt lakes to develop over most of the country (as evidenced by sandy sandstones common across Britain and the salt deposits of Cheshire and Yorkshire). 50 million years later, Pangea had broken into Laurasia (the northern continents) and Gondwanaland (the southern continents), and Britain was mostly underwater again. Only Cornwall, Wales, and Scotland survived as islands.

The last 150 million years have seen seas rise and fall over Britain, dinosaurs disappear, and the North Atlantic open up after a line of volcanoes unzipped Scotland from America and Greenland.

Britain and France were still well connected half a million years ago, by a chalk plateau from Dover to Cap Griz Nez. A glacial ice sheet extended from Scandinavia, across the North Sea, to the Norfolk coast at this time. At its southern edge was a huge lake into which the Thames and the rivers of northern Europe drained. Eventually, and catastrophically, the soft chalk on the east side of this lake gave way with the resulting torrent scouring out the English Channel.

Camping:
Inny Vale Holiday Village, Davidstow, Ph 01840 261248, T£7 ✦ Chapmanswell Caravan Park, St Giles on the Heath, Launceston, Ph 01409 211382, T£10 ✦ Yertiz Campground, Exeter Rd, Okehampton, Ph 01837 52281, T£7 ✦ Others; Bridestowe, Okehampton (see Hostel)

Hostel:
Okehampton YHA, Klondyke Rd, Okehampton, Ph 01837 53916, Dorm£12 (also Camping)

B&B:
Tyne Wells House, Pennygillam, Launceston, Ph 01566 775810, S£20, D£36 ✦ Tinhay Mill Resturant, Lifton, Ph 01566 784201, S£39, D£60 ✦ Meadowlea, 65 Station Rd, Okehampton, Ph 01837 53200, S£20, D£40 ✦ Heathfield House, Klondyke Rd, Okehampton, Ph 01837 54211, S£35, D£50 ✦

Others; Launceston, Okehampton

Hotel:
Eagle House, Castle St, Launceston, Ph 01566 772036, S£25, D£50 ✦ Lifton Hall Country House Hotel, New Rd, Lifton, Ph 01566 784863, S£50, D£80 ✦ White Hart Hotel, Fore St, Okehampton, Ph 01837 52730, S£35, D£50 ✦ Others; Launceston, Lifton, Okehampton

i:
TIC, Market St, Launceston, Ph 01566 772321 ✦ TIC, 3 West St, Okehampton, Ph 01837 53020

Bike Shops:
John Towl 2-Wheel Centre, Newport Ind. Estate, Launceston, Ph 01566 774220 ✦ Okehampton Cycles, Bostock Garden Centre, North Rd, Okehampton, Ph 01837 53248

Addresses, phone numbers, and rates for a selection of accommodation along the route (see p.17-18).
T = Tent
Dorm = Dormitory Bed
S = Single
D = Double
Note: rates are approximate - check when booking. Inclusion is not a recommendation.

Also lists tourist information centres (i:) and bike shops.

Photos of the stage, taken every 25 miles, give an idea of the terrain on the tour. Note: the accumulated distance for these photos includes the minor detours required to ride to and from accommodation and nearby shops.

100mi 1m before St. Stephens

51

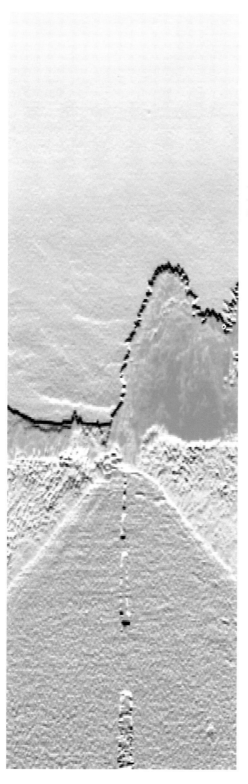

PART II
THE JOURNEY

PENZANCE

Trains and buses into Penzance drop you off next to the main street - **Market Jew St**. To head directly to Land's End go up Market Jew St, which becomes Alverton Rd, then joins the A30. But if you have time, Penzance is an interesting place to spend the day.

Sitting on the edge of pretty **Mount's Bay**, the town has a history linked to seafaring and mining. As the most western town on the mainland, Penzance has been raided repeatedly. The Spanish burned the town in 1595, it was besieged again during the Civil War - by the King's army before he fled to the Scilly Isles, then visited regularly by pirates from France and the Mediterranean. Gilbert and Sullivan used the town's background as the setting for their 1879 comic opera "The Pirates of Penzance", making the town a familiar name around the world.

Penzance's seafaring history is documented at the **Maritime Museum** on Chapel St and at the **National Lighthouse Centre** on Wharf Rd. The Maritime Museum is imaginatively decked out as an 18th century man-of-war, and has many artifacts recovered from wrecks in the area. The National Lighthouse Centre has one of the world's largest collection of lighthouse equipment, and a theatre which shows a film on the dangers of this coastline (the numerous shipwrecks gave the peninsula its Cornish name - Penwith, meaning "Promontory of Blood".

The town's links to the tin mines, which once dotted the countryside, are remembered in a statue of Humphry Davy (a Penzance local who invented the miner's safety lamp to prevent methane explosions underground) which stands in front of **Market House** (1837) at the head of the main street. There is a **geological museum**, in the west wing of St. John's Hall on Alverton St, which explains the origins of the area's mineral wealth and has specimens of the relevant rocks.

Most of Penzance's older buildings, including the **Egyptian House**, date from the 19th century and are located around Chapel St, Regent Sq, and Clarence Tce. The Penzance **Library** has a collection of old Cornish books and lithographs.

Cornwall's, mostly, mild climate - wishfully billed as the "Cornish Riviera" - means there are some interesting gardens around Penzance, with sub-tropical specimens not usually found in English gardens (check at the TIC for details).

The **Tourist Information Centre** is off Wharf Rd near the train station. The **Museum and Art Gallery** are on Morrab Rd, and the **ferry** to the Isles of Scilly leaves from the end of South Pier, off Wharf Rd.

Nearby attractions include the island castle of **St. Michael's Mount**, and the villages of **Newlyn** and **Mousehole**.

At St. Michael's Mount, or the "Holy Rock", the Archangel Michael reportedly appeared to fishermen in the 5th century. Latterly it was the location of fortifications and sieges. The St Aubyn family owns the current mansion, which can be accessed via a causeway at low tide or small ferry boats at high tide.

Newlyn is a fishing village that has been a centre for open-air artists since the 1880's. Newlyn also has Britain's last salt pressing pilchard factory (open to the public), a remnant from an industry that was once a mainstay of the Cornish economy.

The delightfully named Mousehole, pronounced "Mousle", is another pretty fishing village. Dolly Pentreath, generally considered to have been the last person to speak Cornish, was buried on a hill near here in 1777.

The South West Coast Path, a 630-mile walkway (Britain's longest) from Poole to Minehead, also passes through Penzance.

Details for getting from Penzance to Land's End are on p.33.

1348 The Black Death appears for the first time. Spreading inland from the ports of Dorset, the plague rapidly reduces England's population by a third

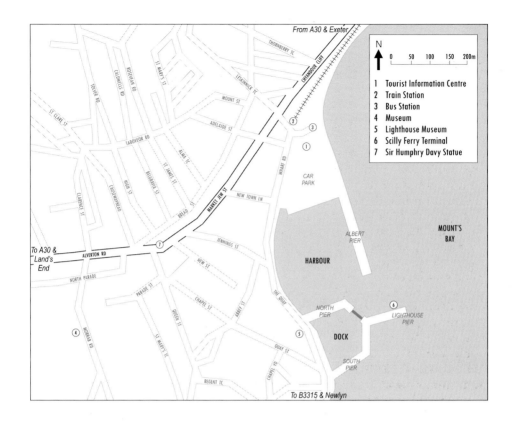

From A30 & Exeter

| N | 0 | 50 | 100 | 150 | 200m |

1 Tourist Information Centre
2 Train Station
3 Bus Station
4 Museum
5 Lighthouse Museum
6 Scilly Ferry Terminal
7 Sir Humphry Davy Statue

MOUNT'S BAY

CAR PARK

ALBERT PIER

HARBOUR

To A30 & Land's End   ALVERTON RD

NORTH PIER

LIGHTHOUSE PIER

DOCK

SOUTH PIER

To B3315 & Newlyn

◆ ◆ ◆ ◆ ◆

Camping;
Wheal Rodney Campsite, Gwallon, Marazion, (3mi E of Penzance), Ph 01736 710605, T£10 ◆ Noongallas Campsite, Gulval (2mi NE of Penzance), Ph 01736 366698, T£8 ◆ Roselands Caravan Park, St Just (6mi W of Penzance, 5mi N of Land's End), Ph 01736 788571, £9 ◆ Trevedra Farm Caravan & Camping Site, Sennen, Ph 01736 871379, T£4 ◆ Others, Penzance /Land's End area

Hostel;
YHA Penzance, Alverton, Penzance, Ph 01736 362666, Dorm£11 ◆ Penzance Backpackers, The Blue Dolphin, Alexandra Rd, Penzance, Ph 01736 363836, Dorm£10 ◆ Whitesands Lodge, Sennen, Ph 01736 871776, Dorm£11 ◆ Others; Land's End area (see p.43)

B&B;
Con Amore, 38 Morrab Rd, Penzance, Ph 01736 363423, £20pp ◆ Dunedin, Alexandra Rd, Penzance, Ph 01736 362652, S£25, D£50 ◆ Carnson House, 2 East Tce, Penzance, Ph 01736 365589, S£20, D£40 ◆ Coth'a Noweth, Catchall, Buryas Bridge, (~½way between Penzance and Land's End on A30), Ph 01736 810572, S£17, D£30 ◆ Homefields Guest House, Mayon,

Sennen, 01736 871418, £19pp ◆ Others, Penzance/Land's End area (see p.43)

Hotel;
The Queens Hotel, The Promenade, Penzance, Ph 01736 362371, S£55, D£110 ◆ Union Hotel, Chapel St, Penzance, Ph 01736 362319, S£37, D£65 ◆ Old Manor Hotel, Sennen, Ph 01736 871280, £25pp ◆ Land's End Hotel, Land's End, Ph 01736 871844, S£65, D£110 ◆ Others; Penzance/Land's End area (see p.43)

i;
TIC, Station Rd, Penzance, Ph 01736 362207

Bike Shops;
The Cycle Centre, Bread St, Penzance, Ph 01736 351671 ◆ Geoff's Bikes, Victoria Pl, Penzance, Ph 01736 363665

1 LAND'S END TO ST. AGNES

Land's End to;

			134300	25000
St Just	5.8mi	c, h, b&b, hotel, bike shop	137100	31400
St Ives	19.5mi	c, h, b&b, hotel, i, bike shop	151700	40400
Hayle	25.5mi	c, b&b, bike shop	155900	37600
Portreath	34.8mi	b&b, hotel	165800	45300
St Agnes	42.6mi	c, b&b, hotel, i	172100	51500

By mid-morning Land's End is usually crowded, or on weekends crammed, with visitors. The southwest tip of England is unashamedly a tourist centre, with souvenir shops, Punch and Judy shows, even a multi-media theatre. There's a fishing trawler and rescue lifeboat on display, that make you appreciate the folk who venture out into these seas, and of course the famous signpost pointing to John O' Groats. Despite the clutter, the most impressive feature of Land's End remains the sheer granite cliffs that drop off into the Atlantic. Battered by the sea and cut by vertical joints, the outcrops have names like Dr Syntax's Head, The Irish Lady, and The Armed Knight.

It's possible, with a short walk, to leave the hubbub behind and find a quiet spot on the cliffs to survey the view before starting the journey northward. The group of rocks 1½ miles off-shore includes Longships Lighthouse. Seven miles off is Wolf Rock Lighthouse, and 25 miles distant, invisible except on clear days, are the Isles of Scilly.

Leaving Land's End follow the A30 for 3 miles, past Sennen with its 13th century church, to the old whitewashed stone marker at the intersection with B3306. Traffic thins after the A30 and fields stretch away in front. Like many B roads in Britain, the route is narrow and stone-walled, and by necessity, cars are generally courteous.

The route passes through St Just, Botallack, and Pendeen - villages that were once the centre of west Cornwall's mining industry. Tin and copper, have been mined here since pre-Roman times. In the 19th century there were hundreds of mines in Cornwall and Devon working to produce a large portion of the world's tin and copper. The discovery of cheaper ores in the Americas, Spain, and Australia put the brakes on Cornish mining, although a few mines still remain, hovering between profit and loss depending on the price of tin. Piles of slag and ruined engine houses with tall chimneys are the most visible reminders of the old industry. These buildings once housed huge steam pumps, used to dewater and ventilate the mines. Museums at Pendeen and Zennor have displays showing the history and hardships of the miners.

The gently rolling B3306, for the most part, traverses a tussock-covered hillside that slopes off to the sea. The route passes diminutive villages, with granite cottages built right to the edge of the narrow road - presumably with people eating and sleeping on the other side of these walls as cars pass a foot or two away.

St Ives is a quintessential English seaside town. A steep descent drops you to a curved promenade lined with hotels. Fishing boats loll behind a seawall. Ice cream, cockles and whelks are on sale, and a rocky headland - The Island - separates the town from Porthmeor, a popular surf beach. The town's back alleys are charming too; crooked and cobbled with small houses squeezed into corners and low doors under stairways. St Ives has a pilchard fishing and mining background, but is known now for its local artists. In 1993 an arm of the Tate Gallery opened here.

After St Ives the A3074 and B3301 lead to Hayle, a port and commercial centre that once produced steam engines for the mines and smelted the ore for export.

Leaving Hayle's suburbs the route follows a line of dunes, or "towans", to Gwithian where the hedge-lined road passes dramatic cliffs overlooking bays with names like

*1403 20,000 die in a battle between Henry IV and Harry
"Hotspur" Percy. Percy is impaled on a spear between
millstones, then cut up and sent to each corner of Britain*

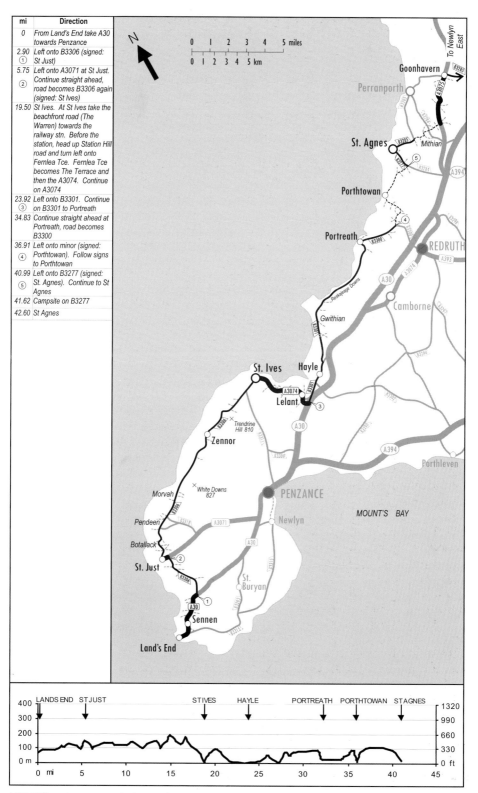

1477 William Caxton prints the first book in England; "The Dictes or Sayengis of the Philosophres"

Hell's Mouth and Deadman's Cove. It's easy to imagine these remote coves linked to the local legends of folks luring smugglers onto the rocks with lanterns, then looting the wreckage. Smuggling was one of Cornwall's biggest industries and seems to have peaked in the 18th century, when government tariffs on luxury imported goods such as tobacco, perfume, and brandy meant huge profits could be made. This pretty clifftop stretch, known as Reskajeage Downs, is now under the control of the National Trust.

A steep switchback leads down to Portreath, giving good views of the village below with its narrow harbour. The jetty here was constructed to offload coal and timber for the mines and load tin and copper ore. Materials were loaded into wagons, which were raised and lowered up the cliff on an inclined rail line, pulled by a cable from a stationary engine, and the system was technically Cornwall's first railway.

The route takes B3300 out of Portreath before following minor roads through Porthtowan to St Agnes. St Agnes is another old mining town, with numerous ruins spotting the landscape and a good museum. It's worth a walk up St Agnes Beacon (¾mi W of town) to view the cliffs stretching from St Ives to Padstow, Brown Willy (the high point of Bodmin Moor), and even St Michael's Mount back in Penzance.

End to End

The name "Land's End" has a romantic quality and travelling from here to John O' Groats has long held a fascination for cyclists - in fact all kinds of travellers, who like the idea of taking the road as far as it goes on mainland Britain (despite the fact that Lizard is further south, and Dunnet Head is further north).

The first two known "End to End" cyclists were a pair of policemen from Leeds, who made the trip in 1882 on penny-farthings, during the cycling boom that occurred soon after working bicycles first appeared. Without the benefit of bridges or high quality roads the trip, of close to 900 miles, took 14 days.

Within a few years the challenge, either for personal reasons or to promote a particular bicycle manufacturer, was to see how fast the journey could be made, and in July 1886 19-year-old G.P. Mills - from the Anfield Bicycle Club - rode his 52-inch wheeled penny-farthing End to End in 5 days, 1 hour, and 45 minutes (a record that still stands). A minor craze for record riding developed, and in 1888 the UK Road Record Association (the RRA) was founded with the aim of standardising and authenticating these efforts. As bridges were built and roads improved, the route became shorter and smoother, but times to beat became dramatically faster. The RRA currently recognises record attempts over various distances from 25 to 1000 miles, and various routes e.g. London to Cardiff, York to Edinburgh, and of course End to End.

In 1990 Andy Wilkinson, known as the "Iron Man" of British long distance cycling, rode from the south door of the Land's End Hotel to the front door of John O' Groats Hotel in the outstanding time of 1 day, 21 hours, 2 minutes, and 18 seconds - a record that remained unbeaten for more than 10 years.

2001 was a banner year for British cycling records. At 8:00am on September 26, 32-year-old Lynee Taylor (already holder of the mixed-tandem End to End record with Wilkinson), set out from Land's End to break the womens solo record - which she did in 2 days, 5 hours, 48 minutes, and 21 seconds. At 10:00am the next day Gethin Butler, a 33-year-old time trialist and racer, set off to break the mens record. Three hours into his attempt he was in Launceston, benefiting from a strong tail-wind, and after 6 hours he was at Taunton (day 5 on this tour) averaging 24 miles an hour. By 4:00am the next morning, after 18 hours in the saddle, he was near his home in Preston, and by the end of his first day he had cycled 509 miles (breaking the UK 24-hour record - a feat his grandfather once achieved). He reached John O' Groats in 1 day, 20 hours, 4 minutes, and 19 seconds - then decided to continue cycling for another 160 miles, in laps to Thurso, to break the 1000-mile record (setting a new time for this distance of 2 days, 7 hours, 53 minutes, and 7 seconds).

For most, the trip is not about speed but the journey itself, and many do it for charity. In addition to cyclists, the locals along the way have seen plenty of other End to Enders over the years; walking, running, driving, as well as the more bizarre - people running backwards, riding unicycles, and on motorised bar-stools and toilets.

Camping;
Lower Numphra Farm (¾mi S of St Just), Ph 01736 788699, T£4pp ◆ Ayr Holiday Park, Ayr Tce, St Ives, Ph 01736 795855, T£7-11 ◆ Beachside Holiday Park, Hayle, Ph 01736 753080, T£10 ◆ Cambrose Touring Park, Portreath Rd, Cambrose (1½mi E of Portreath on B3300), Ph 01209 890747, T£10 ◆ Presingoll Farm, Penwinnick Rd, St Agnes, Ph 01872 552333, T£4pp ◆ Others; St Just, Hayle, Nancekuke, St Agnes

Hostel;
Whitesand's Lodge, Sennen, Ph 01736 871776, Dorm£10 ◆ Land's End YHA, Letcha Vean, St Just (access via Kelynack Farm, ½mi S of St Just), Ph 01736 788437, Dorm£10 (also camping) ◆ Old Chapel Backpackers, Zennor, Ph 01736 798307, Dorm£10 ◆ St Ives Backpackers, St Ives, Ph 01736 799444, Dorm£12 ◆ Others; St Just, St Ives, Perranporth (3.5mi N of St Ives on B3285)

B&B;
Boswedden House, (1mi W of St Just), Ph 01736 788733, S£25, D£50 ◆ Anchorage Guest House, 5 Bunkers Hill, St Ives, Ph 01736 797135, S£20, D£50

◆ The Portreath Arms, Portreath (see Hotel) ◆ Elm Farm, Nancekuke (between Portreath & Porthtowan), Ph 01209 891498, £17pp (also camping) ◆ Beach Cottage, Quay Rd, St Agnes, Ph 01872 553802, £25pp (no single nights in August) ◆ Others; St Ives, Hayle, St Agnes

Hotel;
Western Hotel, Royal Sq, St Ives, Ph 01736 795277, S£27, D£54 ◆ The Portreath Arms, Portreath, Ph 1209 842259, £20pp ◆ St Agnes Hotel, Churchtown, St Agnes, Ph 01872 552307, S£30, D£55 ◆ The Driftwood Spars, Trevaunance Cove, St Agnes, Ph 01872 552428, £34pp ◆ Others; St Ives, St Agnes

i;
St Ives TIC, Street-an-Pol, Ph 01736 796297 ◆ St Agnes Tourist Info. Line, Ph 01872 554150

Bike Shops;
Land's End YHA, St Just (see Hostel) ◆ Richardson's Cycles, St Ives, Ph 01480 463127 ◆ Hayle Cycles, 36 Penpol Tce, Hayle, Ph 01736 753825

0mi Land's End

25mi Lelant

1554 Britain reconciles with Rome. Within a year persecution of Protestants begins

43

2 ST. AGNES TO CAMELFORD

St. Agnes to;

Goonhavern	5.4mi	c, b&b	*178800 53700*
St Columb Major	18.4mi	c	*191300 63500*
Camelford	40.4mi	c, b&b, hotel, i	*210500 83500*

Soon after St Agnes the tour leaves B3285 and takes minor roads through the village of Mithian to connect with the A3075. The route rejoins B3285 at Goonhavern, heading past the "World in Miniature", before connecting with minor roads to Newlyn East, St Columb Major, and Nanstallon. There are no information centres or bike shops along this route to Camelford, however the nearby centres of Newquay and Wadebridge - detours to the west - have a full range of services.

Newlyn East is a small village with a large, sadly dilapidated, old church. About a mile past here the road passes the Lappa Valley Steam Railway. This track opened in 1849 to run silver-bearing lead ore from the East Wheal Rose Mine, about 1½ miles south of here, to ships at Newquay. The line closed in 1963, but this segment was restored in 1974 and now runs tourists to the old mine from mid-spring to mid-autumn. The introduction of rail in the 19th century gave Cornwall a much-needed boost after wool prices, which had previously made the county quite well off, plummeted.

Between Newlyn East and St Columb Major the tour follows narrow minor roads. In places cars touch the hedgerows on both sides of the road and it pays to find a farm gate to stand in when traffic approaches.

St Columb Major was founded in 1332 when Edward II gave permission for a weekly market (a seat in the main street, unveiled in 1983 by the then Duke and Duchess of Cornwall - Charles & Di, marks the town's 650th anniversary).

After St Columb Major the tour rolls along, mostly on minor roads, with some short but steep climbs, to Nanstallon. The little hill on the left on the way into Nanstallon was the site of a Roman fort built around AD50, overlooking the River Camel, then abandoned 30 years later. The Camel is one of Cornwall's longest rivers, flowing from Bodmin Moor 30 miles inland, and is popular for sea trout and salmon fishing. A walking, cycling, and riding path (The Camel Trail) has been created along an old rail line next to the river, for 11 miles, from Padstow to Poley's Bridge. [An alternative route to Camelford from the one shown here, is to take The Camel Trail (unsealed) to Poley's Bridge, then follow the minor roads at the edge of Bodmin Moor to Camelford. Local information centres can provide details on this route].

At Nanstallon the route crosses the Camel and heads up a particularly steep hill, through the tiny settlement of Boscarne, to the A389 (the turnoff at Nanstallon to Boscarne is easy to miss - look for the sign "Boscarne 0.75, Wadebridge 6"). After Boscarne cross the A389 and join B3266, which follows pleasant, gently rolling, countryside to Camelford.

Camelford sits beside the River Camel in the shadow of Bodmin Moor. From the information centre, which incorporates a museum and art galley, you can get a trail map and take a walk up onto the moor. According to local legend, although non-locals will disagree, Camelford was King Arthur's Camelot and Slaughterbridge, 1½ miles north, is the spot where Arthur was killed battling his evil nephew Modred (a granite slab is said to mark his grave). Just west of Slaughterbridge, on Old Station Rd near the intersection of B3314/B3266, is the British Cycling Museum (one of several cycling museums in Britain), with bikes and cycling memorabilia dating from 1818.

Granite and slate have historically been the two most important building materials

1563 A quarter of Londoners die of the plague

mi	Directions
0	At St Agnes Right onto B3285 (signed: Perranporth)
0.96 ①	Left onto minor (signed: Mithian)
1.42 ②	Left onto minor (signed: Perranporth 2.75, Truro 7.5)
1.57	Right onto minor (signed: Truro 7.25), Continue 0.15mi then Left onto B3284 (signed: Perranporth)
1.72 ③	Right onto minor (signed: Penhallow). Continue straight ahead on minor (crosses B3284)
2.95 ④	Left onto A3075
5.35 ⑤	At Goonhavern take B3285 (signed: Bodmin)
7.53 ⑥	Left onto minor just before A30 (signed: Fiddlers Gn. 1)
8.82	Veer Right onto minor (signed: Newland E 0.75). Go str. through Newland East. Left onto "The Butts" (signed: Trerice 2, Lane 2.5). Follow signs to Lappa Valley Railway. Continue straight ahead (signed: Mitchell, St Columb 7)
11.35 ⑦	Right onto minor (signed: St Columb 6). Cont. str. following St Columb signs
16.92	Veer Right on minor (signed: St Columb Major)
17.09 ⑧	Right onto A3059 (signed: Wadebridge (A39) 9), Continue 0.18mi then hard Left at round about onto minor (signed: St Columb)
18.37	Veer Left at Northern end of St Columb Major (Do not take St Mawgan road), Continue str. ahead under A39 (signed: Wadebridge)
18.96 ⑨	Right onto minor (signed: St Wren 3.5)
19.56 ⑩	Right onto B3274 (unsigned)
20.85 ⑪	Straight ahead onto minor (signed: St Wren 1.5). Follow signs for Bodmin
24.35 ⑫	Left onto minor (signed: Bodmin 4.5, Ruthern 2)
25.51 ⑬	Left onto minor at cross roads (signed: Ruthern)
25.85 ⑭	Veer Right onto minor at traffic island (signed: Nanstallon). Continue str.
27.37 ⑮	Sharp Left onto minor (signed: Boscarne 0.75, Wadebridge 6). Road immediately crosses river
29.12 ⑯	Left onto A389 (signed: Wadebridge 4.5), then immediate Right onto B3266 (signed: Camelford)
38.86	Right onto A39 (signed: Camelford 1)
40.39	Camelford

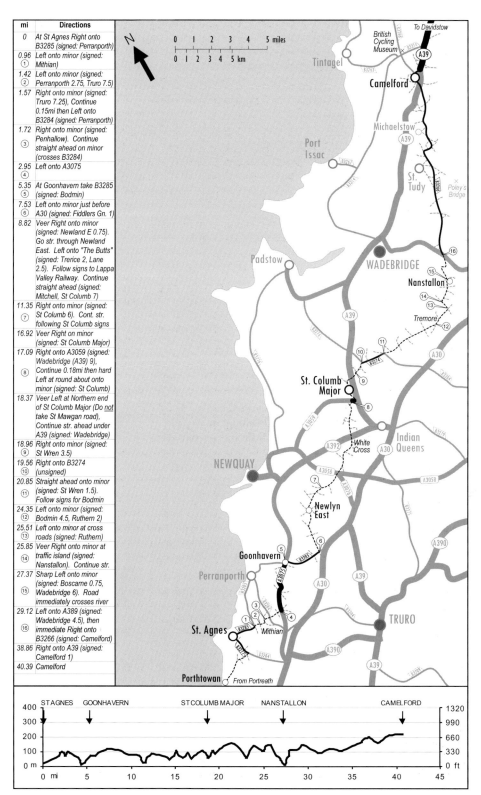

1577 Francis Drake leaves England, with the Golden Hind and 4 other ships, on a circumnavigation

in Cornwall, as seen in the many stone cottages with slate hung windows and doors. Delabole, a couple of miles west of Camelford, has the deepest slate quarry in England. The owners run tours, and there is a viewing platform overlooking the huge hole that has been producing slate continuously since the 14th century.

Celtic Cornwall and King Arthur

Whether or not Camelford was the location of Arthur's Camelot, if Camelot ever existed, will never be known. But the legend itself says something about Celtic Briton's hopes for a leader in the turbulent times after Roman rule. In the Dark Ages of the 5th century until the 7th century, when a king was first installed over a united England, Cornwall was part of the Celtic kingdom known as Dumnonia.

The Celts had themselves invaded southern Britain, around 800BC, and when they got here the land was already inhabited. Small groups of hunters and fishermen had settled as early as 6000BC. They were followed, 2000 years later, by stone tool using Neolithic tribes including a mysterious people known as the Beaker Folk (due to the shape of their pottery) who were responsible for many of southern England's great megaliths.

In Cornwall, the earliest settlers seem to have lived between Land's End and St Ives from about 2500BC, and were joined later by the Beakers. When the Bronze Age arrived, around 1500BC, Cornish tin became a valuable commodity (bronze is an alloy of copper and tin) and an international trade developed, bringing merchants and new ideas into the area. Farming advanced around this time and at Gwithian the early use of ploughs is preserved in prehistoric furrows in the sandy soils.

At the start of the Iron Age (~700BC), when the ability to heat and forge this more common metal (the most abundant in the Earth's crust after aluminium), was developing, the Celts started arriving. Three main migrations occurred, spanning 500BC to 50BC, and an extensive fort-building programme was undertaken in Cornwall. By Roman times Cornwall was a major centre in Celtic Britain.

When Roman control ended it was a chance for Celtic culture to reassert itself, although other influences were also starting to take an interest in the island. An influx of Christian missionaries was embraced by the Celts, their crosses still dot the Cornish landscape. Other invaders had war-like intentions. Angle, Saxon, and Jute tribes arrived from northwest Germany - the first Saxons actually being invited as mercenaries against the Picts and Scots, before they turned on their Celtic hosts. In the south, the Britons of Dumnonia held out the longest against these new invaders.

This is where legend and the poorly recorded history of the Dark Ages start to blend. According to legend Arthur won a major victory against the Saxons at Mons Badonicus, in the first few decades of the 6th century - although no one knows exactly where that was. According to the oral history of the Dumnonia Celts, a great warring leader did rise up against the Saxons in the south and was victorious in halting their advance. What is known is that it was another 500 years before Cornish Celts truly acknowledged a Saxon overlord. [This isolation meant the Celtic dialect of Cornish survived until the last speaker, Dolly Pentreath of Mousehole, died in 1777 and the last person to grow up understanding the language, John Davey of Zennor, died in 1891].

Tintagel, on the coast 5 miles northwest of Camelford has been proposed as the birthplace of Arthur. The 12th century author Geoffrey of Monmouth compiled a fanciful "History of the Kings of Britain" which tells of King Uther Pendragon lusting after the beautiful wife of the Duke of Cornwall. While the Duke was away the enchanter Merlin transformed Uther into the Duke's likeness and an unholy union at Tintagel produced Arthur. Today, most of the ruins are 13th century but excavations do reveal pottery common to the 5th century and Tintagel's location, on a precipitous headland with a narrow land bridge, would have made it an excellent seat of power.

There are plenty of other locations in Cornwall associated with the legend of Arthur, and his knights' quest for the Holy Grail. In one version Arthur was given the sword *Excalibur* at Dozmary Pool, a remote spot on Bodmin Moor, by the Lady of the Lake (on his deathbed, as the sword was thrown back into the lake an arm rose up to catch it, brandishing the sword before disappearing). A granite slab known as "Table-men" near Sennen church is the spot Arthur reportedly rested after a battle with the Danes so fierce that the local waterwheel ran with blood. Between Sennen Cove and the Scilly Isles the Arthurian land of Lyonesse is said to be 40 fathoms down, and Arthur is rumoured to have roamed near the hill-fort of Castle-an-Dinas, 3km southeast of St Columb Major.

If Arthur was a great warrior, the Celts embellished him into an even greater king and he now has legendary links to places all across the country.

Camping;
Perran Springs Touring Park, Goonhavern, Ph 01872 540568, T£11 ◆ Trewan Hall Camp Site, St Columb Major, Ph 01637 880261, T£10 ◆ Juliot's Well Holiday Park, Camelford, Ph 01840 213302, T£10 ◆ Others; Goonhavern, Newquay, Wadebridge, Camelford

Hostel;
Nearest; Newquay, Tintagel

B&B;
Tremor, Halt Rd, Goonhavern, Ph 01872 571287, £15pp ◆ The Old Manse, Victoria Rd, Camelford, Ph 01840 211066, £18pp ◆ Others; Camelford,

Newquay, Wadebridge, St Tudy

Hotel;
The Countryman Hotel, Victoria Rd, Camelford, Ph 01840 212250, £20pp ◆ Others; Camelford, Newquay, Wadebridge

i;
North Cornwall Museum, The Clease, Camelford, Ph 01840 212954 ◆ Others; Newquay, Wadebridge

Bike Shops;
Nearest; Newquay, Wadebridge

50mi Just before Goonhavern

75mi On B3266 to Camelford

1594 Bad weather causes poor harvests over the next 4 years, resulting in inflation and famine

3   CAMELFORD TO OKEHAMPTON

Camelford to;

Launceston	17.1mi	c, b&b, hotel, i, bike shop	*233100 84700*
Lifton	20.7mi	hotel	*238600 85100*
Okehampton	37.1mi	c, h, b&b, hotel, i, bike shop	*258800 95200*

Follow the busy A39 north from Camelford for about 3 miles, then take the A395 past the tiny villages of Davidstow and Hallworthy (there is a campground at Davidstow). About 2 miles past Hallworthy the route diverts onto minor roads through pretty countryside. About 13 miles from Camelford is Egloskerry - another diminutive rural village. Egloskerry has pretty cottages and a 15th century church, although a 19th century "restoration" has obscured much of the original building. A 2½ mile detour northeast from here is North Petherwin, and the Tamar Otter Sanctuary. Many English school children are familiar with these loveable creatures thanks to Tarka the Otter, in Henry Williamson's classic book by the same name. The sanctuary cares for injured otters (unfortunately, many are run over) and has a breeding programme that re-introduces Eurasian otters into the wild. Otter numbers are on the increase in Britain, after a decline in the 1950's and 60's that some link to the increased use of pesticides.

Launceston is dominated by the ruins of its 11th century castle, perched on a conical hill overlooking the town. The town was the ancient capital of Cornwall and hill-top fortifications were first built by the Celts. The existing structure was started by the Saxons and used by King Harold, before being added to considerably by Brian de Bretagne - the first Norman Earl of Cornwall. It then passed into the hands of Robert de Mortain, William the Conqueror's half brother and Duke of Cornwall (the castle is technically still owned by the Duchy of Cornwall). You can enter the castle walls through the north or south gates, and look at the ruins of the kitchen and administration building for free. There is a small charge to cross the moat and climb the old keep - which was never breached.

Other notable buildings in Launceston include the churches of St Mary Magdalene and St Thomas the Apostle. St Mary's is built on a site chosen by the Black Prince, and has retained its 14th century tower. The chapel walls are 16th century carved granite (stones originally destined for the church benefactor's new manor, until a death in the family made him reconsider). St Thomas' is located next to the ruins of a priory that were discovered in 1886 during railway construction (the priory was founded in 1126, but destroyed in the 16th century when Henry VIII dissolved all monasteries). The church has an impressive stone font (reportedly from the priory), a porch with a "leper squint" where the unclean could watch from, and a graveyard where the castle's deceased prisoners were buried. Slate plaques mark other interesting sites around town and the TIC has a town tour map (No. 5 Southgate St, for example, was home to Philip King, 3rd Governor of NSW, Australia). Leave town through Southgate Arch - the one remaining arch from 3 originals - and cross the River Tamar into Devon.

The road climbs in fits and spurts before dropping into Okehampton, another southern English town that changed character after the Normans invaded. This was a small Saxon settlement till the new Norman Sheriff of Devon arrived, built a castle, and moved the town next to it to establish a market. The town grew nicely until the local landlord crossed purposes with Henry VIII, resulting in the castle being wrecked.

Okehampton is on the edge of Dartmoor National Park, the largest undeveloped area in southern England. There is good walking up on the moor, including the remains of an Iron Age fort near East Hill - although check routes with the tourist

1605 Guy Fawkes is caught with 36 barrels of gunpowder under the House of Lords in a conspiracy to blow up James I and Parliament

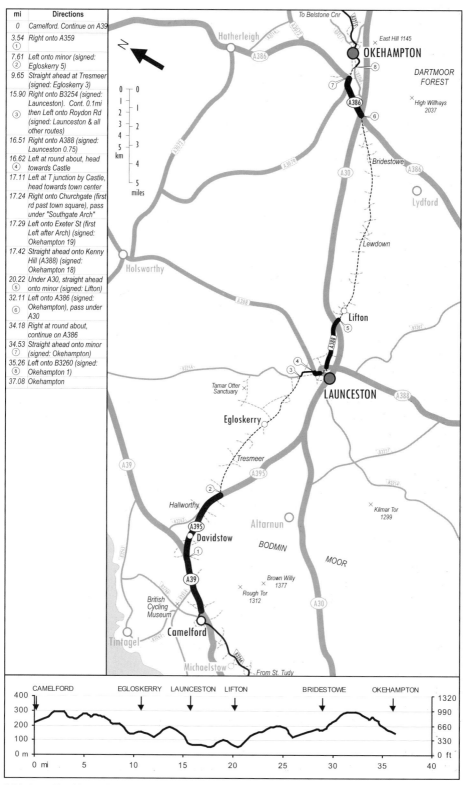

mi	Directions
0	Camelford. Continue on A39
3.54 ①	Right onto A359
7.61 ②	Left onto minor (signed: Egloskerry 5)
9.65	Straight ahead at Tresmeer (signed: Egloskerry 3)
15.90 ③	Right onto B3254 (signed: Launceston). Cont. 0.1mi then Left onto Roydon Rd (signed: Launceston & all other routes)
16.51	Right onto A388 (signed: Launceston 0.75)
16.62 ④	Left at round about, head towards Castle
17.11	Left at T junction by Castle, head towards town center
17.24	Right onto Churchgate (first rd past town square), pass under "Southgate Arch"
17.29	Left onto Exeter St (first Left after Arch) (signed: Okehampton 19)
17.42	Straight ahead onto Kenny Hill (A388) (signed: Okehampton 18)
20.22 ⑤	Under A30, straight ahead onto minor (signed: Lifton)
32.11 ⑥	Left onto A386 (signed: Okehampton), pass under A30
34.18	Right at round about, continue on A386
34.53 ⑦	Straight ahead onto minor (signed: Okehampton)
35.26 ⑧	Left onto B3260 (signed: Okehampton 1)
37.08	Okehampton

1611 James I's Bible is published after 50 scholars spend 7 years translating "as consonant as can be to the original Hebrew and Greek"

centre, as there is also an airforce bombing range nearby. The name Dartmoor is inextricably linked with Dartmoor Prison, a bleak establishment holding about 650 inmates at Princetown in the middle of the moor. Built in 1809 to hold French prisoners during the Napoleonic wars, by 1812 it was also housing American prisoners from their War of Independence. Appalling treatment and poor conditions at Dartmoor led to the deaths of 1,500 inmates in just 4 years from 1812 to 1816. An inquiry was eventually held and the prison closed, before being reopened in 1850 as a civilian prison. It currently holds about 700 prisoners.

Britain's Geology

In broad terms, Britain's rocks tend to be younger and softer in the southeast, and older and harder in the northwest (e.g. the extensive 115 million-year-old chalks of southern England vs. the 2,000 million-year-old gneisses of the Outer Hebrides). This is a result of the more recent, vigorous, geologic events along England's southern edge.

Cornwall's oldest rocks are relatively young geologically speaking - predominantly slates, grits, and limestones from the Devonian period (400 million years ago). The origins of these rocks are linked to events millions of years earlier, when, according to the Theory of Plate Tectonics, pieces of Britain were deep in the Southern Hemisphere, moving imperceptibly northward as if on a giant conveyor belt. According to Plate Tectonics, pieces of continental and oceanic crust jostle and scrape against each other as they slowly slide over the molten mantle. The oceanic plates, which are made up of basalt, are continually being added to at spreading centres along the world's mid-ocean ridges. New crust is generated at submarine volcanoes along the crests of these ridges and spreads out on either side. The continental crust is made up mostly of granite and is thicker (about 25 miles vs. 5 miles for oceanic crust) but lighter, so these pieces effectively float higher in the mantle. Most of the Earth's tectonic activity occurs along the edges of these plates as they slip past, or get squashed into, each other.

540 million years ago England and Wales were on the Northern European Plate, while Scotland was truly independent on the Canadian Plate - a completely different landmass. An ancient sea known as the Iapetus Ocean separated the two pieces. Volcanoes around the edges of this ocean resulted in the igneous highlands of the Lake District and Snowdonia. 500 million years ago the Iapetus started shrinking, and 80 million years later, as the ocean closed, Scotland and England collided and were welded together - the collision pushing up Scotland's Central Highlands. As parts of Scotland went up, much of England - Cornwall included - went down, under another sea that acted as a bathtub for the deposition of sediment and vegetation, materials that eventually formed limestones, slates, and coal measures.

Back at the mid-ocean ridges, new plate material was still being generated and with nowhere to go the Canadian Plate began bulldozing Northern Europe, with the latter, for the most part, heading underground (a portion of ocean floor did get scraped off before disappearing; these are the unusual and beautiful grey-green serpentines of the Lizard Peninsula - rocks streaked with hornblende, and the green mineral olivine). As this plate got pushed into the Earth's mantle it melted, with some of the molten rock rising. This material formed the Cornubian Batholith; molten magma squeezed upward into the existing rocks below Cornwall and Devon about 280 Million years ago - left to slowly cool in an insulated environment just below the surface. This slow cooling allowed the characteristically large crystals of granite time to grow - clear quartz, pink and white alkali feldspars with distinctive cracks along their cleavage planes, plagioclase feldspars, and the platy mica crystals of biotite (black) and muscovite (white). The intrusion gave Cornwall its backbone of granitic highlands, including Wendron Moor (near Redruth), the St Austell granite, and Bodmin Moor.

1611 William Shakespeare retires from play writing and returns to Stratford

There were economic benefits from this slow-baking igneous intrusion. Contact metamorphism resulted in soft rocks around the edges being heated into slates, and, hot, metal bearing, fluids being pushed upwards from the magma and depositing dissolved metals in fissures. These veins contain combinations of tin, copper, lead, and zinc, which are still mined today. The most important mineral for Cornwall has been Cassiterite, an oxide of tin, which has been mined here for thousands of years.

By the time Cornwall's granites had formed, Britain was in the middle of the super-continent Pangaea, a landmass consisting of all the land and covering half the globe.

200 million years before present, Britain was still land-locked, and close enough to the equator for a sandy desert, dotted with salt lakes, to develop over most of the country (as evidenced by orange sandstones common across Britain and the salt deposits of Cheshire and Yorkshire). 50 million years later, Pangea had broken into Laurasia (the northern continents) and Gondwanaland (the southern continents), and Britain was mostly underwater again. Only Cornwall, Wales, and Scotland survived as islands.

The last 150 million years have seen seas rise and fall over Britain, dinosaurs disappear, and the North Atlantic open up after a line of volcanoes unzipped Scotland from America and Greenland.

Britain and France were still well connected half a million years ago, by a chalk plateau from Dover to Gap Griz Nez. A glacial ice sheet extended from Scandanavia, across the North Sea, to the Norfolk coast at this time. At its southern edge was a huge lake into which the Thames and the rivers of northern Europe drained. Eventually, and catastrophically, the soft chalk on the east side of this lake gave way, with the resulting torrent scouring out the English Channel.

Camping;
Inny Vale Holiday Village, Davidstow, Ph 01840 261248, T£7 ◆ Chapmanswell Caravan Park, St Giles on the Heath, Launceston, Ph 01409 211382, T£10 ◆ Yertiz Campground, Exeter Rd, Okehampton, Ph 01837 52281, T£7 ◆ Others; Bridestowe, Okehampton *(see Hostel)*

Hostel;
Okehampton YHA, Klondyke Rd, Okehampton, Ph 01837 53916, Dorm£12 *(also Camping)*

B&B;
Tyne Wells House, Pennygillam, Launceston, Ph 01566 775810, S£20, D£36 ◆ Tinhay Mill Resturant, Lifton, Ph 01566 784201, S£39, D£60 ◆ Meadowlea, 65 Station Rd, Okehampton, Ph 01837 53200, S£20, D£40 ◆ Heathfield House, Klondyke Rd, Okehampton, Ph 01837 54211, S£35, D£50 ◆

Others; Launceston, Okehampton

Hotel;
Eagle House, Castle St, Launceston, Ph 01566 772036, S£25, D£50 ◆ Lifton Hall Country House Hotel, New Rd, Lifton, Ph 01566 784863, S£50, D£80 ◆ White Hart Hotel, Fore St, Okehampton, Ph 01837 52730, S£35, D£50 ◆ Others; Launceston, Lifton, Okehampton

i;
TIC, Market St, Launceston, Ph 01566 772321 ◆ TIC, 3 West St, Okehampton, Ph 01837 53020

Bike Shops;
John Towl 2-Wheel Centre, Newport Ind. Estate, Launceston, Ph 01566 774220 ◆ Okehampton Cycles, Bostock Garden Centre, North Rd, Okehampton, Ph 01837 53248

100mi Near Launceston

1620 The Pilgrims sail for New England

4 OKEHAMPTON TO WELLINGTON

Okehampton to;

Bow	10.0mi	*272100 101800*
Crediton	17.0mi b&b, i, bike shop	*283300 100600*
Wellington	43.0mi b&b, hotel, i, bike shop	*313900 120500*

Leave Okehampton by continuing up the main street (which used to be the main road to Cornwall, and hideously busy, before the A30 bypass was built), turning left onto Northfield St, then right onto Crediton Rd.

The road climbs Appledore Hill and passes through Belstone Corner, then rolls through Bow, which has a cheese factory thoughtfully built into a 19th century thatched cottage, and Coleford, a pretty little village with agricultural roots and whitewashed houses.

Continuing on the minor roads shown here bypasses Crediton, a commercial town of about 6,500, although Crediton does have an interesting history. At one time the town was bigger than Exeter, due to a thriving market charter, unfortunately a series of disastrous fires set the town back. The worst one was on a Sunday in August 1743, when the whole High St burned in 10 hours - 16 people died and 2,000 were left homeless. Crediton was also the birthplace of St Boniface, a famous missionary in the 8th century (a chapel in town keeps one of his bones in a silver box).

Thorverton is a quiet village with a stream running through a pretty town garden. Things may change here though - an Irish company, Minmet PLC, has been drilling at Thorverton Quarry with an eye to opening a gold and silver mining operation. The company is focusing on 250 million-year-old basalts, contained in an east-west trending slice of rocks referred to as the Crediton Trough. The basalt has veins, formed by the migration of hot, metal bearing water, which give the rock gold concentrations of up to 7 grams per ton - enough to make them economically viable.

After Thorverton the route crosses a weir over the River Exe and starts climbing. There is a steep hill out of Bradninich - a dilapidated, tough looking town lined with long grass (apparently unchanged since 1850, when William White described it as "a decayed borough and market town" in his Devonshire Directory).

At Cullompton the tour joins B3181 and starts one last gradual climb before Wellington. Cullompton is another market town, this one on the River Culm, which flows down off the Blackdown Hills. Textiles were the town's stock and trade in the 18th century and tourists can visit a restored cloth and paper mill by the river.

From Uffculme, continue via the minor roads shown to Wellington [Note: take the high road out of Uffculme - if you drop below the town and end up crossing the River Clum, you've gone the wrong way]. The route passes Five Fords Farm before climbing out of the Culm Valley, crossing the M5 and descending into Wellington.

Wellington is a sizeable town of about 10,000, which has been in existence since at least the 9th century, and latterly lent its name to Arthur Wellesley, Napoleon's nemesis at Waterloo, who became the Duke of Wellington and eventually Prime Minister.

The Duke of Wellington
On his death in September 1852 Queen Victoria described the Duke of Wellington as "the greatest man this country ever produced". Not bad for an Irish born lad with little interest in school and whose parents had to buy a commission in the Army - to give "poor Arthur" something to do.

Born in 1769, Arthur Wellesley rose to become the "Iron Duke", victorious

1626 England is at war with both France and Spain

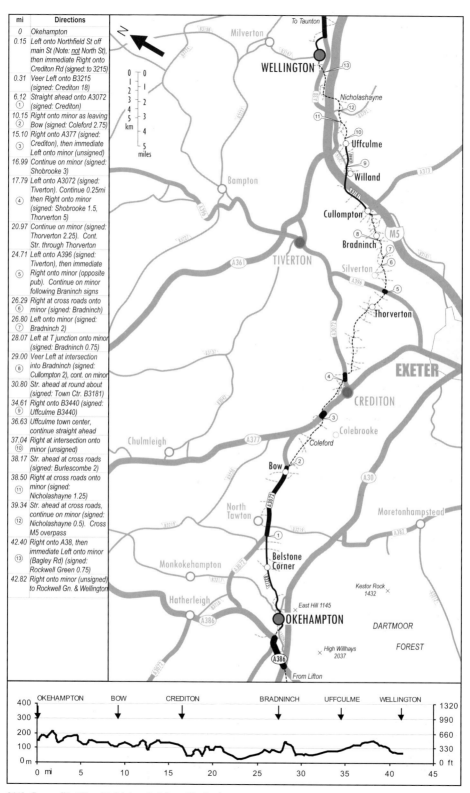

mi	Directions
0	Okehampton
0.15	Left onto Northfield St off main St (Note: *not* North St), then immediate Right onto Crediton Rd (signed: to 3215)
0.31	Veer Left onto B3215 (signed: Crediton 18)
6.12 ①	Straight ahead onto A3072 (signed: Crediton)
10.15 ②	Right onto minor as leaving Bow (signed: Coleford 2.75)
15.10 ③	Right onto A377 (signed: Crediton), then immediate Left onto minor (unsigned)
16.99	Continue on minor (signed: Shobrooke 3)
17.79 ④	Left onto A3072 (signed: Tiverton). Continue 0.25mi then Right onto minor (signed: Shobrooke 1.5, Thorverton 5)
20.97	Continue on minor (signed: Thorverton 2.25). Cont. Str. through Thorverton
24.71 ⑤	Left onto A396 (signed: Tiverton), then immediate Right onto minor (opposite pub). Continue on minor following Braninch signs
26.29 ⑥	Right at cross roads onto minor (signed: Bradninch)
26.80 ⑦	Left onto minor (signed: Bradninch 2)
28.07	Left at T junction onto minor (signed: Bradninch 0.75)
29.00 ⑧	Veer Left at intersection into Bradninch (signed: Cullompton 2), cont. on minor
30.80	Str. ahead at round about (signed: Town Ctr. B3181)
34.61 ⑨	Right onto B3440 (signed: Uffculme B3440)
36.63	Uffculme town center, continue straight ahead
37.04 ⑩	Right at intersection onto minor (unsigned)
38.17	Str. ahead at cross roads (signed: Burlescombe 2)
38.50 ⑪	Right at cross roads onto minor (signed: Nicholashayne 1.25)
39.34 ⑫	Str. ahead at cross roads, continue on minor (signed: Nicholashayne 0.5). Cross M5 overpass
42.40 ⑬	Right onto A38, then immediate Left onto minor (Bagley Rd) (signed: Rockwell Green 0.75)
42.82	Right onto minor (unsigned) to Rockwell Gn. & Wellington

1645 Cromwell's "New Model Army" defeats Charles I at Naseby

commander of the British Army and Prime Minister of Britain and Ireland. In war he was a hero, but during periods of his political career he was hugely unpopular - regularly receiving death threats, and having mobs break the windows of his home.

As the son of the Earl of Mornington he had a privileged upbringing, attending Eton and, ironically, a French military school before joining the infantry. After a brief stint back in Ireland, where he proposed to and was rejected by Catherine Pakenham, daughter of an Irish Baron, he headed off on tours of duty that covered battlefields from Europe to Asia.

Eight years after his French training, Wellesley was fighting against France's expansion into Holland. After his Dutch sortie, he was sent to India to put down native rebellions. His leadership in India impressed his commanders to the extent that he was made local governor for the areas he subjugated (the fact that his brother was Governor-General of India, would not have hurt his career). After eight years on the sub-continent he returned home, now Sir Wellesley, and entered politics as a Tory Member of Parliament for Sussex. He also reversed the rebuff from Catherine Pakenham, marrying her in 1806 (although during the ceremony he reportedly got cold feet, saying, "She has grown ugly by jove"). He then spent a couple of years in Ireland as Irish Secretary, and the family had two sons.

Although an MP, he remained in the Army, where his exploits included leading a brief attack on the Danes to capture their navy at Copenhagen. By 1808 Napoleon's grip over Europe was tightening and Wellesley was sent south to fight the French in Portugal - where he pushed Napoleon's Army back to Spain. After years of fighting, the French were eventually squeezed back into France and by 1814 Napoleon had abdicated, Louis XVIII was crowned King, and Wellesley was a hero in Portugal and Spain. At home, Wellesley was made a Duke and chose the name Wellington, although no one is quite sure why (he had an estate nearby but is thought to have visited it only once). He was also was given £500,000 cash and made ambassador to France.

Unfortunately for Wellington, Napoleon managed to escape from the island of Elba, and return for a final showdown at Waterloo in June 1815. Just south of Brussels, Napoleon's forces of 105,000 faced off against Wellington and his Prussian supporters, who totalled 157,000. At a crucial moment, in a battle that could have easily gone either way, Wellington summoned all his reserves in an attempt to hold his position. At this point Bonaparte sent in his elite Imperial Guard to finish the battle. Waiting until the Guards had almost reach their line, Wellington ordered 1,500 of his men to stand and shoot. The point-blank shots stunned, then stopped, the onslaught, and in a moment of panic forced a disorderly retreat. Wellington and the Prussians advanced and Napoleon was unable to reorganise his forces - the rout was completed and Bonaparte's fate sealed; abdication and exile again. Both sides suffered terrible losses (the French over 30,000 and the British over 20,000), and Wellington is said to have wept "I hope to God that I have fought my last battle". For three years after Waterloo he remained in France, in charge of the occupying forces until Britain finally withdrew.

Wellington's later battles were political. In 1818 he returned to Parliament for a period, and in 1828 the King asked him, during a period of political turmoil, to become Prime Minister. The two big challenges facing Wellington were Catholic Emancipation and Parliamentary Reform. After threatening to resign he successfully passed the Catholic Emancipation Bill, a measure to ease tensions in his Irish homeland. His handling of Parliamentary Reform was not so astute. As farming and manufacturing became more and more mechanised, migration to cities increased, along with unemployment and political tensions. Opposition groups were calling for reform

1658 Oliver Cromwell, Lord Protector and Head of State, dies and is buried in Westminster Abbey

of a parliamentary system that elected country aristocrats based on outdated legal rights and denied many working people the vote. The Duke saw no need at all for changing the system and as a result was hissed, booed, and hit by stones in public. In the face of a possible French-style revolution Wellington's government was ousted in 1830. Wellington stayed in Parliament - still against reform and hated by the reformers - but was not present in the House in June 1832 when a Reform Act was finally passed [with this Act 20% of English adult males could now vote]. Wellington remained a political force though, and was widely respected - even being asked by the King to become Prime Minister again during a later political crisis (he declined).

Wellington died of a stroke at his favourite estate near Deal, in Kent, and was buried at St Paul's following a state funeral. A monument to Arthur Wellesley has been built a couple of miles south of Wellington on the highest point in the Blackdown Hills. The obelisk is the tallest in Europe, although a lack of funds prevented it from being crowned by a statue of Wellington. The bronze plaques around the base depicting scenes from Wellington's life are cast from French cannon captured at Waterloo.

Camping;
Forest Glade Holiday Park, Kentisbeare (5mi E of Cullompton), Ph 01404 841381, T£6 ◆ Gamlins Farm Caravan Park, Greenham (4mi W of Wellington), Ph 1823 672596, T£7 ◆ Others; Exeter

Hostel;
Nearest; Exeter

B&B;
Fircroft, George Hill, Crediton, Ph 01363 774224, S£32, D£44 ◆ Monument House, 41 High St, Wellington, Ph 01823 661484, £18pp ◆ Others; Crediton, Uffculme, Wellington

Hotel;
The Cleve Country House Hotel, Mantle St, Wellington, Ph 01823 662033, S£48, D£60 ◆ Others; Wellington, Cullompton

i;
TIC, The Old Town Hall, High St, Crediton, Ph 01363 772006 ◆ TIC, 30 Fore St, Wellington, Ph 01823 663379 ◆ Others; Exeter, Tiverton

Bike Shops;
The Bikeshed Bike Shop, Union Rd, Crediton, Ph 01363 774773 ◆ Perrys, 33 Tan Bank, Wellington, Ph 01952 244802 ◆ Others; Exeter, Wellington

125mi 1.5mi after Okehampton

150mi 2mi before Bradninch

1660 Parliament offers Charles II the throne. Cromwell's body is exhumed from Westminster Abbey and thrown in a common pit

5 WELLINGTON TO BATH

Wellington to;

Taunton	7.2mi	c, b&b, hotel, i, bike shop	*322600*	*125900*
Othery	11.3mi		*338300*	*131600*
Glastonbury	24.4mi	c, b&b, hotel, i	*349800*	*139200*
Wells	28.2mi	b&b, hotel, i, bike shop	*355000*	*146000*
Paulton	44.9mi	c, h, b&b, hotel, i, bike shop	*365000*	*156600*
Bath	53.9mi	c, h, b&b, hotel, i, bike shop	*375000*	*164800*

Leave town via B3187 and join the A38 towards Taunton. 5 miles from Wellington the A361 and A358 provide a bypass around downtown Taunton, a city of 40,000. The route passes through pretty rural countryside, and is pleasantly flat.

Between Lyng and Othery the road passes a small hill on the right known as Burrow Mump. The spot is believed to have been a fort belonging to Alfred the Great, who hid from the advancing Vikings in the undrained Somerset moors in 878. He emerged later that year to win a decisive battle on Salisbury Plain, and negotiate a treaty with the Danes at Wedmore (about 7 miles north of Street). The settlement resulted in the Vikings leaving Wessex and agreeing to stay on the other side of a line between Chester and London (known as the "Danelaw"). Alfred's skills gave his descendants the opportunity to win back more land from the Norsemen and establish themselves as the first rulers over a united England.

A couple of miles past Othery the road crosses Greylake Bridge, over King's Sedgemoor Drain - one of the many "rhines" (ditches) constructed in the area from the 14th century to drain these boggy moors into productive farmland. The last battle to be fought in England occurred on this moor a few miles west of here, when James II quashed the Duke of Monmouth's rebellion in 1685. These days reeds are planted in the rhines to support a 200-year-old wickerwork industry.

The tour turns left at a traffic island, marked by an ancient stone, on the outskirts of Glastonbury, and continues on the A39 to Wells. A detour straight ahead here takes you straight to Glastonbury and Glastonbury Abbey in the main market. The Abbey is the oldest church in England, having survived numerous invasions, wars, and ecclesiastical crises.

In the Bible, Matthew 26:27-28 says "...then he took the cup, gave thanks and offered it to them, saying, "Drink from it, all of you. This is my blood of the new covenant, which is poured out for many for the forgiveness of sins...". Romantic legend has Joseph of Arimathea bringing this cup to Glastonbury and building a church from wattle - the "Vetusta Ecclesia". The little church was supposedly added to and survived until 1184, when the whole site burnt to the ground. It was rebuilt, but became neglected after Henry VIII had the Abbot hung during the Reformation (the stones being plundered for local buildings until the 1830's).

Even if you don't detour into Glastonbury to see the Abbey, you can still see Glastonbury Tor rising in the distance, capped by the ruins of St Michael's chapel (which was destroyed by a 13th century landslide) - Joseph is said to have hidden the Holy Grail somewhere on the Tor.

Wells is another ecclesiastical town. There is an impressive cathedral here, and a good grassed area out front to rest on. The cathedral was started in the 12th century and the outside walls have perches for over 400 carved figures. The apostles are featured on the west wall, with St Andrew slightly taller than the rest due to the fact that the cathedral is dedicated to him. Inside the church is the world's second oldest

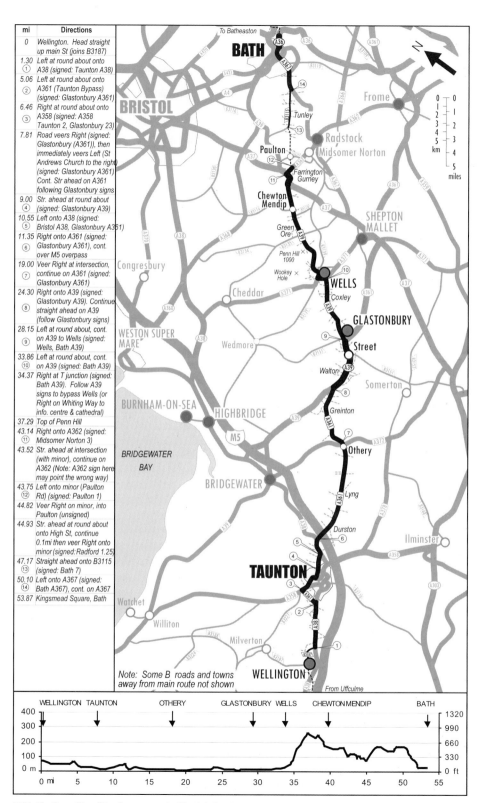

mi	Directions
0	Wellington. Head straight up main St (joins B3187)
1.30 ①	Left at round about onto A38 (signed: Taunton A38)
5.06 ②	Left at round about onto A361 (Taunton Bypass) (signed: Glastonbury A361)
6.46 ③	Right at round about onto A358 (signed: A358 Taunton 2, Glastonbury 23)
7.81	Road veers Right (signed: Glastonbury (A361)), then immediately veers Left (St Andrews Church to the right) (signed: Glastonbury A361) Cont. Str ahead on A361 following Glastonbury signs
9.00 ④	Str. ahead at round about (signed: Glastonbury A39)
10.55 ⑤	Left onto A38 (signed: Bristol A38, Glastonbury A361)
11.35 ⑥	Right onto A361 (signed: Glastonbury A361), cont. over M5 overpass
19.00 ⑦	Veer Right at intersection, continue on A361 (signed: Glastonbury A361)
24.30 ⑧	Right onto A39 (signed: Glastonbury A39). Continue straight ahead on A39 (follow Glastonbury signs)
28.15 ⑨	Left at round about, cont. on A39 to Wells (signed: Wells, Bath A39)
33.86 ⑩	Left at round about, cont. on A39 (signed: Bath A39)
34.37	Right at T junction (signed: Bath A39). Follow A39 signs to bypass Wells (or Right on Whiting Way to info. centre & cathedral)
37.29	Top of Penn Hill
43.14 ⑪	Right onto A362 (signed: Midsomer Norton 3)
43.52	Str. ahead at intersection (with minor), continue on A362 (Note: A362 sign here may point the wrong way)
43.75 ⑫	Left onto minor (Paulton Rd) (signed: Paulton 1)
44.82	Veer Right on minor, into Paulton (unsigned)
44.93	Str. ahead at round about onto High St, continue 0.1mi then veer Right onto minor (signed: Radford 1.25)
47.17 ⑬	Straight ahead onto B3115 (signed: Bath 7)
50.10 ⑭	Left onto A367 (signed: Bath A367), cont. on A367
53.87	Kingsmead Square, Bath

Note: Some B roads and towns away from main route not shown

1666 The Great Fire of London starts at the King's bakers in Pudding Lane

mechanical clock, with jousting characters that appear every 15 minutes. Next door is the Bishop of Bath and Wells' Palace, and nearby, Vicars Close - the oldest inhabited street in Europe. A tea and scone stop in Wells is a good idea as there is a serious climb out of town before the tour descends into Bath.

Continuing on the A39 out of Wells the road winds up Penn Hill towards the radio masts. The road is quite narrow, so watch for speeding traffic coming in either direction. A statue of Remus and Romulus suckling from a she-wolf marks the crest of the hill. There is a nice undulating descent from here to Paulton, then another, not so tough, climb up Tunley Hill before the route joins the busy A367. From here the grey brick expanse of Bath opens out below.

Bath is a very popular tourist town and accommodation can be hard to find. The campground in town is for campervans (RV's) only, so if you are tenting you'll need to stay on the outskirts of town at Newton Mill [turn left (west) onto Lower Bristol Rd just before the A367 crosses the River Avon into Bath. Follow this road for about a mile, then turn left onto Newton Rd - the campground is on the right about half a mile down the road]. There is a regular bus service that runs from near the Newton Mill campground into downtown Bath.

Bath is a pleasant surprise - visiting the Roman Baths is actually free (although there is a charge for the behind-the-scenes tour and museum), and in the central square, next to the Cathedral, there are excellent classical musicians busking for change. A spot Kiwis and Aussies will want to visit is Sally Lunn's original bakery (although they may be disappointed to find that their familiar cream topping is not part of the original). Other famous Bath attractions include the shop-lined Pulteney Bridge, one of Britain's first post offices, and The Circus (a 1750's set of curved apartments built in Palladian style by famous local architect John Wood the Elder).

Bath Spa

In the 18th century Bath was the place to party. Queen Anne visited in 1702, the year she was crowned, and Bath instantly became a fashionable hang-out for balls and banquets. Anne's visit may have been prompted by her poor health - she was unable to walk up the aisle at her Westminster Abbey coronation due to gout. She was met on the border of Somerset and travelled to Bath on a road specially built up the Avon Valley for the occasion.

According to legend, another royal - King Bladud, the father of King Lear - founded Bath in 863BC. A leper, Bladud had been banished to tend swines, which unfortunately also contracted the disease. When the pigs bathed in the steaming swamps next to the Avon they were healed, so Bladud followed them in and was cured as well - returning to take up the Crown.

In reality, the Romans were the first to develop these 49°C natural springs; lining them with lead and naming the place Aquae Sulis, after the fertility goddess Sulis Minerva. For the next 350 years convalescing legionnaires, and their well-off friends, frequented the baths, until they were recalled to Rome in the early 5th century.

The Saxons and Normans both built churches at the site, and royals from King Offa to King Charles II visited to "take the waters". But by the time Anne visited, the baths had become run down and largely built over. Her visit was the stimulus the town needed and over the next 100 years the rich and famous flocked to Bath. The influx in gentry spurred an impressive building programme and in 1755 the original Roman baths were rediscovered.

Like Ibiza, Cancun, and Thailand today, Bath was a trendy getaway in the 18th century. Beau Nash, the country's leading "dandy" at the time was based here and

1671 Thomas Blood, dressed as a parson, is apprehended leaving the Tower of London after stealing the Crown Jewels. He is pardoned after a meeting with the King

made a career out of over-the-top etiquette that appealed to the wealthy. Visitors could pay half a guinea for the Abbey bells to be rung as they entered town, or for invites to one of Nash's famous balls, or for entry to the private gardens by the river. Jane Austin spent time in Bath in the early 19th century, after her father retired there, and satirized the pompous social institutions of such places in her novels "Persuasion" and "Northanger Abbey".

Camping;
Broughton Park, Shoreditch, <u>Taunton</u>, Ph 01823 257144, T£10 ◆ Old Oaks Touring Park, Wick Farm, <u>Glastonbury</u>, Ph 01458 831437, T£10 ◆ Newton Mill Camping, Newton Rd, <u>Bath</u>, Ph 01225 333909, T£10 ◆ Others; <u>Taunton</u>, <u>Glastonbury</u>, Near <u>Wells</u>

Hostel;
Street YHA, Ivythorn Hill, <u>Street</u>, Ph 01629 592707, Dorm£10 ◆ Bath Backpackers, 13 Pierrepont St, <u>Bath</u>, Ph 01225 446787, Dorm£12 ◆ Bath YHA, Bathwick Hill, <u>Bath</u>, Ph 01225 465674, Dorm£11 ◆ Others; <u>Bath</u>

B&B;
Brookfield House, 16 Wellington Rd, <u>Taunton</u>, Ph 01823 272786, S£25, D£45 ◆ The Flying Dragon, 12 Hexton Rd, <u>Glastonbury</u>, Ph 01458 830321, S£22, D£44 ◆ Infield House, 36 Portway, <u>Wells</u>, Ph 01749 670989, S£31, D£42 ◆ Kinlet Guest House, 99 Wellsway, <u>Bath</u>, Ph 01225 420268, S£20, D£40 ◆ The Hollies, Hatfield Rd, <u>Bath</u>, Ph 01225 313366, S£40, D£50 ◆ Others; <u>Taunton</u>, <u>Glastonbury</u>, <u>Wells</u>, <u>Bath</u>

Hotel;
Blorenge House, 57 Staple Grove Rd, <u>Taunton</u>, Ph 01823 283005, S£27, D£45 ◆ George & Pilgrims Hotel, 1 High St, <u>Glastonbury</u>, Ph 01458 831146, S£40, D£65 ◆ Sydney Gardens, Sydney Rd, <u>Bath</u>, Ph 01225 464818, D£75 ◆ Others; <u>Taunton</u>, <u>Glastonbury</u>, <u>Wells</u>, <u>Bath</u>

i;
TIC, Paul St, <u>Taunton</u>, Ph 01823 336344 ◆ TIC, 9 High St, <u>Glastonbury</u>, Ph 01458 832954 ◆ TIC, Town Hall, Market Pl, <u>Wells</u>, Ph 01749 672552 ◆ TIC, Abbey Church Yard, <u>Bath</u>, Ph 01225 477101 ◆ Others; <u>Radstock</u>

Bike Shops;
Bikezone, 25 Bridge St, <u>Taunton</u>, Ph 01823 327006 ◆ On Your Bike, 128A High St, <u>Street</u>, Ph 01458 443048 ◆ Trevors Cycles, 49B St Cuthberts St, <u>Wells</u>, Ph 01749 670868 ◆ Avon Valley Cyclery, Bath Spa Railway Stn, Dorchester St, <u>Bath</u>, Ph 01225 461880 ◆ Others; <u>Taunton</u>, <u>Street</u>, <u>Bath</u>

175mi 1mi before Taunton

200mi Between Glastonbury and Wells

1671 The outlaw Rob Roy McGregor is born

6 BATH TO NEWENT

Bath to;

Nettleton	11.3mi	hotel	*381900 178400*
Nailsworth	26.5mi	hotel, bike shop	*385000 199400*
Stroud	30.5mi	b&b, hotel, i, bike shop	*385100 205500*
Gloucester	40.3mi	b&b, hotel, i, bike shop	*383500 218700*
Newent	49.3mi	b&b, hotel, i	*372200 225900*

Leave Bath by crossing the three-arched Pulteney Bridge. The bridge is one of only a handful in the world that are lined with shops, and was built in 1773 for rich local Frances Pulteney, to connect Bath with her 600 acre estate across the Avon. The bridge suffered a partial collapse during flooding in 1800 but was rebuilt and survived to become a national monument in 1936. At the end of Great Pulteney St the road forks around fine Georgian buildings onto Beckford Road and continues as Warminster Rd. About a mile down Warminster Rd, Bathampton Lane splits off to the left. Continue on Bathampton Lane, which becomes High St, before turning left down Mill Lane and crossing the Avon on a series of low bridges (the last one has a toll for cars, but bikes are free). Turning right at the junction of Toll Bridge Rd and London Rd West takes you to Batheaston and Fosse Lane, where there is a tough climb up "The Mount" to Banner Down and the Roman route known as Fosse Way.

This was once a major Roman highway connecting Exeter (known as Dumnoniorum) and Lincoln (Lindum), with Bath (Aquae Sulis) as a stop en-route. The road was paved, remarkably straight over long distances, and dotted at intervals by Roman villas, forts, and temples. Unfortunately much of the route was later plundered for stone, with the locals hoarding the antiquities they found while digging. The best-preserved piece of the Fosse is a 4-mile stretch near Hinckley (90 miles northwest of Bath).

The present road, flanked by wheat fields, rolls gently along towards Nettleton, passing a lean-to of ancient rocks known as "Three Shire Stones" on the left, and the runways and radio masts of Colerne airfield on the right.

Around Acton Turnville a number of old barns have been modified into subdued but affluent homes, many with expensive looking horses in the front paddock. The area is a centre for horse breeding and signs point to nearby Badminton Estate, where a prestigious 3-day horse-trailing event has been held since 1949 (although the March 2001 event was cancelled, due to the Foot and Mouth Disease outbreak).

The route continues on quiet roads through the pretty villages of Luckington, Sopworth, and Leighterton. The countryside all along this stretch is dotted with the tumuli (earth burial mounds, also called "tumps" or "barrows") of the Neolithic people that lived in the Cotswolds for thousands of years before the Romans arrived. The Long Barrow, just west of Leighterton is a particularly good example - about 300 feet long with a false entrance and three burial chambers.

Past the duck pond at Leighterton the route joins the busy A46 northward. There is a 1 mile downhill after Nailsworth, before the road gets even busier through Stroud. After Stroud there is a steep climb over Scottsquar Hill, with good views of the Cotswold farms below, then a great downhill sweep, over the M5 into the Severn valley. The road bends around the base of Robins Wood Hill just before entering Gloucester.

Gloucester is another ancient town [the local Council has dug up the old Roman latrine, in the middle of the main street, and covered it in glass as an open-air museum]. The nearest camping to Gloucester is about halfway between here and

1688 James II is forced to leave for France, throwing the Great Seal of England in the Thames as he departs

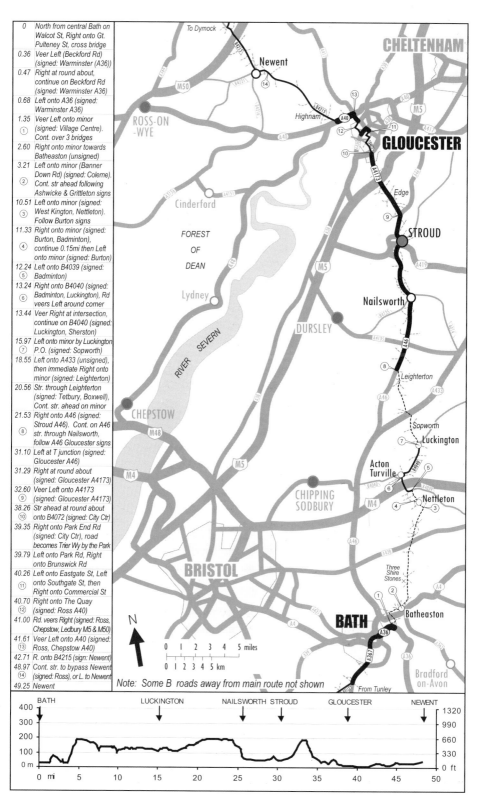

0	North from central Bath on Walcot St, Right onto Gt. Pulteney St, cross bridge
0.36	Veer Left (Beckford Rd) (signed: Warminster (A36))
0.47	Right at round about, continue on Beckford Rd (signed: Warminster A36)
0.68	Left onto A36 (signed: Warminster A36)
1.35 ①	Veer Left onto minor (signed: Village Centre). Cont. over 3 bridges
2.60	Right onto minor towards Batheaston (unsigned)
3.21 ②	Left onto minor (Banner Down Rd) (signed: Colerne). Cont. str ahead following Ashwicke & Grittleton signs
10.51 ③	Left onto minor (signed: West Kington, Nettleton). Follow Burton signs
11.33 ④	Right onto minor (signed: Burton, Badminton), continue 0.15mi then Left onto minor (signed: Burton)
12.24 ⑤	Left onto B4039 (signed: Badminton)
13.24 ⑥	Right onto B4040 (signed: Badminton, Luckington), Rd veers Left around corner
13.44	Veer Right at intersection, continue on B4040 (signed: Luckington, Sherston)
15.97 ⑦	Left onto minor by Luckington P.O. (signed: Sopworth)
18.55	Left onto A433 (unsigned), then immediate Right onto minor (signed: Leighterton)
20.56	Str. through Leighterton (signed: Tetbury, Boxwell), Cont. str ahead on minor
21.53 ⑧	Right onto A46 (signed: Stroud A46). Cont. on A46 str. through Nailsworth, follow A46 Gloucester signs
31.10	Left at T junction (signed: Gloucester A46)
31.29	Right at round about (signed: Gloucester A4173)
32.60 ⑨	Veer Left onto A4173 (signed: Gloucester A4173)
38.26 ⑩	Str ahead at round about onto B4072 (signed: City Ctr)
39.35	Right onto Park End Rd (signed: City Ctr), road becomes Trier Wy by the Park
39.79	Left onto Park Rd, Right onto Brunswick Rd
40.26 ⑪	Left onto Eastgate St, Left onto Southgate St, then Right onto Commercial St
40.70 ⑫	Right onto The Quay (signed: Ross A40)
41.00	Rd. veers Right (signed: Ross, Chepstow, Ledbury M5 & M50)
41.61 ⑬	Veer Left onto A40 (signed: Ross, Chepstow A40)
42.71	R. onto B4215 (sign: Newent)
48.97 ⑭	Cont. str. to bypass Newent (signed: Ross), or L. to newent
49.25	Newent

Note: Some B roads away from main route not shown

N

0 1 2 3 4 5 miles
0 1 2 3 4 5 km

(Elevation profile)

BATH LUCKINGTON NAILSWORTH STROUD GLOUCESTER NEWENT

400 1320
300 990
200 660
100 330
0 m 0 ft

0 mi 5 10 15 20 25 30 35 40 45 50

1694 The Bank of England is founded

Newent (a local farm that offers camping in a back paddock). To get to Newent follow the busy A40 west out of Gloucester to B4215. A short distance south of Newent, on a minor road west of B4216, is the National Birds of Prey Centre, which has over 80 species of these birds and offers tours and falconry displays.

The gate to the aforementioned camping area is on the right, beside a monument marking the site of a 1643 battle. For more formal accommodation stay in Gloucester or Newent.

England and Football

Every town and almost every decent sized village in England has a football field. Football, which to the English naturally means soccer - rather than rugby football, American football, or some other variation - is a truly English invention and is the country's most popular game in terms of the numbers of players and spectators. It is effectively the nation's national sport.

There was a soccer-like game being played in China before the time of Christ, and ball sports in ancient Greece and Rome that consisted of kicking and throwing, but it was the English who perfected the version played around the world today.

Some have tried to trace the roots of the English game to medieval hordes kicking the head of a defeated Danish raider around, but the basics of the game had probably arrived even earlier - with the Romans in AD43. Regardless, by the Middle Ages a game was being played in England (and Europe where they were called mêlées) involving an inflated animal bladder and two highly motivated teams. The goal was to get the ball to the opponent's end of town, and both mobs played the game with a passion, few - or flexible - rules, and often violent or fatal results. To the authorities the sport was seen as a dangerous distraction from the more important pastimes of military training and religious duties, and starting in 1389, when Richard II banned "mob football" which was wasting his archers' time, futile efforts were made to suppress or ban it.

Of course, the sport survived, with Shrove Tuesday becoming a traditional game day. In the suburbs of London, street games played on Shrove Tuesday lasted all day, with several hundred players on each side and goals at each end of the borough. There were plenty of injuries, but the game kept going.

By the 18th century a toned-down version of the mob game that prohibited handling the ball while running was being played at English schools, and further efforts to standardise the sport soon followed. Cambridge University laid down a preliminary set of rules for "football" in 1848, and by 1857 the first club had formed in Sheffield. Six years later, on October 26 1863, representatives from Sheffield and 10 other clubs met at London's Freemason Tavern to lay down uniform rules and form the Football Association (FA), although the new rules did not stipulate the length of the game or the number of players on each team. By 1871 it had become apparent that the two most popular styles of play (a version originating at Rugby School, in Warwickshire, that encouraged running with the ball, versus a style that emphasised use of the feet) could never be united, and the FA hardened its rules against handling the ball. [The Rugby Football Union (RFU) formed that same year and held its first rugby international between England and Scotland]. The first official FA international, England vs. Scotland, was held on November 30 1872 in Glasgow.

The game developed rapidly in the late 19th century, with the addition of a cross-bar to the goal in 1875 and the development of a professional league in 1888. In 1901 attendance for a game exceeded 100,000 for the first time. Soon, soccer was an international sport with (starting in 1930) a World Cup Tournament every 4 years.

England's finest moment in international soccer came in 1966 when they got to

1700 Britain's population is about 6½ million

host the World Cup Tournament. Rated as underdogs, in a competition Brazil had won on the previous two occasions, they survived the early rounds then defeated Argentina and Portugal to make the final. Led by Bobby Moore they faced West Germany at Wembley Stadium in front of a crowd of 97,000 that included the Queen. In the last minute of regulation time West Germany scored an equaliser, to level the game at 2-2 and send the match into over-time. Ten minutes later England scored a controversial goal (some claiming the ball never crossed the line), then sealed the victory in the closing minutes when Geoff Hurst scored his third goal to make the score to 4-2. One of the players that day was Sir Bobby Charlton - probably England's most famous footballer.

Camping;
The Red Lion Caravan Park, Norton (5mi N of Gloucester), Ph 01452 730251, T£10 ◆ Haywood Farm Camping Park, Gorsley (3mi W of Newent), Ph 01989 720453, T£7 ◆ Newton Mill Camping Park, Nr. Newent, Ph 01989 720453, T£5 ◆ Others; Stonehouse (3mi W of Stroud), Near Cheltenham

Hostel;
Nearest; Slimbridge (7mi W of Stroud)

B&B;
The Crown Inn Inchbrook, Stroud, Ph 01453 832914, S£30, D£45 ◆ Alston Field Guest House, 88 Stroud Rd, Gloucester, Ph 01452 529170, S£18, D£36 ◆ Sandyway Countryside, Redmarley Rd, Newent, Ph 01531 820693, S£20, D£40 ◆ Others; Newent, Nailsworth, Gloucester

Hotel;
Fosse Farmhouse Country Hotel, Nettleton, Ph 01249 782286, S£55, D£85 ◆ Egypt Mill Hotel, Nailsworth, Ph 01453 833449, S£50, D£75 ◆ The George Hotel, Church St, Newent, Ph 01531 820203, S£22, D£32 ◆ New Country Hotel, 44 Southgate St, Gloucester, Ph 01452 307000, S£60, D£70 ◆ Others; Nailsworth, Stroud, Gloucester

i;
TIC, George St, Stroud, Ph 01453 760960 ◆ TIC, 28 Southgate St, Gloucester, Ph 01452 421188 ◆ TIC, 7 Church St, Newent, Ph 01531 822468

Bike Shops;
The Cycle Clinic, Bath Rd, Nailsworth, Ph 01453 835200 ◆ Cytek, 59 Westward Rd, Stroud, Ph 01453 753330 ◆ Discount Cycles, 24A Hatherley Rd, Gloucester, Ph 01452 381699 ◆ Others; Gloucester

225mi Pultney Bridge leaving Bath

250mi 6mi before Stroud

1712 Thomas Newcomen invents "an engine for raising water with a power made by fire" (an atmospheric stream engine)

7 NEWENT TO TENBURY WELLS

Newent to;

Ledbury	8.0mi	b&b, hotel, i, bike shop	*371100 237700*
Bromyard	20.5mi	b&b, hotel, i	*365300 254700*
Tenbury Wells	31.8mi	c, b&b, hotel, i	*359500 268000*

After Newent the route continues north, through fields of grain, over the M50, and into the county of Herefordshire. The stage gradually climbs, in fits and spurts, into the low hills around Bromyard, then finishes with a mostly downhill section for 8½ miles into Tenbury Wells.

At Dymock the route turns left by St Mary's Church, off B4215 and onto B4216. The church is open daily and has a display dedicated to the Dymock Poets, a group who frequented the area before the Great War. Two "Poets Paths" leave from the churchyard and take in local spots associated with the poets (the church has leaflets). This area is also famous for the wild daffodils that bloom every spring in the fields and woods around the town.

The first town of any size is Ledbury, mentioned in the Doomsday Book as "Ledeberge". The town is centred around its 16th century Market House, which sits on sixteen chestnut stilts and still hosts markets twice a week. Ledbury also has a 12th century church (St Michael's) with Norman windows, and has retained many of its black and white Tudor buildings, including Feathers Hotel (1570) which was a coach inn on the old Royal Mail route between Cheltenham and Aberystwth (on the Welsh coast). Other notable buildings include the tourist information centre in a 16th century half-timbered house near Market House, and a fine bakery in the main which sells traditional buns, rolls and cakes (there is a bike shop opposite the bakery).

Leaving Ledbury, B4214 crosses the route of the old Hereford to Gloucester canal, a system that once linked Newent, Dymock, and Ledbury, before being abandoned during the rail boom of the late 19th century and being partially built over by the Great Western Railway Company. Sections of this canal are now being restored by a group of local enthusiasts.

The tour passes through the villages of Castle Frome and Bishop's Frome, then Bromyard. The rich farmland in this part of Herefordshire is famous for its ability to produce cattle and hops (a widow from Bishop's Frome - whose grandfather, Farmer Pudge, was a local hops grower - died recently and left a £47,000,000 trust fund for local improvements).

Bromyard is a busy town of about 3,500, with a good café at the leisure centre in the main street and a combined tourist information centre and heritage centre nearby. The last 11 miles to Tenbury Wells include a moderate uphill for a couple of miles after Bromyard, then a gradual decent as the route enters Shropshire just past the tiny village of Collington.

Tenbury Wells sits by the Teme River (according to some Britain's prettiest river) on the border of Shropshire and Worcestershire. In 1839 a mineral spring was discovered here and the town briefly became a spa resort. The town is a pleasant mix of newer brick buildings and crooked old half-timbered houses. For about £25 you can sleep under the blackened beams of the 16th century coaching inn.

A local bicycle maker in Tenbury Wells, T.J. Cycles, builds frames here with a unique rear end configuration called the "Flying Gate". For the last few years the company has also run an annual Flying Gate weekend, where riders of these peculiar bikes get together and do local rides.

1720 Investors recklessly speculating on the South Sea Company are ruined

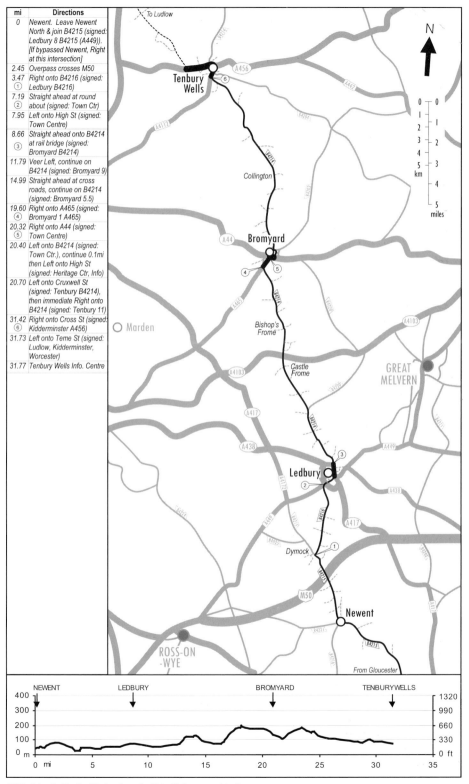

mi	Directions
0	Newent. Leave Newent North & join B4215 (signed: Ledbury 8 B4215 (A449)). [If bypassed Newent, Right at this intersection]
2.45	Overpass crosses M50
3.47 ①	Right onto B4216 (signed: Ledbury B4216)
7.19 ②	Straight ahead at round about (signed: Town Ctr)
7.95	Left onto High St (signed: Town Centre)
8.66 ③	Straight ahead onto B4214 at rail bridge (signed: Bromyard B4214)
11.79	Veer Left, continue on B4214 (signed: Bromyard 9)
14.99	Straight ahead at cross roads, continue on B4214 (signed: Bromyard 5.5)
19.60 ④	Right onto A465 (signed: Bromyard 1 A465)
20.32 ⑤	Right onto A44 (signed: Town Centre)
20.40	Left onto B4214 (signed: Town Ctr.), continue 0.1mi then Left onto High St (signed: Heritage Ctr, Info)
20.70	Left onto Cruxwell St (signed: Tenbury B4214), then immediate Right onto B4214 (signed: Tenbury 11)
31.42 ⑥	Right onto Cross St (signed: Kidderminster A456)
31.73	Left onto Teme St (signed: Ludlow, Kidderminster, Worcester)
31.77	Tenbury Wells Info. Centre

To Ludlow

Tenbury Wells

N

0 — 0
1
1
2
3 — 2
4
5 — 3
km
— 4
— 5
miles

Collington

Bromyard

Marden

Bishop's Frome

Castle Frome

GREAT MELVERN

Ledbury

Dymock

Newent

M50

ROSS-ON-WYE

From Gloucester

NEWENT   LEDBURY   BROMYARD   TENBURYWELLS

400 — 1320
300 — 990
200 — 660
100 — 330
0 m — 0 ft

0 mi   5   10   15   20   25   30   35

*1729 John & Charles Wesley form the Holy Club, to worship &
help the needy, while attending Oxford. Their adherence to
the Book of Prayer earns them the nickname "Methodists"*

65

The Dymock Poets

In 1914, as the full horrors of the first World War were unfolding, Dean Ange of St Paul's Cathedral read a stirring poem by a young soldier on the way to front lines in Gallipoli.

> If I should die, think only this of me:
> That there's some corner of a foreign field
> That is forever England. There shall be
> In that rich earth a richer dust concealed...
>
> *from "The Soldier", R. Brooke (1887-1915)*

The author was by Rupert Brooke, one of the six poets who lived in, or visited, the peaceful Cotswold village of Dymock in the years before WWI, who became known the Dymock Poets. Brooke was not a complete unknown before this poem, he had previously published two volumes of poetry, was Cambridge educated (being part of the "Bloomsbury Set" with Virginia Woolf, EM Forster, TS Elliot and others), and was described as "the most handsome man in England" by WB Yeats, but his death, soon after Dean Ange's St Paul's address, drew national attention. Brooke did not die on the battlefield, but on a Navy ship - from blood poisoning due to an infected mosquito bite. The patriotic sentiment of the poem and the timing of his death lead to Brooke becoming known as a war poet, although most of his verse was on other subjects and he never experienced the full horrors of trench warfare, which lead to the terrifying poems of poets such as Siegfried Sasson and Winfred Owen.

The other Dymock poets were Lascelles Abercrombie, Wilfred Gibson, John Drinkwater, Robert Frost, and Edward Thomas. Abercrombie moved to Dymock in 1911, staying at The Gallows, a Tudor cottage by Ryton Wood, 2 miles east of Dymock. In 1913 Gibson, who lived in London writing poetry and editing the work of Katherine Mansfield and other prominent writers, moved into a thatched cottage in Dymock called The Nail Shop, a place that was to become a central meeting point for the Dymock Poets. [The route passes by this privately owned house]. A year later Frost, a successful American poet from the East Coast, was on a book tour with his family when Abercrombie and Gibson invited him to move into another local cottage - Little Iddens.

Thomas was a poet, critic, and close friend of Frost (he had reviewed several of Frost's books) so he started visiting the Frost's at Dymock, eventually staying at Old Fields farmhouse nearby. Drinkwater, was involved in poetry and theatre in the Midlands and moved in the same London literary circles as the others, and was also invited to visit the village, and Brooke made several visits as well.

At Dymock the poets dwelt on the beauty and peacefulness of the Costwolds, and Abercrombie and Gibson started publishing a subscription magazine called "New Numbers" with works by all 6 poets.

Prior to the war the beauty of Dymock's daffodils were the focus of a poem by Drinkwater, but by 1914 the golden times at Dymock were being overshadowed by new realities. In 1917 Gibson wrote a poem, called Daffodils, that remembers this time, lost and never to return.

Brooke was the first of the Dymock poets to be killed. He was hastily buried on the Greek island of Skyros - fitting for a man who, in 1908, had been described as "Young Apollo, golden-haired" in a friend's poem. Winston Churchill wrote Brooke's obituary in The Times, including the words; "A voice had become audible, a note had been struck, more true, more thrilling, more able to do justice to the nobility of our youth engaged in arms in this present war, than any other".

Edward Thomas died in the trenches of France in April 1917, while a book including his poems was in press.

Much of the Dymock Poets work has faded with time, although The Soldier remains a famous verse in England. The used bookshop in Ledbury's main street has a corner dedicated to the Dymock Poets.

Camping;
The Millpond, Little Tarrington, (5mi NE of Ledbury), Ph 01432 890243, T£7 ◆ Palmers Meadow, c/- Tenbury Town Council Offices, Teme St, Tenbury Wells, Ph 01584 810118, T£7 ◆ Knighton On Teme Caravan Park, Tenbury Wells (4mi W of Tenbury Wells), Ph 01584 781246, T£9 ◆ Others; Near Bromyard

Hostel;
Nearest; Near Great Melvern

B&B;
Wall Hills Country House, Hereford Road, Ledbury, Ph 01531 632833, S£40, D£55 ◆ Park House, 28 Sherford St, Bromyard, Ph 01885 482294, £23pp ◆ Redgate House, Bromyard Rd, Tenbury Wells, Ph 01584 810574, £17pp ◆ The White House, White House Ln, Kyrewood, Tenbury Wells, Ph 01584 810694, £21pp ◆ Others; Ledbury, Bromyard, Tenbury Wells

Hotel;
The Feathers Hotel, High St, Ledbury, Ph 01531 635266, S£72, D£95 ◆ The Falcon Hotel, 4 Broad St,

Bromyard, Ph 01885 483034, S£40, D£60 ◆ The Ship Inn, Teme St, Tenbury Wells, Ph 01584 810269, S£20 ◆ The Bridge Hotel, Teme St, Tenbury Wells, Ph 01584 810434, £20pp ◆ Others; Ledbury, Bromyard, Tenbury Wells,

i;
TIC, 3 The Homend, Ledbury, Ph 01531 636147 ◆ TIC/Heritage Centre, 1 Rowberry St, Bromyard, Ph 01885 482033 ◆ TIC, 21 Teme St, Tenbury Wells, Ph 01584 810136 (Summer only)

Bike Shops;
Saddle Bound Cycles, 3 Southend, Ledbury, Ph 01531 633433 ◆ Others; Ledbury

275mi Near Newent on B4215

300mi Between Ledbury and Bromyard

Tenbury Wells to;

Ludlow	8.5mi	c, b&b, hotel, i, bike shop	*351700 275500*
Church Stretton	23.2mi	c, b&b, hotel, i, bike shop	*345300 293700*
Shrewsbury	38.7mi	c, h, b&b, hotel, i, bike shop	*349100 312500*

Leave Tenbury Wells via the town's historic stone bridge over the River Teme (the middle of the bridge marks the Shropshire/Worcestershire county line), and turn left onto the A456. The route passes a pre-Roman earthen fort on the left, continues briefly, then turns off the A456 to take country lanes towards Ludlow. Follow the A49 bypass around Ludlow and take B4365 north, which crosses the town's race track and heads north towards Culmington [if you do want to stop in Ludlow signs point the way]. Ludlow is a very pretty town dominated by a massive sandstone castle, started by the Normans in 1085 to guard the Welsh Marches. To subdue the troublesome Welsh, William the Conqueror encouraged any baron that could, to march an army into Wales and keep the land they conquered - hence the Welsh Marches.

After Culmington the route crosses B4368 and starts up Siefton Batch, a pretty valley on a tiny minor road. The road passes grazing land, wheat fields and forest, climbing all the way. Just after Westhope the road crests a limestone ridge known as Wenlock Edge and sweeps down to Byne Brook in Ape Dale. After the tiny villages of Ticklerton and Hope Boulder the road climbs again, through a gap between Hazler Hill on the left and Helmeth Hill on the right, before dropping into Church Stretton.

There are actually three Strettons strung out along B4370, Church Stretton being the largest. The town has long attracted tourists, initially as a health spa and more recently for the good walking the area offers. The Long Mynd (Long Mountain) to the west of town has many good hikes, with numerous tumuli and pre-historic structures dotting the hillsides, including Bodbury Ring about a mile northwest of the town. Halfway up the rounded hill of Caer Caradoc, east of All Stretton, is a cave where the Celtic King Caractacus is said to have fought his last battle with the Romans in AD50.

At All Stretton the tour turns east onto a branch of the Roman Road named Watling Street by the Anglo-Saxons. This stretch of road was surveyed and constructed by the Legions to allow the rapid movement of troops, required to deal with the Celts. The road is remarkably straight and includes several fords at low points (generally dry, except during heavy rain). Roman roads were typically constructed to a high standard, with flat paving stones laid on a base of compacted gravel, and completed with kerbs and drainage ditches. Forts were stationed strategically along the road.

The terrain along this stretch is generally flat or gently downhill, making for easy cycling. Turn left off Watling Street at Frodesly and continue to Condover. The Royal National Institute for the Blind purchased the 16th century mansion here after WWII and it is now a school for the blind and deaf.

Shrewsbury is almost an island, surrounded on three sides by the River Severn and guarded by a castle on the fourth. Because of the town's proximity to Wales it has witnessed battles, sieges, and the comings and goings of numerous kings and queens. Through the turmoil the town has managed to retain a good number of its historic buildings and half-timbered houses. The town site may have been a fort for the Welsh as early as the 5th century. The Saxon Kings; Offa, Alfred, and Athelstan won lands in the area in the 8th and 9th centuries before the Normans arrived. Roger de Montgomery founded the castle in 1070 and it has been extensively added to since then.

To enter town, pass Abbey Church, also founded by Roger de Montgomery, cross

1764 James Hargreaves invents the "Spinning Jenny" to efficiently produce thread

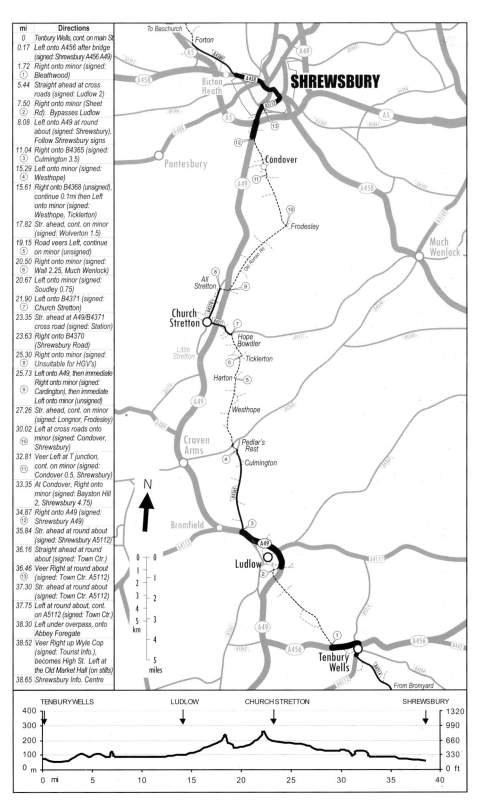

mi	Directions
0	Tenbury Wells, cont. on main St
0.17	Left onto A456 after bridge (signed: Shrewsbury A456 A49)
1.72 ①	Right onto minor (signed: Bleathwood)
5.44	Straight ahead at cross roads (signed: Ludlow 2)
7.50 ②	Right onto minor (Sheet Rd). Bypasses Ludlow
8.08	Left onto A49 at round about (signed: Shrewsbury), Follow Shrewsbury signs
11.04 ③	Right onto B4365 (signed: Culmington 3.5)
15.29 ④	Left onto minor (signed: Westhope)
15.61	Right onto B4368 (unsigned), continue 0.1mi then Left onto minor (signed: Westhope, Ticklerton)
17.82	Str. ahead, cont. on minor (signed: Wolverton 1.5)
19.15 ⑤	Road veers Left, continue on minor (unsigned)
20.50 ⑥	Right onto minor (signed: Wall 2.25, Much Wenlock)
20.67	Left onto minor (signed: Soudley 0.75)
21.90 ⑦	Left onto B4371 (signed: Church Stretton)
23.35	Str. ahead at A49/B4371 cross road (signed: Station)
23.63	Right onto B4370 (Shrewsbury Road)
25.30 ⑧	Right onto minor (signed: Unsuitable for HGV's)
25.73 ⑨	Left onto A49, then immediate Right onto minor (signed: Cardington), then immediate Left onto minor (unsigned)
27.26	Str. ahead, cont. on minor (signed: Longnor, Frodesley)
30.02 ⑩	Left at cross roads onto minor (signed: Condover, Shrewsbury)
32.81 ⑪	Veer Left at T junction, cont. on minor (signed: Condover 0.5, Shrewsbury)
33.35	At Condover, Right onto minor (signed: Bayston Hill 2, Shrewsbury 4.75)
34.87 ⑫	Right onto A49 (signed: Shrewsbury A49)
35.84	Str. ahead at round about (signed: Shrewsbury A5112)
36.16	Straight ahead at round about (signed: Town Ctr.)
36.46 ⑬	Veer Right at round about (signed: Town Ctr. A5112)
37.30	Str. ahead at round about (signed: Town Ctr. A5112)
37.75	Left at round about, cont. on A5112 (signed: Town Ctr.)
38.30	Left under overpass, onto Abbey Foregate
38.52	Veer Right up Wyle Cop (signed: Tourist Info.), becomes High St. Left at the Old Market Hall (on stilts)
38.65	Shrewsbury Info. Centre

1771 Cook sails the Endeavour back to England after discovering Australia and New Zealand

the Severn and head up Wylie Cop past the half-timbered houses. In the heart of Shrewsbury is The Square with the Old Market Hall, built on stilts in 1596 (the lower floor for grain, the upper for wool). The Tourist Information Centre is also in The Square.

To see more of Shrewsbury continue up High St onto Pride Hill, towards the castle. On the corner of Castle Hill and St Mary's St, Hotspur, the rebel son of the Earl of Northumberland, was hung, drawn, and quartered in 1403, after being killed in the Battle of Shrewsbury. St Mary's church nearby dates from 970. At the top of the hill is the castle. The museum, library, and 17th century Council House, where the Council of the Marches voted 12-4 to side with the King during the Civil War, are all nearby.

A good way to endear yourself with the locals is to casually pronounce the towns name as they do; "Shrowsbury" (as in "Shropshire"). Other interesting facts about Shrewsbury; the pop idol violinist Paganini played here in 1832, the town is famous for its Shrewsbury biscuits, and 5 miles to the east are the ruins of Wroxeter (Viroconium) the fourth largest Roman city in Britain.

The nearest campground is Oxen Touring Park, several miles out of town and a short detour off the route to Chester (directions are in the next stage on p.82). [Note: the camp requires a key deposit which cannot be regained until 8:30am the next morning when the office opens].

Civil War

In September 1642 Charles I came to Shrewsbury to assemble his army before the opening battle of the English Civil War. Trouble had been brewing since Charles' father, James Stuart, had proclaimed his "Divine Right" to govern without interference from Parliament. Charles dramatically inflamed the conflict in 1629, a few years after becoming King, by ruling without Parliament for 11 years - the "Eleven Years Tyranny". Facing a Scottish invasion and bankruptcy, he reluctantly reconvened Parliament which, unsurprisingly, refused to provide him any funds. Political and religious conflicts continued for several years until things came to a head in August 1642 when the King raised his standard at Nottingham and towns across the country were forced to take sides.

The King was not overly popular with the towns folk of Shrewsbury because of a ship-money tax he had imposed on people living in coastal and river areas to fund his navy. However the local gentry were pro-Royal, with 12 of the 16 Shropshire Members of Parliament supporting the King, so the town prepared for war. The city walls were reinforced and night watchmen sealed and guarded the town gates at night.

Charles himself arrived in Shrewsbury on September 20, with an army of about 7,000 lead by the Earl of Forth. One of his first tasks was to address the locals at a meadow on the outskirts of town (where the present football field is). The appeal was for money and recruits. Donations and promises of funds flowed (Shrewsbury school loaning several hundred pounds), and his army grew to about 14,000. The soldiers were billeted out with the locals and an emergency mint was set up in the castle where silver objects were melted into coins bearing the slogan "Let God arise, Let his enemies be scattered".

On October 12, Charles and the army (known as the "Cavaliers") marched out of Shrewsbury headed for London. The Earl of Essex mobilised a similar sized Parliamentary force (known as the "Roundheads") and the two armies met on the afternoon of October, 23 at Edgehill, near Derby. The Royal cavalry made brutal advances into the Parliamentary army, but the royal troops suffered badly in hand to hand combat. At dusk, after three hours of stalemate fighting, Essex called his forces off leaving the route to London open. Charles' army headed south but by the time

1776 James Watt installs his newly developed steam engine in several Cornish mines to pump water

they reached Reading, Essex had reinforcements and Charles was never able to capture the capital.

Civil war continued for 9 years with towns being sacked, raids, murder, and wastage by both sides. At the Battle of Naseby (1645) Parliament won a decisive victory and Charles was captured, although the fighting continued on and off until 1651. As resistance weakened, Shrewsbury Castle was also captured, with little effort, by a Parliamentary force in 1645.

Charles was executed at Whitehall on a cold morning in January 1649 - he wore two shirts because he was afraid if he shivered people would think he was scared. His decorum to the end - "subjects do not have the power to judge a king" - gained the respect of the people and was considered a propaganda victory for the Royalists. Oliver Cromwell, an MP, and commander in the Parliamentary cavalry who had risen as leader of the "New Model Army" ruled the new Commonwealth, with virtual Divine Right, until his death in 1658. Cromwell's son Richard ("Tumbledown Dick") succeeded him but was not the statesman his father was. In 1660 Parliament recalled Charles' son (Charles II) from the Netherlands, and Britain became a kingdom again.

Camping;
Sparchford Farm Camping Site, Culmington, Ludlow, Ph 01584 861222, T£7 ◆ Springbank Camping Park, 62 Shrewsbury Rd, Church Stretton, Ph 01694 723570, T£4pp ◆ Oxen Touring Park, Welshpool Rd, Shrewsbury, Ph 01743 340868, T£11 (3mi W of Shrewsbury) ◆ Severn House, Montford Bridge, Shrewsbury, Ph 01743 850229, T£5 (4mi NW of Shrewsbury) ◆ Others; Shrewsbury

Hostel;
Shrewsbury YHA, The Woodlands, Abbey Foregate, Shrewsbury, Ph 01743 360179, Dorm£10

B&B;
Number 28, 28 Lower Broad St, Ludlow, Ph 01584 876996, S£35, D£65 ◆ Sayang House, Hope Bowdler, Church Stretton, Ph 01694 723981, S£28, D£55 ◆ Jinlye Guest House, Castle Hill, All Stretton, Ph 01694 723243, S£45, D£70 ◆ College Hill Guest House, 11 College Hill, Shrewsbury, Ph 01743 365744, From £18pp ◆ Abbey Court House, 134 Abbey Foregate, Shrewsbury, Ph 01743 364416, £18pp ◆ Others; Ludlow, Church Stretton, Shrewsbury

Hotel;
Overton Grange Hotel, Hereford Rd, Ludlow, Ph 01584 873500, S£45, D£58 ◆ Longmynd Hotel, Cunnery Rd, Church Stretton, Ph 01694 722244, S£40, D£80 ◆ Sydney House Hotel, Coton Crs, Shrewsbury, Ph 01743 354681, S£38, D£50 ◆ The Castle Vaults Inn, 16 Castle Gates, Shrewsbury, Ph 01743 358807, S£30, D£49 ◆ Abbots Mead Hotel, 9 St Julian's Friars, Shrewsbury, Ph 01743 235281, S£37, D£54 ◆ Others; Ludlow, Church Stretton, Shrewsbury

i;
TIC, Castle St, Ludlow, Ph 01584 875053 ◆ TIC, Church St, Church Stretton, Ph 01694 723133 ◆ TIC, The Square, Shrewsbury, Ph 01743 281200

Bike Shops;
Climb On Bikes, 22 Bull Ring, Ludlow, Ph 01584 872173 ◆ Longmynd Cycles, Sandford Court, Sandford Ave, Church Stretton, Ph 01694 722367 ◆ Shrewsbury Cycles, 43 Ditherington Rd, Shrewsbury, Ph 01743 232061 ◆ Others; Ludlow, Shrewsbury

325mi 1mi before Westhope

1781 Britain loses control of US Territories

British beef

Land's
End
sign

Penzance

Marker on the A30 between
Penzance and Land's End

Land's End

On B3301
between Hayle
and Portreath

Sennen
church

Portreath

Wells Cathedral

Directions to the
British Cycling Museum
near Camelford

Launceston
Castle

*1793 Drunken members of the Hell Fire Club burn down St
Mary's Church in Glasgow*

1796 Poet Robert Burns dies at age 38

Statue of Remus and Romulus, Penn Hill, near Wells

County Line on the Tenbury Wells Bridge

The Ledbury Cake Shop

Bath's spring water

Chester

Roman Baths at Bath

Runcorn Bridge over the River Mersey

A cream tea

Classic phone box

Kirkstone Pass, between Windermere and Patterdale

KEY:

0mi	25mi	50mi
75mi	100mi	125mi
150mi	175mi	200mi
225mi	250mi	275mi
300mi	325mi	350mi
375mi	400mi	425mi
450mi	475mi	

1807 The British slave trade is abolished

KEY:

500mi	525mi	550mi
575mi	600mi	625mi
650mi	675mi	700mi
725mi	750mi	775mi
800mi	825mi	850mi
875mi	900mi	925mi
950mi	958mi	

1816 John MacAdam develops a durable road surface - a later version being named "tarmac" in his honour

The Royals

Country home

Fish 'n chips

Erskine Bridge over the
River Clyde

Rannoch Moor

Loch Ness Visitor
Centre,
Drumnadrochit

Highland
cattle

Urquhart Castle &
Loch Ness

Lock on The Caledonian Canal

Cycle
crossing

1818 The "dandy-horse", an expensive lightweight version
of the early bicycle, the hobby-horse, is released

*1829 At the opening ceremony for the first passenger rail
line, from Liverpool to Manchester, an MP is knocked
down and killed by Stephenson's "Rocket" engine*

Siberian Owl, Dunrobin Castle Falconry

Road sign

Dunrobin Castle, near Golspie

Sleepy man

Sutherland coastline, north of Wick

Sign at the end of the road

John O' Groats

Stacks of Duncansby, east of John O' Groats

Scapa Flow, Orkney Is.

Skara Brae, Orkney Is.

1831 A major cholera outbreak occurs, spurred by unsanitary conditions in many major cities

9 SHREWSBURY TO CHESTER

Shrewsbury to:

Ellesmere	20.0mi	b&b, hotel, i, bike shop	*340000 335000*
Farndon	35.3mi	hotel	*342000 354300*
Chester	43.9mi	h, b&b, hotel, i, bike shop	*340600 366500*

The roads leaving The Square in Shrewsbury are a bit confusing (directions are given opposite). Leaving town the tour passes Rowley's Mansion (with displays of Roman history and Shropshire geology) on Bridge St, and crosses Welsh Bridge, named sensibly because it lead to Wales. The road continues up Frankwell Rd to The Mount (the start of the A458), then joins B4380. [Oxen Touring Park Campground is reached by continuing straight on A458, towards Bicton Heath. The campground is on the left].

The tour follows flat to gently rolling country lanes to Ellesmere, passing horse studs and wheat fields. Off to the right near Little Ness is Adcote School, in a large mansion built in 1879 for a relative of Abraham Darby, a rich iron manufacturer.

The village of Baschurch consists of a garage and several shops, it was included in the Domesday Book and apparently got its name from the Church of Bassa, a 6th century Saxon chief. About a mile north of Baschurch, but not readily visible from the road, is a hill-fort site known as "The Berth", where the Saxons apparently besieged the local Celts. After Baschurch the route continues on minor roads, crossing a rail overbridge at Stanwardine in the Fields, and passing through several small villages.

Ellesmere is a lake and canal town with pleasant Georgian and timber-framed houses. There are seven lakes, or "meres", east of town (the largest is over 100 acres) that allow the locals to call the area Shropshire's Lake District. The lakes are popular for boating and fishing. The canal is the Shropshire Union, another Telford construction.

Between Ellesmere and Penley the tour briefly enters Wales - the first indication being the road signs in Penley, which are in both Welsh and English. After the village of Worthenbury, the route leaves B5069 and heads north on a minor road. The route traverses gently rolling farmland along tree lined roads, with glimpses of the industrial edge of Wrexham off to the west. After only 5 or so miles in Wales the tour is back in England, in the county of Cheshire.

Farndon has a stone bridge that, miraculously considering the border disputes, has linked England and Wales for 800 years, and is still in use. Interestingly, the town was home to John Speed, one of Britain's foremost mapmakers in the early 17th century. In 2000 the town hosted the National 24-hour Cycling Championships, with the winning trio totalling 1,235 miles (each rider logging over 400 miles).

From here the route heads directly north to Chester, paralleling the River Dee which the road briefly nears at the "Crook of Dee" just after Aldford. Chester's long history includes being a major Roman town, the last English city to fall to William the Conqueror, and during the Elizabethan era - a place for pageants and plays. Nowadays, the town brims with tourists. The TIC is on Union St. Near here is the semi-circle of a partially excavated Roman amphitheatre, discovered in 1929, and the reconstructed columns of a Roman garden. Steps at Pepper St, by the garden, lead onto the city walls - a great way to see Chester. A complete circuit takes about an hour.

The walls were started by the Romans in AD76 and have been variously added to and demolished through the ages until the present walkway was completed in Victorian times. The walls themselves carry much of Chester's history; cannonball holes, a tower in the northeast corner from which Charles I watched his troops loose the battle of Rowton Moor in 1645, a water tower in the northwest corner that has stood dry since

1838 Charles Dickens "Oliver Twist" is published

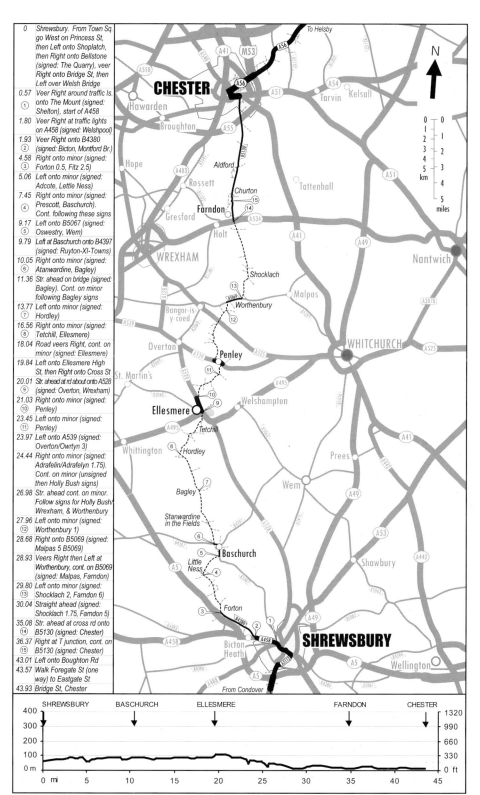

Mile	Direction
0	Shrewsbury. From Town Sq. go West on Princess St, then Left onto Shoplatch, then Right onto Bellstone (signed: The Quarry), veer Right onto Bridge St, then Left over Welsh Bridge
0.57 (1)	Veer Right around traffic Is. onto The Mount (signed: Shelton), start of A458
1.80	Veer Right at traffic lights on A458 (signed: Welshpool)
1.93 (2)	Veer Right onto B4380 (signed: Bicton, Montford Br.)
4.58 (3)	Right onto minor (signed: Forton 0.5, Fitz 2.5)
5.06	Left onto minor (signed: Adcote, Little Ness)
7.45 (4)	Right onto minor (signed: Prescott, Baschurch). Cont. following these signs
9.17 (5)	Left onto B5067 (signed: Oswestry, Wem)
9.79	Left at Baschurch onto B4397 (signed: Ruyton-XI-Towns)
10.05 (6)	Right onto minor (signed: Atanwardine, Bagley)
11.36	Str. ahead on bridge (signed: Bagley). Cont. on minor following Bagley signs
13.77 (7)	Left onto minor (signed: Hordley)
16.56 (8)	Right onto minor (signed: Tetchill, Ellesmere)
18.04	Road veers Right, cont. on minor (signed: Ellesmere)
19.84	Left onto Ellesmere High St, then Right onto Cross St
20.01 (9)	Str. ahead at rd about onto A528 (signed: Overton, Wrexham)
21.03 (10)	Right onto minor (signed: Penley)
23.45 (11)	Left onto minor (signed: Penley)
23.97	Left onto A539 (signed: Overton/Owrtyn 3)
24.44	Right onto minor (signed: Adrafelin/Adrafelyn 1.75). Cont. on minor (unsigned then Holly Bush signs)
26.98	Str. ahead cont. on minor. Follow signs for Holly Bush/ Wrexham, & Worthenbury
27.96 (12)	Left onto minor (signed: Worthenbury 1)
28.68	Right onto B5069 (signed: Malpas 5 B5069)
28.93	Veers Right then Left at Worthenbury, cont. on B5069 (signed: Malpas, Farndon)
29.80 (13)	Left onto minor (signed: Shocklach 2, Farndon 6)
30.04	Straight ahead (signed: Shocklach 1.75, Farndon 5)
35.08 (14)	Str. ahead at cross rd onto B5130 (signed: Chester)
36.37 (15)	Right at T junction, cont. on B5130 (signed: Chester)
43.01	Left onto Boughton Rd
43.57	Walk Foregate St (one way) to Eastgate St
43.93	Bridge St, Chester

1839 A Scot, Kirkpatrick Macmillan, advances bicycle design by adding pedal rods to crank the rear wheel. The bicycle can now be ridden with feet off the ground

the river silted up and moved, and a couple of breaches where Victorian rail bridges were put through (one disastrously collapsing in the 1860's). There is a set of steps in the southeast corner called The Wishing Steps. Local legend says that if you can run up, down, and back up these steps without taking a breath your wish will be granted.

Roman Britain

In AD76, 33 years after their invasion of Britain, the Romans established a camp on a low sandstone ridge - now the site of Chester - overlooking the River Dee, in order to tackle the troublesome Welsh. The camp, known as Deva (pronounced "Dewa"), grew into a walled fortress that housed over 5,000 soldiers and cavalry from the 20th Legion - named *Valeria Victrix* in honour of the wife of the invading Emperor Claudius.

The Romans had had an eye on Britain since Julius Caesar led an exploratory force to the South Coast in 55BC. He returned the following year en masse, crossing the Thames and forcing the Britons to surrender, provide hostages, and agree to payment of an annual tribute. But he left the same year before cementing his position and Britain never became part of the Roman Republic.

Britain did become a province of the new Roman Empire 97 years later when Claudius, the 4th Emperor, sent an invasion force consisting of 5 Legions and auxiliaries (totalling over 40,000 men) to Richborough, in Kent. Within a short time the southern tribes had succumbed and Claudius himself arrived, in a procession with elephants, to accept the surrender and install client kings.

The Romans stayed another 400 years but their occupation was never without resistance. In AD60 Roman officials who wanted to extend their landholdings had Boudicca, the widow of one of the client kings, flogged and her daughters raped. Her revolt lasted over a year and resulted in 70,000 Roman citizens being killed and several major cities, including Colchester and London, being burnt. At this time the Romans were also pushing into Wales in an attempt to subdue powerful Welsh tribes, such as the Silures and Ordovices, and gain control of the metal mines there. Suetonius Paulinus, the 3rd governor of Britain, led the 20th Legion from Chester to conquer North Wales, but it took 20 years before the whole of Wales was added to the province.

As Chester grew the original clay and wooden walls were replaced with stone, and the Romans effectively integrated the locals into the Empire by building major public works and offering citizenship for military service (soldiers were given a bronze citizenship plaque and a copy was sent to Rome).

The 2nd century saw the Romans consolidate their hold on the Britain, even pushing deeper into Scotland (to the Firth of Clyde) and starting another wall - although this only lasted 10 years before they were beaten back to their previous position. By the 3rd century Britain had been split into Britannia Superior and Britannia Inferior (south and north) and was being ruled by two governors, to avoid the temptation for local officials to usurp power - although this did happen on several occasions, requiring Rome to intervene.

The 4th century saw Christianity become the official religion and Britain face a major "barbarian conspiracy" with co-ordinated attacks by the Scots and Picts. As a result of this renewed threat, Chester's walls were refurbished in AD367 (a headstone from Deanery Field, the city cemetery, was uncovered in the north wall in 1883, indicating the haste with which these repairs were undertaken). The general Flavius Theodosius was dispatched from Rome to restore order, which he did with the help of his son (also named Theodosius), although the old general ended up being killed in a conspiracy. Two years later the military skills of Theodosius II were called on again to save the Emperor Gratian in Gaul. As a reward he was named Emperor of the East. When Gratian was murdered by his own troops and his 21-year-old half-brother

Valentinian II was also found dead in suspicious circumstances, Theodosius became sole Roman Emperor - the last to govern a united Empire. On his deathbed in AD395 Theodosius split the Roman world in two, giving each half to a son; Britain was included in west under Honorius, with the east going to Arcadius.

Honorius had his hands full elsewhere in his empire and in AD410, when Britain appealed for help against Pict and Saxon attacks, he directed Britons to "defend themselves", effectively ending Rome's control of the Province. A generation later Rome itself fell to the Ostrogoths, and Britain along with the other western provinces was reduced to a collection of warring kingdoms (the eastern provinces endured for another 1,000 years as the Byzantine Empire until the Ottoman conquest of 1453).

By the early 5th century the Legionaries had deserted Chester, although today traces are occasionally unearthed, e.g. a lead water pipe found under Eastgate in 1899 was stamped with the name of Julius Agricola, governor of the Province in AD79.

Hostel;
Chester YHA, 40 Hough Green, Chester, Ph 01244 680056, Dorm£11 ◆ Chester Backpackers, 67 Boughton, Chester, Ph 01244 400185, Dorm£13

B&B;
Mereside Farm, Ellesmere, Ph 01691 622404, S£25, D£40 ◆ Derry Raghan Guest House, 54 Hoole Rd, Chester, Ph 01244 318740, S£22, D£42 ◆ Others; Ellesmere, Chester

Hotel;
Black Lion Hotel, Scotland St, Ellesmere, Ph 01691 622418, £25pp ◆ Greyhound Hotel, High St, Farndon, Ph 01829 270244, S£30, D£40 ◆ Dene Hotel, 95 Hoole Rd, Chester, Ph 01244 321165, S£47, D£60 ◆ Others; Ellesmere, Farndon, Chester

i;
TIC, The Mere, Ellesmere, Ph 01691 622981 ◆ TIC, Northgate St, Chester, Ph 01244 402111

Bike Shops;
Butler Cycles, 37 Scotland St, Ellesmere, Ph 01691 622101 ◆ Action Bikes, 104 Northgate St, Chester, Ph 01244 310077 ◆ Others; Chester

350mi 2mi after Shrewsbury

375mi Between Penley and Worthenbury

1844 A potato famine in Ireland causes many Irish to emigrate to England

10 CHESTER TO CROSTON

Chester to;

Prescot	24.0mi	hotel, bike shop	*347100 392600*
Up Holland	34.0mi	hotel	*351900 405300*
Eccleston	43.8mi	b&b	*352000 417000*
Croston	46.1mi	c, hotel	*350300 418900*

This stage passes through England's industrial heartland, squeezing between the sprawling manufacturing centres of Liverpool and Manchester. Traffic is heavy through this area and cyclists require extra vigilance.

The A56 leaves Chester's suburbs and rolls through pleasant fields with the power plant stacks of Ellesmere Port away in the distance. After Frodsham, the route enters Halton County and joins the busy A557 to Runcorn. The A557 carries a lot of commercial traffic and feels like a motorway, although it does at least have a wide shoulder to ride on. The pale green Runcorn Bridge forms a frenetic arterial route over the Manchester Ship Canal and the murky Mersey River. You can brave the left-hand lane or take the pedestrian walkway on the east side of the bridge.

The rail bridge, next to Runcorn Bridge, was built first (in 1868). This bridge, which included a footpath, drastically reduced the ferry traffic across the Mersey. Then, in 1905, an impressive Transporter bridge was opened for road traffic. The Transporter consisted of a gantry with a moving trolley high above the river. A platform, called "the car", hung below the trolley near ground level and was used to carry traffic back and forth. This bridge was cheaper than a full suspension bridge and allowed tall ships to pass below. Unfortunately, the system was slow and the car was subject to alarming swinging in high winds. Eventually, in 1961, the Transporter was replaced by the present Runcorn Bridge and demolished.

On the other side of the river, at Widnes, the A557 passes chemical plants and car wreckers, before joining the quieter A57 at a roundabout over the M62 in Merseyside. Widnes has a long history as a chemical producing area. During the second half of the 19th century an alkali industry was established in the West Bank area, following the perfection of the Leblanc process [which turned table salt (sodium chloride) into the soda ash (sodium carbonate) required to make soap and glass]. Canal barges and rail lines brought salt from Cheshire and coal from Lancashire, for processing at Widnes' factories. Unfortunately, the factories also produced thousands of tons of toxic waste, which were disposed of into the air, on land, and in the river. Legislation, first introduced in the 1860's, gradually curtailed this dumping and the environment has now recovered significantly. In 1926 an amalgamation of 4 of the largest local companies resulted in the formation of Imperial Chemical Industries Ltd (ICI), which eventually became the UK's biggest chemical producer. The Catalyst Museum on the West Bank ("the only museum in Europe solely devoted to the chemical industry") has more information on the history of local chemical manufacturing.

The A57 passes through the brick-housed suburbs of Rainhill and Holt, before the route heads back into fields as the tour turns northward on B5201. Continue on B5201 through the intersection with the A580, and briefly join B5205 at Crank. From here the tour follows mostly minor roads through Up Holland to Appley Bridge, where the road crosses the Leeds and Liverpool Canal, briefly entering Manchester County. Cross the A5209 into Lancashire and join B5250 to Eccleston [there are 2 Ecclestons, and an Eccleston Park near Prescot, on this stage - the one on B5250 is the last].

At the B5250/A581 intersection, about a mile north of Eccleston, you can turn left

1848 Following European revolutions, rumours of a 1,000,000 person riot in London circulate, however only 30,000 turn out in the rain to demonstrate

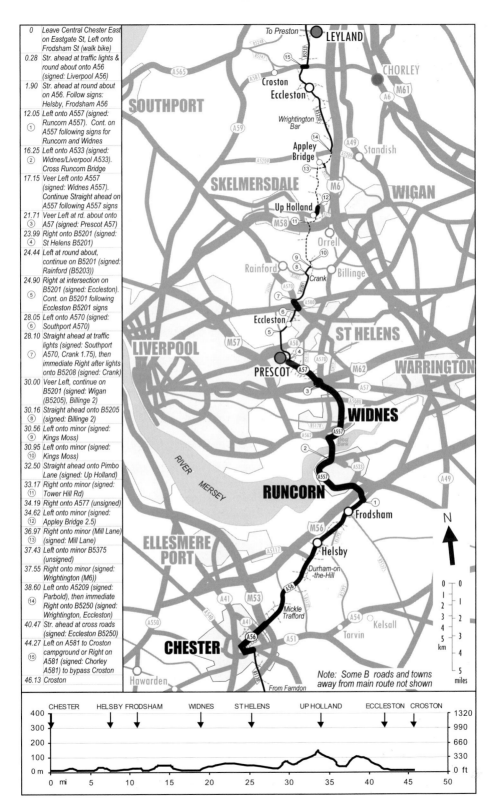

0	Leave Central Chester East on Eastgate St, Left onto Frodsham St (walk bike)
0.28	Str. ahead at traffic lights & round about onto A56 (signed: Liverpool A56)
1.90	Str. ahead at round about on A56. Follow signs: Helsby, Frodsham A56
12.05 ①	Left onto A557 (signed: Runcorn A557). Cont. on A557 following signs for Runcorn and Widnes
16.25 ②	Left onto A533 (signed: Widnes/Liverpool A533). Cross Runcorn Bridge
17.15	Veer Left onto A557 (signed: Widnes A557). Continue Straight ahead on A557 following A557 signs
21.71 ③	Veer Left at rd. about onto A57 (signed: Prescot A57)
23.99 ④	Right onto B5201 (signed: St Helens B5201)
24.44	Left at round about, continue on B5201 (signed: Rainford (B5203))
24.90 ⑤	Right at intersection on B5201 (signed: Eccleston). Cont. on B5201 following Eccleston B5201 signs
28.05 ⑥	Left onto A570 (signed: Southport A570)
28.10 ⑦	Straight ahead at traffic lights (signed: Southport A570, Crank 1.75), then immediate Right after lights onto B5208 (signed: Crank)
30.00	Veer Left, continue on B5201 (signed: Wigan (B5205), Billinge 2)
30.16 ⑧	Straight ahead onto B5205 (signed: Billinge 2)
30.56 ⑨	Left onto minor (signed: Kings Moss)
30.95 ⑩	Left onto minor (signed: Kings Moss)
32.50	Straight ahead onto Pimbo Lane (signed: Up Holland)
33.17 ⑪	Right onto minor (signed: Tower Hill Rd)
34.19	Right onto A577 (unsigned)
34.62 ⑫	Left onto minor (signed: Appley Bridge 2.5)
36.97 ⑬	Right onto minor (Mill Lane) (signed: Mill Lane)
37.43	Left onto minor B5375 (unsigned)
37.55	Right onto minor (signed: Wrightington (M6))
38.60 ⑭	Left onto A5209 (signed: Parbold), then immediate Right onto B5250 (signed: Wrightington, Eccleston)
40.47	Str. ahead at cross roads (signed: Eccleston B5250)
44.27 ⑮	Left on A581 to Croston campground or Right on A581 (signed: Chorley A581) to bypass Croston
46.13	Croston

Note: Some B roads and towns away from main route not shown

for Croston (2 miles west), which has a campground and pubs, or continue north on B5253 to the bigger towns of Leyland and Preston. Croston is a good place to stop for a rest day as it has a rail service into Liverpool (p90 has more details on Croston).

Liverpool, the busiest European port on the Atlantic, is an interesting place. Over the last 400 years, millions of people have come and gone through the city's wharves. The Dockyards museum, near the landmark twin towers of the Royal Liver Building, has good displays on the city's history. For soccer fans there is Goodison Park; home to Everton, and Anfield; home to Liverpool - two of the powerhouses of English football. For culture there is the Walker Art Gallery and The Cavern (an early Beatles' hangout which still hosts musical acts).

Liverpool and the Blitz

Liverpool's dockland area suffered some of the heaviest bombing of the Blitz during the first week of May 1941. For 7 nights the Luftwaffe rained bombs and mines on Liverpool's port facilities, shipping channels, and industry in an effort to cut Britain's supply lines with North America. By the end of the week 3,000 people had been killed and 75,000 left homeless, but the danger that persisted was the numerous unexploded bombs and mines that had to be cleared. This was the job of the RAF's bomb disposal officers and the Navy's RMS (Rendering Mines Safe) Unit. These brave souls had to defuse or dispose of these bombs to prevent more damage or loss of life.

The mine then, as today, was a particularly nasty and indiscriminate weapon. The ones the Luftwaffe dropped during the Biltz floated down by parachute, sank, then lay, waiting for a ship to pass and trigger the magnetic or acoustic firing mechanism that was connected to up to a ton of high explosive (specifically, hexanitrodiphenylamine). The allies had some success in degaussing their ships (neutralizing the magnetic field) and installing loud hammers in the bows (to fire acoustic mines at a distance), but by early 1940 mines had effectively closed London Port and Trans-Atlantic supplies were being directed to Bristol, Glasgow, and Liverpool. The largest of these was Liverpool.

Ivan Southall wrote a great biography of the men who had to delouse these mines in "Softly Tread the Brave" *(Angus and Robertson, 1961)*. The book tells the story of officers from the Torpedo and Mine School "HMS Vernon" in Portsmouth, who went around the country defusing unexploded mines that accidentally fell on land or in tidal estuaries. The Germans jealously guarded their mine technology, and each of these mines should have self-destructed on hitting land - except for a design flaw that meant the self-destruct mechanism sometimes stuck, delicately, mid-sequence. Once a mine was located it was the RMS officer's job to remove his watch and everything metal from his pockets and approach the mine with his bag of non-magnetic (usually bronze) tools.

The officer's first task was to remove the self-destruct fuse with a mechanical "gag". The gag simulated the water pressure that normally turned the self-destruct fuse off. Any mistake in the gag procedure, or slight knock to the mine, could set off the barely audible whir of a 17-second clock that exploded the mine. Hearing this fuse run meant a terrifying dash, hopefully to safety, or if the mine was in an inaccessible location - certain death. After the self-destruct fuse was disabled, the main detonator had to be removed and its wires cut, then finally the primer and hydrostatic clock were removed. This was the normal sequence, although many men died when the mine they where working on inexplicably just blew, or when they encountered a booby trap in the mine. In cases where access to the fuse was not available, or the mine was buried too deep, the charge was burnt or steamed out of the mine, or a small charge was set off a few feet from the mine to wreck the firing mechanism.

There were also new, more ingenious, mines that the Germans developed which

1860's Use of the French designed Velocipede, a front wheel drive wooden bike with iron wheels, on England's cobble streets earns it the nickname "Boneshaker"

had to be defused for the first time by someone. Some had both magnetic and acoustic triggers, and one, nicknamed "George", had photoelectric cells that caused it to explode when it was opened during daylight. The disposal teams sometimes got lucky when new weapons were damaged on landing, making them safe for inspection, and there were several cases of mines deliberately being dropped on land to assist the allies (an action that required the collusion of both the pilot and navigator).

The Mersey Maritime Museum has a German mine on display, rendered safe by one of these heroic officers. There are still bombs and mines buried below Liverpool, and around Britain - some known and some unknown (in 1996 the Armed Forces Minister released a list of known UXB's in London). In 1998 a live 750kg bomb was unearthed in Wiltshire, forcing the evacuation of over 1,000 people from nearby homes for several days while a bomb disposal officer unsuccessfully tried to defuse it. It was eventually blown up in a controlled explosion.

Camping:
Royal Umpire Caravan Park, Southport Rd, Croston, Ph 01772 600257, T£11

Hostel:
Nearest; Liverpool

B&B:
Woodside, 44 Tennyson Dr, Billinge (1mi S of Up Holland), Ph 01942 519647, S£30, D£50 ◆ Parr Hall Farm, Parr Ln, Eccleston, Chorley Ph 01257 451917, S£25, D£40 ◆ Others; Frodsham

Hotel:
Premier Lodge, 804 Warrington Rd, Rainhill (1½mi SE of Prescot), Ph 0870 7001430, D£47 ◆ Quality Hotel Skelmersdale, Prescott Rd, Up Holland, Ph 01695 720401, S£79, D£89 ◆ Mill Hotel, Moor Rd, Croston, Ph 01772 600110, S£50, D£65 ◆ Others; Frodsham, Prescot

i:
TIC, 6 Church St, Runcorn, Ph 01928 576776 ◆ Others; Wigan

Bike Shops:
Rimmer Cycles, 13 Warrington Rd, Prescot, Ph 0151 426 5399 ◆ Others; Prescot, Chorley

400mi Helsby

425mi Just before Up Holland

11 CROSTON TO TEWITFIELD

Croston to;

Preston	9.7mi	b&b, hotel, i, bike shop	*353400 429500*
Garstang	24.7mi	b&b, hotel, i	*349100 445500*
Cockerham	29.1mi	c	*346500 452300*
Lancaster	36.3mi	b&b, hotel, i, bike shop	*347600 461800*
Nether Kellet	39.5mi	c	*350500 468200*
Tewitfield	45.2mi	c, hotel	*352100 473600*

Croston got its name as a "cross town" when St Aidan came here in the 7th century and erected one as a point of worship (the current stone cross in Church St was placed, in 1953, at the spot thought to be the site of original wooden one). The town, which is on the banks of the River Yarrow, suffered severe flooding in 2000 when heavy rain caused the river to rise to the bottom of the old Town Bridge and flow down Town Rd, inundating several homes.

From Croston, retrace the route eastward 2 miles to the A581/B5253 intersection and head north on B5253. The road passes through the suburbs of Leyland, a town synonymous with the British motor-vehicle industry, and joins the A582 leading to Preston in Lancashire County. The 300-foot spire of St. Walburge's Church dominates the horizon around Preston (which derived its name from "Priests town"). Richard Arkwright was born here in 1732. He developed a spinning machine that produced stronger yarn than the earlier Spinning Jenny machine and the town became a leading textile producer in the 19th century.

The road crosses the River Ribble and the tour briefly joins the A583, then the A5085. Soon after joining the A5085, take the minor road heading north, through Catforth, to St Michael's on Wyre.

Between Preston to Tewitfield the tour crosses back and forth over the Lancaster Canal. The canal was designed by John Rennie who is best known for building London bridges - including the 1831 London Bridge (which was sold for £1.5 million to a US developer, moved to Lake Havasu, Arizona and reopened in 1971). The Canal was opened in 1797 and provided an important link for many of the towns along its route. Coal was sent north from Preston, and limestone from small quarries around Tewitfield, went south, earning the canal the nickname "The Black and White".

The tour joins the A586, then the busy A6, before Garstang. A market has been held in Garstang since 1310 and if you arrive on a Thursday you'll find stalls with local crafts and produce lining the High Street. Luckily, the A6 skirts the edge of Garstang and many of the old town's narrow alleys and historic buildings have been preserved.

B5272, then the A588, lead through Cockerham to Lancaster. The route passes through Lancaster town centre, past the town's cathedral and historic Mitre House, before crossing the River Lune. Overlooking the Lune is one of England's best preserved castles (it is owned by the Queen). The castle is largely Norman and was built on the site of an earlier Roman fort (the name Lancaster is a derivation of "Lun-Castrum" - fort on the Lune). Lancaster is now a university town with a pleasant collection of Georgian buildings.

Continue briefly on the A6 after Lancaster, before taking minor roads through Nether Kellet and Over Kellet to the tiny stop of Tewitfield. There is a small campground and a pub (which serves good meals) next to the Lancaster Canal, pleasantly surrounded by hedge-rowed fields and stone cottages. In the 19th century

1870 James Starley, designs the Penny-Farthing or "Ordinary" bicycle

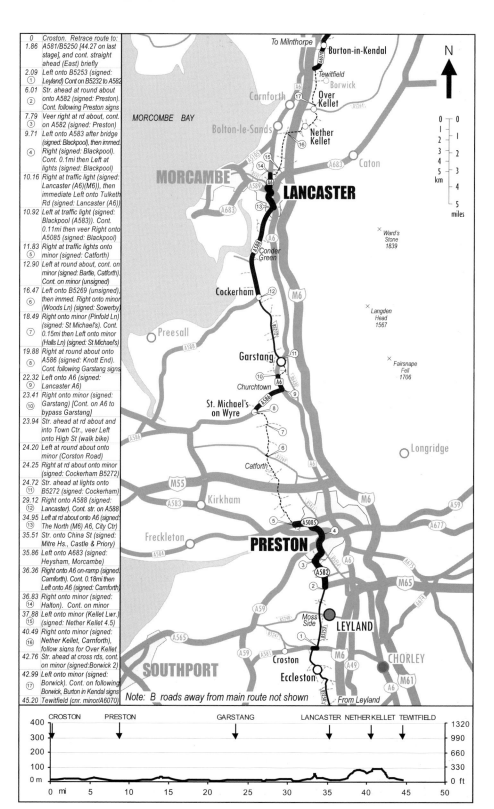

Dist		Directions
0		Croston. Retrace route to:
1.86		A581/B5250 [44.27 on last stage], and cont. straight ahead (East) briefly
2.09	(1)	Left onto B5253 (signed: Leyland) Cont on B5232 to A582
6.01	(2)	Str. ahead at round about onto A582 (signed: Preston). Cont. following Preston signs
7.79	(3)	Veer right at rd about, cont. on A582 (signed: Preston)
9.71	(4)	Left onto A583 after bridge (signed: Blackpool), then immed. Right (signed: Blackpool). Cont. 0.1mi then Left at lights (signed: Blackpool)
10.16		Right at traffic light (signed: Lancaster (A6)(M6)), then immediate Left onto Tulketh Rd (signed: Lancaster (A6))
10.92		Left at traffic light (signed: Blackpool (A583)). Cont. 0.11mi then veer Right onto A5085 (signed: Blackpool)
11.83	(5)	Right at traffic lights onto minor (signed: Catforth)
12.90		Left at round about, cont. on minor (signed: Bartle, Catforth). Cont. on minor (unsigned)
16.47	(6)	Left onto B5269 (unsigned), then immed. Right onto minor (Woods Ln) (signed: Sowerby)
18.49	(7)	Right onto minor (Pinfold Ln) (signed: St Michael's). Cont. 0.15mi then Left onto minor (Halls Ln) (signed: St Michael's)
19.88	(8)	Right at round about onto A586 (signed: Knott End). Cont. following Garstang signs
22.32	(9)	Left onto A6 (signed: Lancaster A6)
23.41	(10)	Right onto minor (signed: Garstang) [Cont. on A6 to bypass Garstang]
23.94		Str. ahead at rd about and into Town Ctr., veer Left onto High St (walk bike)
24.20		Left at round about onto minor (Corston Road)
24.25		Right at rd about onto minor (signed: Cockerham B5272)
24.72	(11)	Str. ahead at lights onto B5272 (signed: Cockerham)
29.12	(12)	Right onto A588 (signed: Lancaster). Cont. str. on A588
34.95	(13)	Left at rd about onto A6 (signed: The North (M6) A6, City Ctr)
35.51		Str. onto China St (signed: Mitre Hs., Castle & Priory)
35.86		Left onto A683 (signed: Heysham, Morcambe)
36.36		Right onto A6 on-ramp (signed: Carnforth). Cont. 0.18mi then Left onto A6 (signed: Carnforth)
36.83	(14)	Right onto minor (signed: Halton). Cont. on minor
37.88	(15)	Left onto minor (Kellet Lwr.) (signed: Nether Kellet 4.5)
40.49	(16)	Right onto minor (signed: Nether Kellet, Carnforth), follow signs for Over Kellet
42.76		Str. ahead at cross rds, cont. on minor (signed:Borwick 2)
42.99	(17)	Left onto minor (signed: Borwick). Cont. on following Borwick, Burton in Kendal signs
45.20		Tewitfield (cnr. minor/A6070)

Note: B roads away from main route not shown

1873 4 men on Ordinaries cycle from London to John O' Groats

the canal was extended northward from here to Kendal and there were 8 locks at Tewitfield that lifted the canal 75ft. Unfortunately, construction of the M6 in 1968 cut the canal at Tewitfield and canal travel northward past here is no longer possible.

There are good walks around Tewitfield, through farm fields and along the old towpaths which horses used to walk along to pull the barges. There are small quarries, overgrown jetties, and rusting loaders that provide interesting reminders of a once busy thoroughfare. The Tourist Information Centre in Lancaster has more information on these walks.

British Leyland

Leyland has been a centre for motor vehicle production since the 1890's when James Sumner, a local blacksmith, put a lawn mower engine on a tricycle and won first prize at the Royal Lancashire Agricultural Show. From there Sumner turned his attention to trucks, and buses, going into business with George and Henry Spurrier, wealthy backers from Preston. They formed the Lancashire Steam Motor Company and in 1896 produced their first steam powered van. A year later they built their first bus, an 18-seater with a top speed under 10mph.

Within 5 years the development of the petrol engine had mostly replaced steam power and the industry was developing rapidly. Soon Leyland's passenger vehicles were carrying paying customers in London, and the company name was changed to Leyland Motors. As business boomed prior to WWI the workforce grew to over 1,500. During the war almost all of Leyland's trucks went to the war effort.

Following WWI the company continued to grow, incorporating new innovations such as pneumatic tyres, aluminium bodywork, and diesel engines on their single- and double-decker buses. In the 1920's Leyland dabbled briefly, and unsuccessfully, in automobile production.

WWII resulted in Leyland again halting commercial production in favour of military vehicles, including the construction of the Centurion tank. After the war the way bus companies ran their routes started changing. Previously, country buses were green, city buses were red, and all buses had conductors. With companies searching for improved profits, Leyland developed buses with the motors in the rear and moved the entrance to the front so the driver could take fares. Over the next decade thousands of Leyland buses went into service, in London and around the country, and combined with its truck output, Leyland became the world's 5th biggest vehicle producer.

In the 1960's Leyland continued expanding, acquiring the car making companies Triumph and Rover (makers of the Mini). Then in 1968 Leyland Motors merged with the other powerhouse of British vehicle production - British Motor Holdings (owners of the Jaguar, Austin, and Morris marques) to form British Leyland Motor Corporation.

The new company now produced cars, buses, and trucks. But, buy the 1970's economic conditions were deteriorating and when British Leyland started losing money the government bought out the company. Hard hitting rounds of rationalisation followed, with heavy job losses. Over the years the car making components of British Leyland, most of them unprofitable, were sold off or wound up. As the market for buses declined Leyland's bus division was also sold, eventually being bought by Volvo in 1988 (the last Leyland bus rolled out of the Leyland factory in 1991).

True to James Sumner's original vision, trucks are still being made locally by Leyland Trucks Ltd, an arm of the company that was sold in 1998 to Paccar, Inc of Bellevue, USA (owners of the Kenworth, Peterbilt, and DAF brands), and over 1000 people are employed at a modern factory in Leyland.

The British Commercial Vehicle Museum, located in the former Leyland Motors

1876 George Bernard Shaw arrives in London, from Dublin, at age 20

south works in King St, Leyland, records the area's contribution to motorised transport in Britain. The collection, of over 60 vehicles, includes an 1896 Thornycroft van that is reputedly the world's first commercial truck, as well as many other historic British Leyland trucks. The museum is open 10:00am to 4:30pm, Sunday, Tuesday, and Wednesday, April to October (Sundays only in November).

Camping;
Claylands Caravan Park, Cabus (2mi N of Garstang), Ph 01524 791242, T£10 ◆ Mosswood Caravan Park , Crimbles Ln, Cockerham, Ph 01524 791041, T£10 ◆ Marina Caravan Park, Conder Green, Glasson Dock, Ph 01524 751787, T£10 ◆ Hawthorns Caravan & Camping Park, Nether Kellett, Ph 01524 732079, T£10 ◆ Detrongate Caravan Park, Bolton-le-Sands (1½mi W of Nether Kellet), Ph 01524 732842, T£6 ◆ Gatelands Caravan Park, Tewitfield, Ph 01524 781133, T£5 ◆ Others; Morcambe (4mi NW of Lancaster), Bolton-le-Sands

Hostel;
None near route

B&B;
Butler's Guest House, 6 Stanley Tce, Preston, Ph 01772 254486, S£30, D£40 ◆ Castle View Guest House, 42 Bonds Ln, Garstang, Ph 01253 602022, £20pp ◆ The Old Station House, 25 Meeting House Ln, Lancaster, Ph 01524 381060, S£15, D£40 ◆ Lancaster House, 11/12 Newton Tce, Caton Rd, Lancaster, Ph 01524 65527, S£25, D£40 ◆ Others; Preston, Lancaster

Hotel;
Holiday Inn, The Ringway, Preston, Ph 0870 4009066, S£60 ◆ Hampson House Hotel, Hampson Ln, Hampson Green, Lancaster, Ph 01524 751158, S£42, D£54 ◆ The Longlands Hotel, Tewitfield, Ph 01524 781256, £22pp ◆ Others; Leyland, Preston, Garstang, Condor Green, Lancaster

i;
TIC, The Guildhall, Lancaster Rd, Preston, Ph 01772 253731 ◆ TIC, Discovery Centre, High St, Garstang, Ph 01995 602125 ◆ TIC, 29 Castle Hill, Lancaster, Ph 01524 32878 ◆ Others; Lancaster, Morcambe

Bike Shops;
The Cycle Cabin, Fox Ln, Leyland, Ph 01772 622823 ◆ Ride Away Cycles, Unit 2 29-33, Berry Ln, Preston, Ph 01772 782828 ◆ Pedalers Bike Shop, 20 King St, Lancaster, Ph 01524 37622 ◆ Others; Leyland, Preston, Lancaster, Morcambe

450mi Just before Catforth

475mi Just before Nether Kellet

1880's The basic format of today's road bike is unveiled in the low or "Safety" bicycle

Tewitfield to;

Milnthorpe	6.9mi	c, b&b, hotel	*349800 481500*
Windermere	21.2mi	c, h, b&b, hotel, i	*341200 498700*
Patterdale	32.6mi	h, b&b, hotel	*339700 515800*
Near Longthwaite	41.2mi	c	*343000 523400*

From Tewitfield the tour continues north to Burton-in-Kendal, in the county of Cumbria. After Holme and Milnthorpe the route briefly joins the congested A6 again, passing the walls of Levens Hall, with its 17th century topiary garden (see p.96), before turning left onto the A590, then onto quiet minor roads via an underpass just before Levens village.

From here the road gradually starts climbing, with Cumbria's dramatic buttressed topography ahead on the horizon. At Brigsteer the tour enters the Lake District National Park. Although William Wordsworth thought the area was the "loveliest spot man hath never found" the Lake District has, ironically, become one of the most popular tourist destinations in UK and the larger towns can get severely congested during summer weekends.

The villages of Brigsteer and Underbarrow are made up of pretty stone cottages sitting amongst stone-walled fields. About a mile after Underbarrow there is a steep climb (beside Beckside Golf Course) that will probably require dismounting and pushing a touring bike. At the top of this hill the road joins B5284, which gradually climbs to the Windermere Golf Course. From here the road is a glorious sweep down to the edge of England's largest lake; Windermere.

During the last glaciation an ice sheet covered much of the Lake District's highlands. Glaciers radiated out from this sheet, carving basins for many of today's lakes. Windermere's lakebed was gouged out by a glacier that moved down from the north, assisted by tributary glaciers that joined from Troutbeck and Esthwaite valleys. The ice finally retreated about 10,000 years ago (although Windermere still freezes over occasionally), leaving a lake 11 miles long and a mile wide. The deepest portions of the lake, to the north and south, are below sea level, separated by Belle Isle, a remnant of more resistant rock that the advancing glacier rode over. The glaciers left 15 other major lakes in the Cumbrian Mountains, radiating out from the central highlands like spokes in a wheel. Other notable glacial features are the dramatic U-shaped valleys, their sides smoothed by the advancing ice, and the small but beautiful mountain lakes, known as tarns or corries, at the heads of these valleys that feed the Lake District's rivers.

Windermere is expensive, with some surly shop attendants who seem to take the tourist trade for granted (several cafés have charming signs notifying patrons that "Customers Eating Take-Out Food At The Dine-In Tables Will Be Asked To Leave"). A better way to appreciate Windermere is to hike the zig-zag path to the top of Orrest Head, at the north end of town. This 700ft climb gives great views out over the lake and the tourists below (the Tourist Information Centre on Victoria St has details on where exactly to find the start of the track).

Almost immediately after Windermere the stone-walled A592 starts climbing through rocky fields towards Kirkstone Pass, with dramatic views back down to the lake. This is the highest mountain pass in England and is the toughest climb of the tour - a 1,300ft gain in elevation over 6 miles - so expect a tough ride. Kirkstone Inn (which dates from 1467) at the top of the pass provides a fantastic panorama of

1894 The Manchester Ship Canal, engineered by James Brindley, is opened linking Manchester's textile industry with the ports of Liverpool

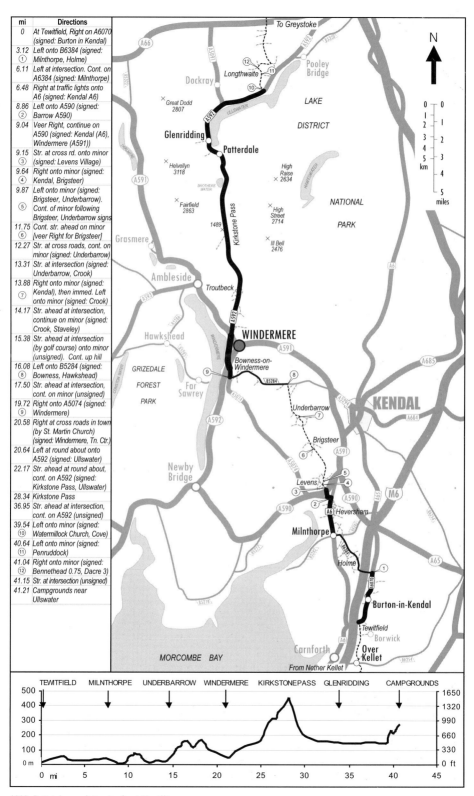

mi	Directions
0	At Tewitfield, Right on A6070 (signed: Burton in Kendal)
3.12 ①	Left onto B6384 (signed: Milnthorpe, Holme)
6.11	Left at intersection. Cont. on A6384 (signed: Milnthorpe)
6.48	Right at traffic lights onto A6 (signed: Kendal A6)
8.86 ②	Left onto A590 (signed: Barrow A590)
9.04	Veer Right, continue on A590 (signed: Kendal (A6), Windermere (A591))
9.15 ③	Str. at cross rd. onto minor (signed: Levens Village)
9.64 ④	Right onto minor (signed: Kendal, Brigsteer)
9.87 ⑤	Left onto minor (signed: Brigsteer, Underbarrow). Cont. of minor following Brigsteer, Underbarrow signs
11.75 ⑥	Cont. str. ahead on minor [veer Right for Brigsteer]
12.27	Str. at cross roads, cont. on minor (signed: Underbarrow)
13.31	Str. at intersection (signed: Underbarrow, Crook)
13.88 ⑦	Right onto minor (signed: Kendal), then immed. Left onto minor (signed: Crook)
14.17	Str. ahead at intersection, continue on minor (signed: Crook, Staveley)
15.38	Str. ahead at intersection (by golf course) onto minor (unsigned). Cont. up hill
16.08 ⑧	Left onto B5284 (signed: Bowness, Hawkshead)
17.50	Str. ahead at intersection, cont. on minor (unsigned)
19.72 ⑨	Right onto A5074 (signed: Windermere)
20.58	Right at cross roads in town (by St. Martin Church) (signed: Windermere, Tn. Ctr.)
20.64	Left at round about onto A592 (signed: Ullswater)
22.17	Str. ahead at round about, cont. on A592 (signed: Kirkstone Pass, Ullswater)
28.34	Kirkstone Pass
36.95	Str. ahead at intersection, cont. on A592 (unsigned)
39.54 ⑩	Left onto minor (signed: Watermillock Church, Cove)
40.64 ⑪	Left onto minor (signed: Penruddock)
41.04 ⑫	Right onto minor (signed: Bennethead 0.75, Dacre 3)
41.15	Str. at intersection (unsigned)
41.21	Campgrounds near Ullswater

1900 Britain's population is about 45 million

Cumbria, assuming it's not rainy or misty. For centuries travellers coming up the Pass would rest at the Inn after getting out of their carriages and walking the last stretch, which was too steep for the horses to pull. Kirkstone Quarry (under the shadow of Raven Crag at the top of pass) exposes the 500 million-year-old Borrowdale Volcanics, which underlie much of the central fells and give the District its dramatic bluffs and crags.

From Kirkstone Pass the road sweeps 5 miles down to Patterdale, a drop that reaches 20% grade in places. Helvellyn, off to the west, dominates the descent. At 3118ft this is the second highest peak in England - and the most popular hike in the Lake District. In fact the seven highest peaks in England are in Cumbria (the highest; Scafell Pike (3205ft) is the second most popular climb. The Park has seen its share of fatalities over the years; climbing accidents and walkers getting caught out ill-equipped for poor weather.

Brothers Water is a picturesque little lake before Ullswater, separated from the latter by alluvial debris eroded off the surrounding slopes after the last glaciation.

Patterdale is named after St Patrick, who is rumoured to have passed through the valley (tradition has it St Patrick's Well, near where the road first touches Ullswater, has healing water). Ullswater is thought by many to be the prettiest Lake District lake.

Glenridding, about a mile past Patterdale, is a centre for walking and hiking in the surrounding hills and has a good information centre with details on accommodation in the valley. Continuing on the A592, the tour hugs the edge of Ullswater, until a minor road heads north to several campgrounds in the hills above the lake. If you plan on staying at a hostel, B&B, or hotel on this stage your best bet is to hang back at Patterdale or Glenridding, and check ahead that accommodation is available.

The Gardens of Levens Hall

The topiary garden at Levens Hall (just north of Milnthorpe on the way into the Lake District National Park) is the oldest and most extensive in the world, and is well worth stopping to admire.

Topiary, which dates from Roman times, is the art of clipping and trimming trees into decorative shapes, and at Levens there are over 100 huge bushes sculpted into peculiar designs. Many of these hedges have been maintained in the same geometric design since the 17th century.

The gardens are predominantly the work of Monsieur Guillaume Beaumont, who spent 23 years as the gardener at Levens Hall from 1689 to 1712. Not much is known about Beaumont's background. He is thought to have trained under André Le Nôtre, (Louis XIV's gardener at Versailles) then come to Britain in the 1680's as a Protestant refugee, possibly spending time in Holland where topiary was popular. Soon after his arrival he was in demand as a designer of the exquisite formal gardens favoured by the wealthy in the late 17th and early 18th centuries. Beaumont's early work in Britain included laying out the gardens at Hampton Court Palace, although these gardens have since been replaced.

Beaumont moved to Levens Hall at the request of Colonel James Grahme, owner of the estate, who as Privy Purse to James II had recently become unemployed, due to the King's abdication.

By 1694, after a period of initial design work, Beaumont had laid out Levens' box-edged beds, beech lined avenue, ha-ha hedges, and 4 hectare yew topiary - creating a garden that has attracted visitor ever since. Despite the topiary being re-cut in the early 18th century and a change in fashion to the so-called natural garden, Beaumont's original layout has, miraculously, survived - complete with individual trimmed

1905 The term "smog" is coined to describe the smoke-laden fog hanging over Britain's industrial areas

specimens such as The Judge's Wig, The Great Umbrellas, and The Howard Lion.

Today the garden is maintained by four full-time gardeners and the topiary alone takes several months to trim from aluminium scaffolds and hydraulic lifts. Interestingly, the cuttings of yew and golden yew (*Taxus baccata* and *Taxus baccata aurea*), which used to be mulched into compost, are now sent away to a medical laboratory for use in the manufacture of a cancer drug.

In addition to the topiary, the gardens also feature a rose garden, a nuttery, and a garden full of 17th century plants.

The grey stone mansion of Levens Hall itself, is Elizabethan, built around an earlier 13th century square pele tower (the house is also open to the public). The whole 80 hectare estate has been in family ownership since Beaumont's time, the present owner, Hal Bagot, being a direct relation of Colonel Grahme.

Levens Hall is open from early April to mid-October. It costs £4.50 to view the gardens, or £6 to visit both the house and garden (the gardens are open from 10:00am, the house from 12:00pm). There is also a gift shop that sells cards and cuttings from the gardens.

Camping;
Hall More Caravan Park, Hale (1½mi W of Holme), Ph 01524 781918, T£8 ◆ Limefitt Park, Windermere, Ph 01539 432300, T£10 ◆ Sykeside Camping Park, Brotherswater (2mi S of Patterdale), Ph 017684 82239, T£3 ◆ The Quiet Camping and Caravan Site, Near Longthwaite, Ph 01768 486337, T£10 ◆ Others; Near Milnthorpe, Windermere, Near Longthwaite

Hostel;
Lake District Backpackers Lodge, High St, Windermere, Ph 01539 446374, Dorm£11 ◆ YHA Windermere, Bridge Ln, Troutbeck (2mi N of Windermere), Ph 01539 443543, Dorm£11 ◆ YHA Patterdale, Patterdale, Ph 01768 482394, Dorm£11 ◆ Others; Arnside, Kendal, Ambleside

B&B;
Crag Brow Cottage, Helm Rd, Bowness-on-Windermere, Ph 01539 444080, S£50, D£70 ◆ Osbourne Guest House, 3 High St, Windermere, Ph 01539 446452, S£32 ◆ Ullswater View, Patterdale, Ph 01768 482175, £25pp ◆ Beech House, Glenridding, Ph 01768 482037, S£23, D£40 ◆ Others; Near Milnthorpe, Bowness-on-Windermere, Windermere, Patterdale, Glenridding

Hotel;
King's Arms Hotel, Hale (1½mi W of Holme), Ph 01539 563203, S£20, D£40 ◆ The Cross Keys Hotel, 1 Park Rd, Milnthorpe, Ph 01539 562115, S£28, D£55 ◆ Cedar Manor Hotel, Ambleside Rd, Windermere, Ph 01539 443192, S£40, D£65 ◆ Hideaway Hotel, Phoenix Wy, Windermere, Ph 01539 443070, S£40, D£70 ◆ Patterdate Hotel, Patterdale, Ph 01845 4584333, S£35, D£65 ◆ Glenridding Hotel, Glenridding, Ph 01768 482228, S£75, D£105 ◆ Others; Bowness-on-Windermere, Windermere, Glenridding, Patterdale, Watermillock (2½ mi SW of Pooley Bridge on A592)

i;
TIC, Victoria St, Windermere, Ph 01539 446499 ◆ TIC, Ullswater, Main Car Park, Glenridding, Ph 01768 482414 ◆ Others; Kendal

Bike Shops;
Nearest; Kendal, Penrith, Keswick

500mi Windermere

13 ULLSWATER TO DUMFRIES

Ullswater (Near Longthwaite) to;

Greystoke	5.4mi	b&b	*344000 530900*
Carlisle	23.3mi	h, b&b, hotel, i, bike shop	*340100 556100*
Annan	43.9mi	c, b&b, hotel	*319400 566600*
Dumfries	61.0mi	b&b, hotel, i, bike shop	*297000 576000*

North of Ullswater the tour crosses the A66, leaving the Lake District behind. The stage is basically downhill for 20 miles, then flat until a minor climb into Dumfries.

Greystoke is a small village with a stately castle behind high walls. The buildings date from 1129, and were added to by the Normans in the 14th century. Cromwell partially wrecked the castle after the owners supported the king, and a fire in the 19th century destroyed much of the interior, although it was rebuilt each time. The present estate covers 3,000 acres and includes farmland, forest, and pre-historic fortifications.

Just up the road at Upthank End there is another impressive manor; Hutton in the Forest, a medieval house with pele tower (a stronghold to resist sieges, common to northern English homes of the period). The gardens are open daily, except Saturday, (11:00am to 5:00pm), the house is open Thursday, Friday, and Sunday (12:30 to 4:00pm).

The minor road north from Upthank End is a fairly direct route to Carlisle paralleling the M6. Enter Carlisle and head into the town square where there is a good tourist information centre. Carlisle was established as a Roman camp (Luguvalium) to support the forts along Hadrian's Wall, and later became a medieval castle town to protect the border, although ownership of the town has historically flip-flopped between the England and Scotland. William II started the castle in the 11th century, but the Scots under David I captured it, in the 12th. Henry VIII expanded the castle as part of his defences when the English had it again, and it was lost, briefly, for the last time to the Jacobites in 1745. Leaving Carlisle, the tour takes an underpass near the castle onto the A7, a narrow and busy road. An alternative is the wider, even busier, A74 direct to Gretna.

The suburb of Stanwix is just after the roundabout onto the A7, on the north side of the River Eden. Hadrian's Wall passed through here on its transect of Britain, which ended near Bowness-on-Solway, 13 miles west of Carlisle. The nearest remnant of the wall is at Brunstock, 2 miles northeast of Stanwix.

The steel bridge over the River Sark at Gretna marks the English-Scottish border. The first house in Scotland is a marriage registry, taking advantage of a 19th century law which allows 16 year olds to marry without parental consent (the legal age is 18 in England). Gretna has seen its share of elopements, and the town has several marriage businesses that will arrange all your wedding details, including witnesses if necessary.

From Gretna (in the border county of Dumfries and Galloway) follow B721 to Annan, then B724 and B725 to Bankend. The road passes a well along this stretch where Robbie Burns sought relief during his final sickness.

At Bankend a minor road heads north to Dumfries. The route passes Burns' house, on Burns St, to White Sands Rd by the River Nith (where there is a TIC). The nearest campground is a couple of miles further on at Newbridge. Burns, now embraced as Scotland's national poet, died in Dumfries in 1796 after spending his last 5 years here. He wrote "Auld Lang Syne" here and is buried in St Michael's churchyard.

Foot & Mouth Disease

Soon after Britain's latest foot and mouth outbreak hit, it became apparent that infected animals all across the country could be linked to England's largest sheep market, at Longtown, near Carlisle. From here the trail led 40 miles east, to Hexham Market, then another 15 miles east to Burnside Farm - the suspected source of the outbreak.

1916 The osprey is hunted to extinction in Scotland and not seen again till 1954 when a pair return to nest at Loch Garten

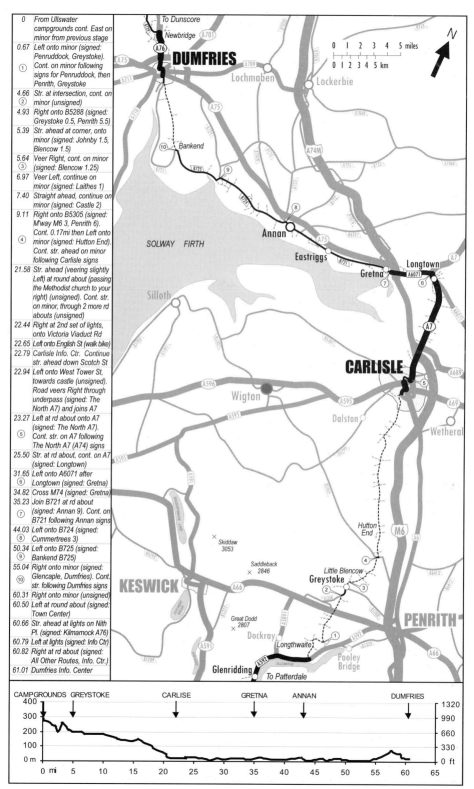

0	From Ullswater campgrounds cont. East on minor from previous stage
0.67	Left onto minor (signed: Penruddock, Greystoke).
(1)	Cont. on minor following signs for Penruddock, then Penrith, Greystoke
4.66	Str. at intersection, cont. on
(2)	minor (unsigned)
4.93	Right onto B5288 (signed: Greystoke 0.5, Penrith 5.5)
5.39	Str. ahead at corner, onto minor (signed: Johnby 1.5, Blencow 1.5)
5.64	Veer Right, cont. on minor
(3)	(signed: Blencow 1.25)
6.97	Veer Left, continue on minor (signed: Laithes 1)
7.40	Straight ahead, continue on minor (signed: Castle 2)
9.11	Right onto B5305 (signed: M'way M6 3, Penrith 6).
(4)	Cont. 0.17mi then Left onto minor (signed: Hutton End). Cont. str. ahead on minor following Carlisle signs
21.58	Str. ahead (veering slightly Left) at round about (passing the Methodist church to your right) (unsigned). Cont. str. on minor, through 2 more rd abouts (unsigned)
22.44	Right at 2nd set of lights, onto Victoria Viaduct Rd
22.65	Left onto English St (walk bike)
22.79	Carlisle Info. Ctr. Continue str. ahead down Scotch St
22.94	Left onto West Tower St, towards castle (unsigned). Road veers Right through underpass (signed: The North A7) and joins A7
23.27	Left at rd about onto A7
(5)	(signed: The North A7). Cont. str. on A7 following The North A7 (A74) signs
25.50	Str. at rd about, cont. on A7 (signed: Longtown)
31.65	Left onto A6071 after
(6)	Longtown (signed: Gretna)
34.82	Cross M74 (signed: Gretna)
35.23	Join B721 at rd about
(7)	(signed: Annan 9). Cont. on B721 following Annan signs
44.03	Left onto B724 (signed:
(8)	Cummertrees 3)
50.34	Left onto B725 (signed:
(9)	Bankend B725)
55.04	Right onto minor (signed:
(10)	Glencaple, Dumfries). Cont. str. following Dumfries signs
60.31	Right onto minor (unsigned)
60.50	Left at round about (signed: Town Center)
60.66	Str. ahead at lights on Nith Pl. (signed: Kilmarnock A76)
60.79	Left at lights (signed: Info Ctr)
60.82	Right at rd about (signed: All Other Routes, Info. Ctr.)
61.01	Dumfries Info. Center

*1916 60,000 British troops are killed or wounded on the first
day of the Battle of the Somme. Army Generals refer to
this a "wastage"*

On February 19, 2001 vets were making a routine check of pigs at Cheale Meats Abattoir near London, when they noticed telltale signs of Foot and Mouth Disease (FMD). The next day the disease was confirmed, and Britain's live animal and meat exports were banned. Over the next few days, as the government scrambled to contain the virus, it became apparent that FMD had already criss-crossed the country and the UK faced a crisis.

For Britain's farmers FMD could not have come at a worse time, after recent outbreaks of swine fever and mad-cow disease. The impact on the rest of the country was significant too; "No-Entry" signs went up across the country and tourism dwindled.

Back at Burnside Farm, at Heddon-on-the-Wall (near Hadrian's Wall), it quickly became apparent that the brothers who ran the 500-head piggery (Bobby and Ronnie Waugh) had not operated a model farm, and that there had been numerous complaints. In December 2000, an animal welfare group complained to the Ministry of Agriculture (MAFF) and the RSPCA about the squalid conditions at Burnside. MAFF visited and issued the brothers a warning to tidy their act up. It appears that the pigs at Burnside contracted FMD from being fed diseased meat in unprocessed swill. Speculation into the source of this diseased meat quickly followed; illegally imported meat from a Chinese restaurant, aircraft meal scraps from Newcastle Airport, and wastes from a local Army camp that imported South American meat, were all suggested. The official report into the outbreak is due for release in mid-2002.

From Burnside the virus looks to have jumped the fence to 7 nearby farms. Animals from one of these farms went to Hexham, and from there to Longtown, where infected sheep were sent around the country for a week before the disease was discovered.

The FMD virus was first identified in the 1890's, and is one of the most contagious viruses known - a ball-shaped micro-organism, that attaches itself to the wall of a healthy cell and injects its own genetic material into the host. This perverts the cell's own genetics so that it starts producing viral proteins which eventually assemble into a multitude of virus clones and rupture out of the, now dead, cell to continue the infection. For an animal the symptoms are miserable - fluid filled blisters in the mouth and on the feet that burst and become raw. Animals develop a fever and often become lame. In cattle, milk production is reduced and miscarriage and sterility are common. In sheep FMD can be more difficult to spot. Interestingly, after 2 or 3 weeks many animals recover, but for farmers this loss of production is disastrous.

The virus can cling to almost anything and be transported; people around infected animals and cars that drive over infected dung become carriers. The virus lurks in frozen carcasses and can even be blown through the air. Thankfully, it is exceptionally rare for humans to contract the disease. Bobby Brewis, a 34-year-old from northern England, is the only person in the UK known to have caught FMD. He contracted it in 1966 during a another FMD epidemic - "I just felt a bit groggy" he is quoted as saying after recovering. During the 1966 outbreak 2,000 farms were affected and over 440,000 animals were slaughtered. There was another scare in 1981 when the virus showed up on a farm on the Isle of Wright, after being blown across the Channel, but this was quickly contained. The 2001 outbreak by comparison resulted in about 4 million animals being slaughtered on 10,000 farms. At its height in early April 2001, up to 50 new cases a day were being reported, although about a month later the number of new cases dropped to under 10 a day, and this number steadily reduced as the Government's controls started taking effect.

By the end of 2001 the "No-Entry" signs had disappeared from most of Britain, and public lands and pathways were generally open again, although people were being requested to avoid contact with animals. In parts of northern England, where FMD hit the hardest, more direct precautions are still in place - with some farmers continuing to step in and out of buckets of disinfectant and scrub the dirt off their vehicle tyres.

1916 The war stalemates. Over ¾ million British soldiers are killed or wounded during the year - many downing in mud or freezing to death

Camping;
The Braids Caravan Park, Annan Rd, <u>Gretna</u>, Ph 01461 337409, T£5 ◆ Parkend Touring Park, <u>Newbridge</u> (2mi NE of Dumfries on A76), T£5 ◆ Others; <u>Blackford</u> (3½mi N of Carlisle on A7), <u>Annan</u>

Hostel;
YHA <u>Carlisle</u>, Bridge Ln, Ph 01228 597352, Dorm£13

B&B;
Lattendales Farm, <u>Greystoke</u>, Ph 017684 83474, £15pp ◆ East View Guest House, 110 Warwick Rd, <u>Carlisle</u>, Ph 01228 522112, S£25, D£40 ◆ Milnfield Farm, Low Rd, <u>Annan</u>, Ph 01461 201811, £20pp ◆ Hazeldean House, 4 Moffat Rd, <u>Dumfries</u>, Ph 01387 266178, £25pp ◆ Others; <u>Carlisle</u>, <u>Gretna</u>, <u>Annan</u>, <u>Dumfries</u>

Hotel;
Cumbria Park, 32 Scotland Rd, Stanwix, <u>Carlisle</u>, Ph 01228 522887, S£75, D£95 ◆ Queensberry Arms, 47 High St, <u>Annan</u>, Ph 01461 202024, S£45, D£60 ◆ Hill Hotel, 18 St Mary's St, <u>Dumfries</u>, Ph 01387 255524, £40pp ◆ Others; <u>Carlisle</u>, <u>Gretna</u>, <u>Annan</u>, <u>Dumfries</u>, <u>Newbridge</u>

i;
TIC, Green Market, <u>Carlisle</u>, Ph 01228 625600 ◆ TIC, 64 Whitesands, <u>Dumfries</u>, Ph 01387 253862 ◆ Others; <u>Longtown</u>, <u>Gretna</u> <u>Green</u>

Bike Shops;
Whiteheads Cycle Centre, 128 Botchergate, <u>Carlisle</u>, Ph 01228 526890 ◆ Nithsdale Cycle Centre, 46 Brooms Rd, <u>Dumfries</u>, Ph 01387 254870 ◆ Others, <u>Dumfries</u>, <u>Penrith</u>, <u>Carlisle</u>

525mi 1.5mi before Greystoke

550mi On the A7 between Carlisle and Longtown

575mi On B725 just before Bankend

1917 One writer describes the war as "an enormous carnival of death"

14 DUMFRIES TO DALMELLINGTON

Dumfries to;

Dunscore	9.0mi	b&b, hotel	*286800*	*584400*
Moniaive	16.8mi	i	*277900*	*590900*
Carsphairn	32.0mi	b&b, hotel	*256200*	*593200*
Dalmellington	41.9mi	b&b, hotel	*248200*	*605800*

This stage rises from an elevation of 50ft to 650ft, in 3 steady climbs and 3 gradual descents. B729 from Newbridge to Kirkland is a beautiful road. A quiet stone-walled lane, lined with trees, fields, and solitary stone homes.

The first village is Dunscore. There is a pretty 19th century toll house at Throughgate, just before Dunscore itself, which has been converted into rental accommodation. Dunscore has several small shops and a Post Office. 4½ miles further on is Maxwelton House, an impressive manor house dating from 1370 [open 11:00am-5:00pm (except Saturday.) May to September]. Originally called Glencairn Castle, the house was owned by the Earls of Glencairn until it was sold to a local noble, Stephen Laurie in 1611. Laurie made extensive additions and changed the name to Maxwelton. His great granddaughter, born in 1682, was apparently an exceptional beauty, and is the subject of a traditional Scottish song, composed by one of her many admirers;

Annie Laurie

Maxwelton's braes are bonnie
Where early falls the dew
And 'twas there that Annie Laurie
Game me her promise true
Game me her promise true
Which ne'er forgot will be
And for bonnie Annie Laurie
I'd lay me doon and dee

Her brow is like the snowdrift
Her throat is like the swan
Her face it is the fairest
That e'er the sun shone on
That e'er the sun shone on
And dark blue is her e'e
And for bonnie Annie Laurie
I'd lay me doon and dee

Like dew on th'gowan lying
Is th' fall o'her fairy feet
And like the winds in summer sighing
Her voice is low and sweet
Her voice is low and sweet
And she's all the world to me
And for bonnie Annie Laurie
I'd lay me doon and dee

Anon.

*1917 The House of Windsor created by George V to replace
the family name Saxe-Coburg-Gotha*

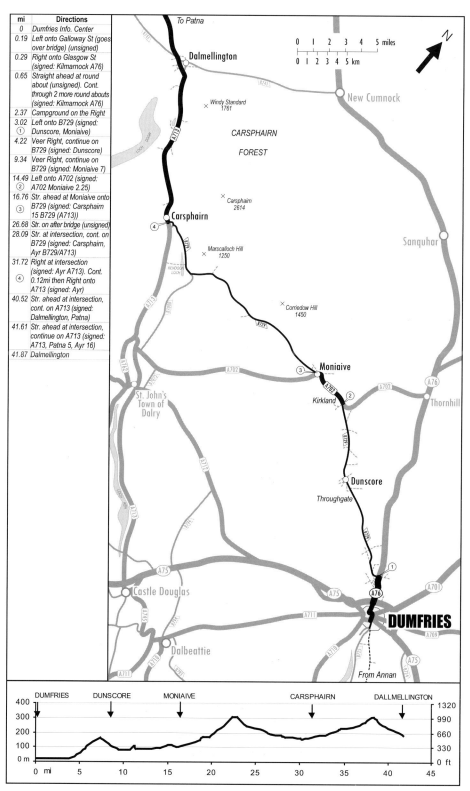

mi	Directions
0	Dumfries Info. Center
0.19	Left onto Galloway St (goes over bridge) (unsigned)
0.29	Right onto Glasgow St (signed: Kilmarnock A76)
0.65	Straight ahead at round about (unsigned). Cont. through 2 more round abouts (signed: Kilmarnock A76)
2.37	Campground on the Right
3.02 ①	Left onto B729 (signed: Dunscore, Moniaive)
4.22	Veer Right, continue on B729 (signed: Dunscore)
9.34	Veer Right, continue on B729 (signed: Moniaive 7)
14.49 ②	Left onto A702 (signed: A702 Moniaive 2.25)
16.76 ③	Str. ahead at Moniaive onto B729 (signed: Carsphairn 15 B729 (A713))
26.68	Str. on after bridge (unsigned)
28.09	Str. at intersection, cont. on B729 (signed: Carsphairn, Ayr B729/A713)
31.72 ④	Right at intersection (signed: Ayr A713). Cont. 0.12mi then Right onto A713 (signed: Ayr)
40.52	Str. ahead at intersection, cont. on A713 (signed: Dalmellington, Patna)
41.61	Str. ahead at intersection, continue on A713 (signed: A713, Patna 5, Ayr 16)
41.87	Dalmellington

1918 An armistice ending WWI is signed on 11 November

Moniaive has a pub that serves good meals, and a marker post in the main street dating from 1638.

After Moniaive B729 gradually climbs, next to Stroanshalloch Burn, through exotic forest until it crests on a remote and exposed tussock plateau dotted with Scottish Blackface sheep and distant whitewashed cottages. 6 miles after Moniaive the road starts a sweet descent, crossing the Southern Upland Way and passing several small streams, including the Water of Ken, which feed Kendoon Loch and becomes the River Dee downstream. The river below the Loch was extensively dammed in the 1930's for the Galloway Hydro-Electric Power Scheme. There is a Youth Hostel on the right hand side of B7000, about 1½ miles south of the B729/B7000 intersection.

Carsphairn sits on the Water of Deugh between barren hills with patches of purple heather. This village grew in the 18th century, partly due to the discovery of copper, lead and zinc nearby. The village has a heritage centre and is now quite a popular base for hiking and fishing. Scotland's largest wind farm, consisting of 36 wind turbines (each one over 100 feet tall with three 50-foot blades) was constructed in the forest north of Carsphairn during the late 1990's. Enough power generated is to supply about 20,000 homes.

The route joins the A713 and gradually climbs again after Carspharin, entering East Ayrshire, before a final drop through Muckwater gorge, past Loch Muck, to Dalmellington in Doon Valley.

Dalmellington was a small rural community until ironstone and coal were discovered in the hills nearby in the 1840's and mining and iron smelting commenced at Waterside, a few miles up the road. The Dalmellington Iron Company moved hundreds of families into the area to run the operation, which reached a peak in the 1870's. By the 1920's iron production had become uneconomic and ended. In the late 1980's coal mining ceased as well and most locals now travel further afield to work.

Today Dalmellington has a population of about 1,500 but, being off the beaten tourist track, does not have a tourist information center or campground. Your best bet for accommodation in Dalmellington is one of the bed & breakfasts. [There is an interesting old Cyclists Touring Club plaque above the front door of the old Eglinton Hotel in Dalmellington (which caters to working men). These plaques were put on hotels, recommended by the club, that offered accommodation to touring cyclists].

Dunscore's Heroine

A small plaque in the village church at Dunscore remembers a very brave local lady - Jane Haining - who went to Hungary before WWII to care for children, chose to stay during the Nazi invasion, and became the only Scot known to have died in the concentration camps.

Born in Dunscore in 1897, Jane grew up an independent, well-adjusted, child despite the death of her mother when she was five. She went on to school at Dumfries Academy where she excelled, becoming dux of her year.

For the next 10 years Jane worked at a threadmakers in Paisley, before discovering her mission in life during a visit to Queen's Park Church in Glasgow. The topic being discussed was the Jewish Mission in Hungary and as the meeting progressed Jane turned to a friend and said "I have found my life work". In 1932, after a crash course in Hungarian, she was sent as a teacher to the Church of Scotland's mission in Budapest.

The mission school catered to about 400 Jewish and Christian children, many of them orphaned or from destitute families. Jane quickly grew to love the children and

1921 At Newlyn, Cornwall, 6 years of tide measurements are completed to calculate a national benchmark, still used, for mean sea level

the work. She was on leave in Scotland during September 1939 when the war broke out and immediately headed back to the school. When the Nazi's arrived in Hungary en-masse in March 1944, Jane chose to stay with the children, despite being recalled by the Church of Scotland. Conditions for Jews in Hungary deteriorated rapidly and in May the Gestapo raided the school. Jane was arrested on charges of assisting Jews and spying.

At this time Hitler and Himmler were accelerating their "final solution" plans. From mid-May to early July nearly half a million Hungarian Jews were sent north by train to Poland's Auschwitz-Birkenau. Jane Haining, accompanied by many of the school's Jewish children, were part of this group. A new rail line, directly into the camp, had recently been constructed by the Germans to increase the efficiency of prisoner transport, and during the summer of 1944 Auschwitz's gas chambers were working around the clock. The killing was on such a scale that the camp's crematoria could not keep up and bodies where being piled in the fields and set alight.

Jane was tattooed with the number 79467, and on August 16 was gassed with a group of Hungarian women. The Nazis forwarded a fake death certificate to the Church of Scotland in a cowardly attempt to cover their tracks. The death certificate indicating, "Miss Haining, who was arrested on account of justified suspicion of espionage against Germany, died in hospital July 17, of cachexia brought on by intestinal catarrh".

Jane Haining was not forgotten after the war, in Queen's Park Church there is a stained-glass window in remembrance of her, and in the late 1990's she was added to the list of "Righteous Among the Nations" by Yad Vashem (the Holocaust Martyrs and Heroes Memorial, in Jeruselum) when a medal was presented to her sister by the Israeli Ambassador to Britain.

Camping;
Nearest; Penpont (5mi NE of Moniaive), Patna (5mi NW of Dalmellington)

Hostel;
Nearest; Kendoon YHA, B7000, Ph 01644 460680, Dorm£9 ◆ Others; Castle Douglas, Ayr

B&B;
Boreland Farm, 2mi NW of Dunscore, Ph 01387 820287, S£19, D£35 ◆ Low Kirkbride Farm, 2mi NE of Dunscore, Ph 01387 820258, £18pp ◆ Woodlea Hotel and Guest House, Moniaive, Ph 01848 200209, S£26, D£40 ◆ Ladywell Guest House, Carspairn Rd, Dalmellington, Ph 01292 550358, £20pp ◆ Bellsbank House, Bellsbank Rd, Dalmellington, Ph 01292 550248, £20pp

Hotel;
The George Hotel, High St, Dunscore, Ph 01848 200203, £22pp ◆ The Craigdarroch Arms Hotel, High St, Moniaive, Ph 01848 200205, £26pp ◆ Eglinton Hotel, 50 Main St, Dalmellington, Ph 01292 550245, £20pp

i;
Carsphairn Heritage Centre, Carsphairn, Ph 01644 460208

Bike Shops;
Nearest; Ayr

600mi Just after Moniaive

1922 Sinn Fein leaders negotiate independence for 26 Catholic counties in S. Ireland. N. Ireland, consisting of 6 largely Protestant counties, remains in Britain

Dalmellington to;

Drongan	11.5mi		*244700 618600*
Tarbolton	17.4mi	hotel	*243000 627200*
Kilmaurs	28.5mi	b&b	*241100 641200*
Neilston	40.7mi	b&b	*248000 657300*

This stage enters an area referred to as Strathclyde; a huge portion of Scotland including Ayr, Glasgow, Oban, and some of the Inner Hebrides, defined in a 1975 local government reorganisation. As the tour nears Glasgow the countryside gets more populated, and the roads busier. Many of the small towns near Glasgow expanded rapidly during the Industrial Revolution but have since struggled economically and several of the towns along this stage have a bleak, hard-nosed edge about them. In terms of topography, the route drops to cross the River Irvine, west of Kilmarnock, before climbing again towards Glasgow. The last 3½ miles to Neilston are downhill.

Leaving Dalmellinngton the A713 follows the River Doon past Waterside, which has the excellent Dunaskin Open Air Museum at the Dalmellington Iron Company's old iron-works. Coal and ironstone were mined here, with iron being produced from 1848 until 1921 - when dwindling ironstone reserves and a strike halted production. Bricks were made at the plant for a few years and coal mining continued until 1988, when the factory finally closed. The museum is open April to October 10:00am to 5:00pm and has displays include an original iron workers cottage, machinery from the Industrial Revolution, steam trains restored by the Ayrshire Railway Preservation Group, and a café.

A couple of miles past Waterside is Patna, a centre for those working the nearby Benquhat and Lethamhill mines and a reminder that coal is still the main mineral resource in Scotland's economy.

After Patna B730 crosses rolling farmland past Drongan, another mining community whose fortunes suffered when the local pit closed in 1986. The town's youth reportedly have a strong and unfriendly rivalry with neighbouring Coylton. Just north of here the route doglegs across the A70, to Tarbolton in South Ayrshire.

Robert Burns moved to the Tarbolton area when he was 12 (after living his early years at Alloway, near Ayr), when his father started work at nearby Lochlea Farm. These were tough times for the Burns' - there was little food on the table, Robert appears to have permanently damaged his health by overworking on the farm, then in 1784 their father died. But, during his time at Tarbolton, Burns also started writing after gaining inspiration from Robert Ferguson, another Scottish poet ("The Tarbolton Lasses" is a disparaging song Burns wrote about some of the drippy local ladies). When he turned 21, Burns co-founded The Bachelor's Club, a debating group open to "every frank, honest, open-hearted man who is a professed lover of one or more of the female sex" although "no mean-spirited, worldly mortals, whose only will is to heap up money" were allowed. The 17th century thatched cottage on Sandgate St, where the Club met, is now a museum.

The town is keen to maintain its strong association with Burns and when a mining company recently proposed an open-cast coal mine near Lochlea Farm the idea was soundly voted down. Tarbolton does have a history before Burns - at the northern edge of town there are the remains of a pre-Roman bailey and motte (now drained). It is thought a wooden castle was once connected to the "mainland" by a walkway of secret planks, just below the water, which could be destroyed when protection was required.

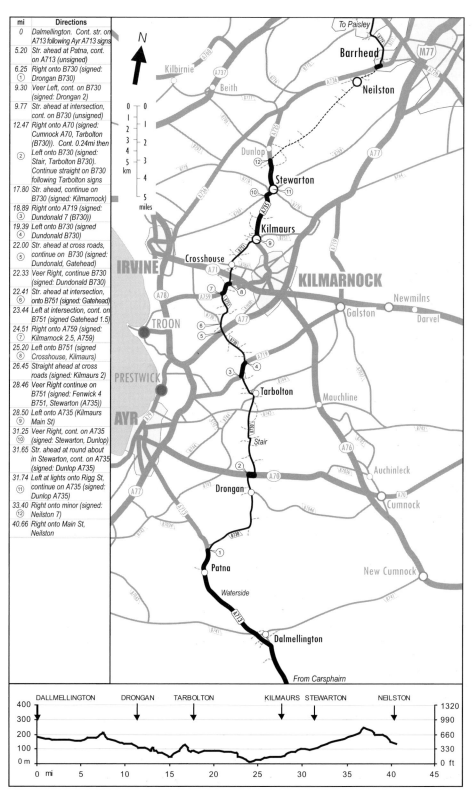

mi	Directions
0	Dalmellington. Cont. str. on A713 following Ayr A713 signs
5.20	Str. ahead at Patna, cont. on A713 (unsigned)
6.25 ①	Right onto B730 (signed: Drongan B730)
9.30	Veer Left, cont. on B730 (signed: Drongan 2)
9.77	Str. ahead at intersection, cont. on B730 (unsigned)
12.47	Right onto A70 (signed: Cumnock A70, Tarbolton (B730)). Cont. 0.24mi then
②	Left onto B730 (signed: Stair, Tarbolton B730). Continue straight on B730 following Tarbolton signs
17.80	Str. ahead, continue on B730 (signed: Kilmarnock)
18.89 ③	Right onto A719 (signed: Dundonald 7 (B730))
19.39 ④	Left onto B730 (signed Dundonald B730)
22.00 ⑤	Str. ahead at cross roads, continue on B730 (signed: Dundonald, Gatehead)
22.33	Veer Right, continue B730 (signed: Dundonald B730)
22.41 ⑥	Str. ahead at intersection, onto B751 (signed: Gatehead)
23.44	Left at intersection, cont. on B751 (signed Gatehead 1.5)
24.51 ⑦	Right onto A759 (signed: Kilmarnock 2.5, A759)
25.20 ⑧	Left onto B751 (signed Crosshouse, Kilmaurs)
26.45	Straight ahead at cross roads (signed: Kilmaurs 2)
28.46	Veer Right continue on B751 (signed: Fenwick 4 B751, Stewarton (A735))
28.50 ⑨	Left onto A735 (Kilmaurs Main St)
31.25 ⑩	Veer Right, cont. on A735 (signed: Stewarton, Dunlop)
31.65	Str. ahead at round about in Stewarton, cont. on A735 (signed: Dunlop A735)
31.74 ⑪	Left at lights onto Rigg St, continue on A735 (signed: Dunlop A735)
33.40 ⑫	Right onto minor (signed: Neilston 7)
40.66	Right onto Main St, Neilston

N

Barrhead
M77
To Paisley
Kilbirnie
Neilston
Beith
Dunlop
⑫
Stewarton
⑩ ⑪
Kilmaurs
⑨
Crosshouse
IRVINE
KILMARNOCK
⑦ ⑧
Newmilns
Galston
Darvel
TROON
⑥
⑤
A719
Tarbolton
Mauchline
PRESTWICK
Stair
AYR
A76
②
A70
Auchinleck
Drongan
Cumnock
A70
①
Patna
New Cumnock
Waterside
Dalmellington
From Carsphairn

DALLMELLINGTON DRONGAN TARBOLTON KILMAURS STEWARTON NEILSTON

The tour continues on B730, past the A719 and the very busy A77, before turning onto B751 which enters East Ayrshire and skirts the city of Kilmarnock. Continue through the towns of Crosshouse (2 miles west of here is Dreghorn, birthplace of John Dunlop the inventor of the pneumatic bicycle tyre), Kilmaurs (in North Ayrshire), and Stewarton, and continue north on the A735. The minor road turnoff to Neilston is about 2 miles past Stewarton. The route enters East Renfrewshire County along this stretch, passing a landfill, then cresting a rise that looks out over Glasgow away in haze.

Neilston is a tough little town with no campground, but there are a couple of B&B's nearby - ask the local butcher for directions. More accommodation options are available just north of here at Paisley, or you could head into Glasgow via the A736 and A761 or quieter minor roads (if you stay in Neilston or Paisley, and want to explore Glasgow, there are regular train services into the city).

Glasgow is an interesting place. In the mid-18th century the population was under 20,000. Thanks to Trans-Atlantic trade, textile making, and the Industrial Revolution, the population exploded and by the mid-19th century the city was home to nearly 400,000. As new coal-fired shipyards and steel works sprang up, soot started smothering Glasgow and living conditions in the city's slums deteriorated rapidly.

Glasgow has now been rejuvenated. The accumulated smoke and grime has been removed from most of the Victorian buildings now, and Glasgow's rough reputation (partly fuelled by violence associated with cross-city football rivalry) has mellowed somewhat. The city is one of the most popular tourist destinations in Britain.

Glasgow and the Industrial Revolution

Prior to the 18th century, Glasgow was a medieval University town with a population under 15,000. With the opening up of the shipping trade with America, Glasgow became an import centre for tobacco, then cotton, and other New World goods, and by the end of the 18th century the population had grown to over 100,000. But it was the so-called "Industrial Revolution" of the late 18th and early 19th centuries that really made Glasgow boom.

From about 1760 to 1840 this Revolution, which had been quietly building through invention and innovation, gained momentum as the use of mechanical power became widespread and Britain's industrial output increased dramatically.

The River Clyde was widened and dredged, and the docks became choked with bales of American cotton that fed factories using newly invented machines to spin cotton and weave fabric. The textile factories of Glasgow and Paisley attracted whole families, many arriving from Ireland during the disastrous Potato Famine of the 1840's. Children put to work in the mills had the dual benefit of being cheap and they could easily crawl between and under the machines. The British still call their woollen pullovers "sweaters" in reference to these sweatshops, although by 1833 the Factory Act had banned the use of under 9 year-olds, and limited 9 to 11 year-olds to 9-hour days, and under 18's to 12-hour days.

Steam, iron, and coal were the other components to the Revolution. James Watt, was working as an instrument maker at the University of Glasgow in 1765 when he was given a Newcomen atmospheric engine to repair. Watt's review of the machine and his addition of a separate condenser led to a much improved engine that was soon being used not only for dewatering mines but powering factories, locomotives, and steamships.

In the 1820's James Neilson was the manager at Glasgow's Gasworks when he started tinkering with the idea of using a pre-heated blast of hot air to improve the efficiency of iron smelting (cold air being the preferred method until them). He ran a test of his theory at the Clyde Ironworks in 1824, and found the method more than

1928 Women are granted the right to vote on the same basis as men

doubled the output of iron per ton of coal. The method also allowed the use of cheaper grades of coal in iron production and became the preferred method of iron making until large-scale industrial methods were developed in the 1850's.

For more information on Scottish discoveries that lead to the Industrial Revolution, visit the Glasgow Science Centre on Pacific Quay, on the south bank of the River Clyde. The site is marked by the 100m tall titanium-clad Glasgow Tower, Scotland's tallest structure, and the only tower in the world that can rotate 360 degrees on its base.

Camping;
Carskeoch House Caravan Park, Patna, Ph 01292 531205, T£5 ◆ Cunninghamhead Estate Caravan Park, 2½mi W of Kilmaurs, Ph 01294 850238, T£8

Hostel;
Nearest; Ayr, Glasgow

B&B;
Aulton Farm, 2mi W of Kilmaurs, Ph 01563 538208, S£20, D£36 ◆ Chapeltoun House Hotel, 2mi SW of Stewarton, Ph 01560 482696, S£70, D£100 ◆ Crumyard Farm, Neilston, £18pp ◆ Greenlaw Guest House, 12 Greenlaw Dr, Paisley, Ph 01418 895359, S£22, D£36 ◆ Others; Neilston, Paisley

Hotel;
Black Bull Hotel, 2 Montgomerie St, Tarbolton, Ph 01292 541909, £42pp ◆ The Crown Hotel, 24 Cunningham St, Tarbolton, Ph 01292 541546, £20pp ◆ Travel Inn, Annadale, Crosshouse, Ph 01563 570534, D£42 ◆ Mill House Hotel, 8 Dean St, Stewarton, Ph 01560 482255, £15pp ◆ Uplawmoor Hotel, Neilston Rd, Uplawmoor (3mi SW of Neilston), Ph 01505 850565, S£40, D£50 ◆ Abbey Hotel, Barrhead Rd, Paisley, Ph 01418 894529, S£35, D£50 ◆ Gleniffer Hotel, Glenburn Rd, Paisley, Ph 01418 842670, S£25, D£45 ◆ Others; Patna, Paisley

i;
TIC, 62 Bank St, Kilmarnock, Ph 01563 539090 ◆ TIC Paisley, 9A Gilmour St, Paisley, Ph 0141 890711 ◆ TIC, 35 Vincent Pl, Glasgow, Ph 01412 044400

Bike Shops;
Thomson Cycles, 11 Lawn St, Paisley, Ph 01418 870834 ◆ Dooleys Cycles, 40 Moss St , Paisley, Ph 01418 870834 ◆ Others; Ayr, Irvine, Glasgow

625mi 0.5mi after Dalmellington

650mi Crosshouse

1930 Arthur Ransome writes "Swallows and Amazons", based on his time in the Lake District

16 NEILSTON TO ARDLUI

Neilston to;

Paisley	5.0mi	b&b, hotel, i, bike shop	*248800 664100*
Alexandria	24.8mi	h, hotel	*239400 679900*
Luss	31.8mi	c, hotel	*235900 693000*
Tarbet	41.9mi	b&b, hotel	*231900 704500*
Ardlui	50.2mi	c, hotel	*231800 715700*

Take the A736 leaving Neilston, then B774 through the suburbs of Barrhead, into Paisley. Once the thread making capital of the world, Paisley started mass-producing copies of Kashmir fabrics in the 1770's, lending it's own name to the distinctive teardrop design (a museum in High St has a history of the pattern and Paisley shawls).

The route to Erskine Bridge, via the A726, is well signposted from Paisley. The bridge spans the River Clyde a few miles upstream from where it becomes tidal at the Firth of Clyde. The river was dredged and widened in the 19th century and a boom in shipbuilding at Clydebank followed. The Queen Mary, Queen Elizabeth, and QEII were all built here, although most of the big shipyards have now closed.

Before Erskine Bridge was built, crossing the Clyde into West Dunbartonshire meant taking the car ferry. In 1971 Princess Anne opened the new bridge, which had taken 4 years to construct. The 36 cables (each 2.5-inches thick) hold the 1000ft central span 180ft-above high tide, although in 1996 an oil rig being towed into Clydebank still managed to hit the bridge, closing it for several days. For cyclists the bridge is free, but cars pay a 60p toll. In 2001 there was a minor panic in the Scottish Parliament, when a civil servant forgot to renew the bridge's licence to take tolls, and traffic travelled free for a week, costing the government £100,000 in lost revenue).

At the northern end of Erskine Bridge the route joins the A82. Taking the A82, then the other roads shown on the map opposite, is a fairly quick way to get to Balloch, beside the first big loch on the tour - Loch Lomond (taking the A82 all the way to Balloch is the quickest route, although this is a busy road).

Another option at the northern end of Erskine Bridge is to join the Glasgow to Loch Lomond Cycleway, which takes dedicated cycle paths and minor roads to Balloch. The cycleway is quiet, avoids the A82, and follows the River Leven in places, however, it is a longer route, has a rough surface in places, and passes behind urban areas not recommended for solo cyclists or cycling at night. To get on the cycleway, exit the bridge to the left and follow the pedestrian path under the bridge, this joins a walkway towards the River Clyde and then the cycle path. The cycleway is well signed (you can also get a brochure from local tourist information centres).

The A82 north from Balloch is a beautiful road. The craggy hills on either side curve down to the waters edge and numerous islands dot the loch. These islands were home to Irish missionaries, who sought sanctuary here, in the 5th century. Inchmurrin, the largest island is named after St Mirren, who is said to have visited. Inchlonaig the next biggest, has a forest of yew trees, planted by Robert the Bruce for bows. The other islands have their own stories; of churches, forts, hideouts, and illegal whisky.

The road hugs the loch edge, passing the villages of Luss, Tarbet, and Ardlui, with the bulk of Ben Lomond looming across the lake. Ardlui, in Argyll & Bute County, has limited services but is a convenient place to stop before tackling the climb to Crianlarich.

Arduli consists of a hotel/pub and a couple of campgrounds. The biggest one is on the lakeside next to the hotel - unfortunately the tent area here for cyclists and walkers is a small barbwire enclosure on the land-locked side of the A82. The area is rocky

1936 Edward VIII is forced to choose between the throne and marriage to the divorced American Mrs Wallace Simpson

mi	Directions
0	Neilston (At minor/Main St 40.66 last stage). Turn Right
1.13	Right onto A736 (signed: Glasgow, Barrhead A736).
①	Cont. 0.29mi then Left onto B771 (signed: Paisley 4)
2.30	Veer Left onto B774
②	(signed: Glenburn B774)
4.97	Right onto A761 (signed: Erskine & Bridge (A726)).
③	Continue straight ahead on A761 following signs: Erskine & Bridge (A726)
6.03	Right at round about by BP Stn. (onto Caledonian St), continue on A761 (signed: Erskine & Bridge (A726))
7.30	Veer Right at major round about onto A726 (signed: Erskine) Note: don't get on M8
④	
8.95	Str. ahead at round about, cont. on A726 (signed: Erskine). Continue on A726 following Erskine and Erskine Bridge A726 signs
12.40	Left at rd about, leads onto bridge (signed: Erskine Bridge (A898)) [or walk up second signed pedestrian walkway onto bridge]
14.08	Left at North end of bridge onto A82 (signed: Crianlarich A82). Continue to Balloch via A82, A814, A812, B857 as shown here, or directly via busier A82. [Another alternative here is to join the Glasgow to Loch Lomond cycleway - see text]
⑤	
[25.35]	[If you took the cycleway to Balloch, exit Left off the cycle path at Balloch, onto Fishermans Road (signed: Town Ctr). Cont. 0.15mi then Left onto minor. At 25.60mi Right at rd. about (signed: Glasgow A811 (A82), Loch Lomond (W), Tarbet 17)]
26.00	At round about cont. North on A82 (signed: Crianlarich)
⑥	
28.55	Straight ahead at round about, continue on A82 to Tarbet (signed: Crianlarich)
41.92	Veer Right at Tarbet, cont. on A82 (signed: Crianlarich, Ft. William A82)
⑦	
50.15	Ardlui

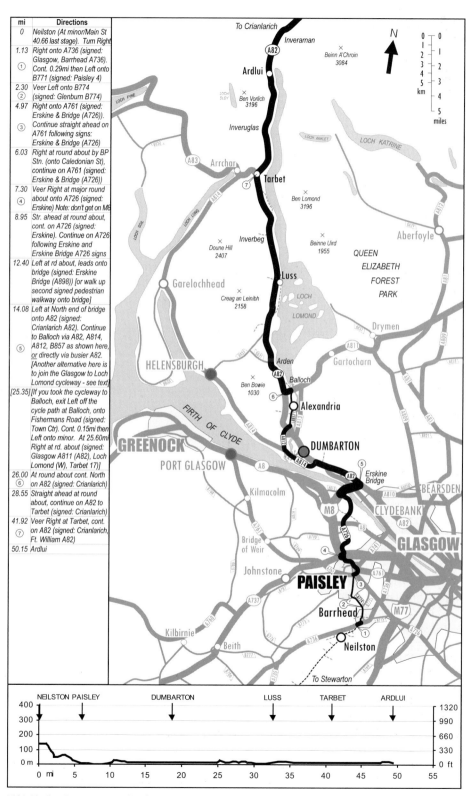

and requires a walk across the road to use the restroom. A more picturesque, and cheaper, alternative is the basic campground located in a field next to the loch, a little before the pub. Be prepared for Scotland's famous midges at these lakeside campsites.

Scotland's Contribution to Bicycle Design

Scotland has long been a land of inventors and innovators. Scottish ingenuity is responsible for the first true bicycle, the development of useable pneumatic tyres and, in the 1990's, the "Superman" aerodynamic position used to break world cycling records until it was banned. That first self-propelled bicycle, completed in 1839, was the work of Kirkpatrick Macmillan, a blacksmith from Thornhill, 14 miles north of Dumfries.

Before Macmillan, the proto-bicycle consisted of two wooden wheels, the front one steerable, with a board between to sit on and was known as "The Running-Machine" in Germany, the "Hobby-Horse" or "Dandy-Horse" in England and the US, and the "Draisienne" in France. Debuting in 1817, The Running-Machine was the invention of Baron Karl von Drais, a German with an aversion to horses and an engineering bent, and was propelled by striding along the ground. The device was actually quite popular, although Drais was unable to successfully market the machine, his patents were stolen, and he lost all his money on the invention - eventually dying penniless.

In 1835 Macmillan started experimenting with levers and cranks, and after 4 years developed the first self-propelled bicycle, complete with pedals connected to crank rods to power the rear wheel. It was manoeuvrable and fast (although with wooden wheels, somewhat heavy). Macmillan regularly rode from Thornhill to Dumfries on the machine, and in 1842 completed a tour to Glasgow in competition against a postal carriage - which he won - completing the last 40 miles or so from Cumnock in 5 hours. Macmillan did get into difficulties at the end of this trip when his bicycle drew crowds of curious onlookers and he accidentally knocked a child down (he was fined five shillings and the child was unhurt). Despite his success, Macmillan seems to have simply enjoyed cycling and had no aspirations to patent or make his invention a commercial venture.

After Macmillan there was a gap in the development of the bicycle until the 1860's, when the Frenchman Pierre Michaux, took the somewhat sideways step of adding pedals directly to the hub of the front wheel on his "Velocipedes", or as they were descriptively known in England "Boneshakers". Although less efficient than Macmillan's mechanism, the Boneshaker was a commercial success that spurred development. Soon metal rims and spokes, ball bearings, freewheels, and tubular frames were appearing. In 1870 a young foreman at the Coventry Machinists Co. (formerly the Coventry Sewing Machine Co.), James Starley, developed the concept of a huge (up to 5ft diameter) front wheel to maximise torque and a much smaller rear wheel. This drastic combination known as the "Ordinary", and nicknamed the "Penny-farthing" (after a large and small coin of the time), became the bike of choice for the next 15 years (although, the height of the handlebars and the restrictive clothing worn by women meant they often had to choose more stable tricycles and quadricycles). Starley is also credited with the revolution of the tangentially spoked wheel.

As bicycles became popular, the next major development was HJ Lawson's 1874 "Safety", a chain-driven machine with two realistically sized wheels. By the late 1880's John Starley, nephew of the developer of Ordinaries, had developed a Safety model known as "The Rover", which was dominating the bicycle market. Although the double diamond frame had not yet become the industry standard, the Safety was basically recognisable as today's modern bicycle - with one exception: it had solid tyres.

In 1845 Robert Thomson, a Scottish inventor from Stonehaven, north of Dundee, patented a vulcanised-rubber pneumatic tyre for steam carriages, but the rubber needed

1936 Frank Whittle founds Power Jets Ltd to develop a feasible jet engine for aircraft

for these "aerial wheels" proved too expensive and they soon fell out of favour. It was another 43 years before John Boyd Dunlop, a Scottish veterinarian living in Belfast, tired of the bumps and uncomfortable ride of solid tyres, experimented with inflated surgical rubber glued to his son's tricycle and came up with a working pneumatic tyre. Despite a legal challenge by Thomson, Dunlop received a patent and formed the Dunlop Rubber Company. The new tyres dramatically reduced rolling resistance, improved braking, and caused a boom in bicycle production that made rapid transport a viable option for many people in a time when automobiles were uncommon.

Dunlop sold his company and patent early on, but by the time of his death in 1921 he had the satisfaction of seeing his development become the standard around the world for motorcycles, cars, trucks, and aeroplanes.

Camping;
Tullichewan Holiday Park, Old Luss Rd, Balloch, Ph 01389 759475, T£9 ◆ Camping & Caravan Club Site, Luss, Ph 01436 860658, T£8 ◆ Ardlui Holiday Home Park, Ardlui, Ph 01301 704243, T£7 ◆ Others; Ardlui

Hostel;
YHA Loch Lomond, Arden, Alexandria, Ph 01389 850226, Dorm£12

B&B;
Kilmalid House, 17 Glenpath, Dumbarton, Ph 01389 732030, D£40 ◆ Ballyhennan Old Toll House, Tarbet, Ph 01301 702203, S£20, D£35 ◆ Others; Paisley (see p.109), Alexandria, Tarbet

Hotel;
The Inverbeg Inn, Inverbeg, Ph 01436 860678, S£70,

D£100 ◆ Milton Inn, Dumbarton Rd, Milton, Dumbarton, Ph 01389 761401, S£34, D£44 ◆ Lomond View Country House, Tarbet, Ph 01301 702477, S£35, D£50 ◆ The Ardlui Hotel, Ardlui, Ph 01301 704243, S£45, D£60 ◆ Others; Paisley (see p.109), Luss, Alexandria

i;
The Old Station Building, Balloch Rd, Balloch, Ph 01389 753533 ◆ TIC, Milton on A82, Dumbarton, Ph 01389 742306 ◆ TIC, Main St, Tarbet, Ph 01301 702260 ◆ Others; Paisley (see p.109)

Bike Shops;
Nearest; Paisley (see p.109), Glasgow

675mi Just before Erskine

700mi On the A82 between Luss and Tarbet

17 ARDLUI TO FORT WILLIAM

Ardlui to;

Crianlarich	8.2mi	h, hotel	*238400*	*725400*
Bridge of Orchy	19.8mi	h, hotel	*229800*	*739600*
Glencoe	⊬ₒ 25.0mi	c, h, b&b, hotel	*209800*	*758800*
Fort William	59.8mi	c, h, b&b, hotel, i, bike shop	*210200*	*773900*

The scenery changes dramatically along this stage as the A82 crosses the northeast-southwest trending Highland Boundary Fault, a line loosely separating the Lowlands from the Highlands. The tour gains elevation significantly after Loch Lomond, crossing the inhospitable Rannoch Moor into Highland County, before dropping, in a glorious sweep, through Glencoe to Loch Leven and Loch Linnhe. Parts of this stage parallel the West Highland Way, a 95-mile walk from Glasgow to Fort William.

The River Falloch flows down Glen Falloch to the head of Loch Lomond, and the stage starts by following the river past Inverarnan, then the Falls of Falloch a couple of miles further on. The Glen has a primordial feel, with thick moss draping the trees and the road cutting through steely schist. The climb to Crainlarich, in Stirling County, crosses country once roamed by the MacGregors. Known as the "The Nameless Clan" and outlawed in 1603 they were forbidden to wear their tartan or own land, and became rebels and mercenaries. Their most famous son was Rob Roy, born in 1671, and later glamorised by Sir Walter Scott and William Wordsworth.

The route continues climbing past the small settlements of Crainlarich, and Tyndrum, before dropping several miles to Bridge of Orchy (prior to 1935 the road to Fort William crossed the river here, hence the name). If it's raining and miserable, Bridge of Orchy is a good place to stop. The hotel/pub here has luxury and budget accommodation and serves a great banoffee pie (a toffee, banana, and cream dessert). If the weather is marginal, or you are particularly tired, consider resting here before the 25-mile journey to Glencoe, which is exposed and gains another 650 feet elevation before dropping.

From Bridge of Orchy the road passes Loch Tulla before climbing a steep 2½-mile switchback, through the Black Mount area, into the true Scottish Highlands. At the end of this climb is Rannoch Moor - a windswept plateau hemmed in by huge bluffs sculpted by glacial action. The road traverses a thick carpet of tussock, cut by streams and dotted with peaty lochs. Apart from the road and a few distant whitewashed houses dwarfed by bluffs, there is little evidence of human habitation. On a fine summer's day this is a beautiful ride - the road lined with purple and white wildflowers and a wide horizon. But when it's misty, wet and windy the crags close in, and a headwind can make this section tough going. Robert Louis Stevenson described this dramatic scenery is his novel "Kidnapped" as being "as waste as the sea", and more recently the hills have been used as backdrops for the movies Rob Roy and Braveheart.

The Kingshouse Hotel in the heart of the Moor has a long history and, probably due to its lack of competition, is actually the oldest inn in Scotland. There is also a mountain rescue post here.

About 16 miles after Bridge of Orchy the A82 starts to descend through Glen Coe. This is another panoramic stretch, as the valley walls close in and the road follows the River Coe down to Loch Leven. Unfortunately, this Glen is most famous for the early morning massacre of MacDonalds in 1692. The Secretary of State for Scotland, John Dalrymple, had ordered the MacDonalds punished for failing to take an oath of loyalty to William III in a timely manner, and Robert Campbell and a group of Campbell troops were dispatched to Glencoe. After enjoying 12 days of hospitality with the MacDonalds,

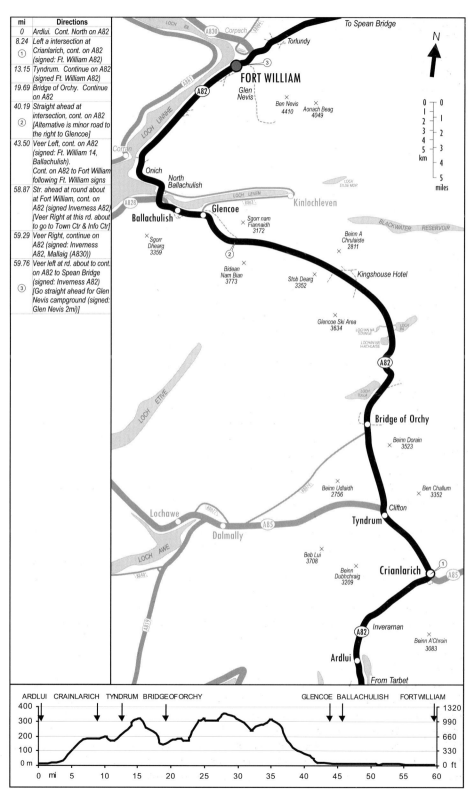

mi	Directions
0	Ardlui. Cont. North on A82
8.24 ①	Left a intersection at Crianlarich, cont. on A82 (signed: Ft. William A82)
13.15	Tyndrum. Continue on A82 (signed Ft. William A82)
19.69	Bridge of Orchy. Continue on A82
40.19 ②	Straight ahead at intersection, cont. on A82 [Alternative is minor road to the right to Glencoe]
43.50	Veer Left, cont. on A82 (signed: Ft. William 14, Ballachulish). Cont. on A82 to Fort William following Ft. William signs
58.87	Str. ahead at round about at Fort William, cont. on A82 (signed Inverness A82) [Veer Right at this rd. about to go to Town Ctr & Info Ctr]
59.29	Veer Right, continue on A82 (signed: Inverness A82, Mallaig (A830))
59.76 ③	Veer left at rd. about to cont. on A82 to Spean Bridge (signed: Inverness A82) [Go straight ahead for Glen Nevis campground (signed: Glen Nevis 2mi)]

1940 The Battle of Britain is fought for aerial supremacy of the skies over Southern England

orders arrived to kill everyone under 70, and 40 men, women, and children were murdered one morning during a snowstorm. An inquiry eventually led to Dalrymple's expulsion from office but the perpetrators were basically pardoned by the King.

At the bottom of Glencoe is Loch Leven and the little town of Ballachulish, sitting beside an old slate quarry. Continuing over Loch Leven, the A82 becomes busier and has little shoulder to ride on as the route follows the edge of Loch Linnhe to Fort William.

Fort William is a decent sized town of about 10,000, with a good selection of shops and services, including a heated pool at the Community Centre. There is a good campground about 2 miles from downtown in beautiful Glen Nevis, near the base of Britain's highest peak Ben Nevis.

The Bonnie Prince

The West Highlands Museum on High St in Fort William has a curious painting of Bonnie Prince Charlie, the charismatic "Young Pretender". The painting looks like a curved smear of paint and is indecipherable until a circular mirror is placed in the centre of the picture - revealing a secret portrait of the handsome young prince.

Charles landed in Scotland to rally the Highland clans and reclaim the throne in the Jacobite Rebellion of 1745. The 25 year old Prince was the son of James Edward (The Old Pretender) and grandson of the last hereditary Stuart King, James II. He was considered by many to be the legitimate Stuart heir to the throne. Unfortunately for Charles, his grandfather's Catholicism and inept dealings with government (he stacked Parliament with Catholic MP's, much to the alarm of the Church of England), had resulted in the Catholic Stuarts becoming increasingly unpopular.

When Charles' father, James Edward, was born, it meant another Catholic in line for the throne, and James II was forced to leave for France (his Protestant daughter Mary and her Dutch husband William became King and Queen). James Edward returned in 1715, to Peterhead near Aberdeen, after a Jacobite Rebellion (the term Jacobite is from Latin for James) was raised in his favour, but was quickly beaten back by the British.

The Young Pretender's 1745 effort was, initially, much more successful. Trained in war growing up in the courts of France and Italy, he landed with only 12 supporters on the tiny island of Eriskay in the Outer Hebrides on July 23. By November 17 he had raised the Highlands in revolt, captured Edinburgh (although Edinburgh Castle and Fort William both held out), and with an army of over 5,000 besieged and took Carlisle on the English border. By December he was in the heart of England, at Derby, only 130 miles from London.

At Derby, Charles' nerve broke. Faced with the prospect of tens of thousands of royalist troops and little support from the English people, his lieutenants urged a retreat and Charles reluctantly agreed. The Duke of Cumberland, son of the Hanoverian King George II, relentlessly pursued and finally cornered Charles on a moor at Culloden, near Inverness, on April 16 1746. The ensuing battle against 9,000 Redcoats lasted less than an hour. An artillery attack decimated Charles' ranks and the outcome was sealed after the Highlanders first charge, when, in a choreographed move, each Redcoat squatted and bayoneted the exposed side of the Highlander to his right. With twenty highlanders killed for every Redcoat the battle was a complete annihilation, and Charles' forces broke up and fled after 1,000 of their number had been killed. Cumberland's dogged pursuit of the fleeing army, over the next few weeks, earned him his nickname "The Butcher", and with a £30,000 price on his head Charles was a wanted man.

For the next 5 months Charles was smuggled from town to town around Scotland's mainland and outer islands, his most famous escape being from the Outer Hebrides to Skye, dressed as Flora MacDonald's maid. He was never betrayed by his hosts but eventually fled to France. A life as a hanger-on followed, first in France then in Italy where he finally died a drunk with his title to the throne disclaimed by the Pope.

For Cumberland, praises flowed, a work was composed by Handel in his honour and a flower was named after him (the "Sweet William" - known in Scotland as the "Sour Billy"). The praises ceased after his later military failures in France caused his father to sack him.

For the Highlanders their support for Charles cost them dearly, with the banning of tartan and the forced break-up of their clan system.

Camping;
Pine Trees Leisure Park, Tyndrum, Ph 01838 400314, T£9 ◆ Invercoe Caravans, Glencoe, Ph 01855 811210, T£6pp ◆ Glen Nevis Caravan and Camping Park, Glen Nevis, Ft William, Ph 01397 702191, T£10 ◆ Others; Luib (7mi E of Crianlarich), Corpach (4mi W of Fort William), Ft William

Hostel;
YHA Crainlarich, Station Rd, Crianlarich, Ph 01838 300260, Dorm£9 ◆ Bridge of Orchy Bunkhouse (bunkroom only), Bridge of Orchy, Ph 1838 400208, Dorm£9 ◆ YHA Glencoe, Glencoe, Ph 01855 811219, Dorm£9 ◆ Fort William Backpackers, Alma Rd, Ft William, Ph 01397 700711, Dorm£11 ◆ YHA Glen Nevis, Glen Nevis, Ft William, Ph 01397 702336, Dorm£13 ◆ Others; Onich (3mi N of Ballachulish), Corpach (4mi W of Fort William)

B&B;
Limetree Studio Gallery, Achintore Rd, Ft William, Ph 01397 701806, £27pp ◆ Others; Glencoe, Ballachulish, Ft William

Hotel;
Ben More Lodge Hotel, Crianlarich, Ph 01838 300210, S£40, D£65 ◆ Bridge of Orchy Hotel, Bridge of Orchy, Ph 1838 400208, £35pp ◆ Kings House Hotel, Rannoch Moor, (14mi N of Bridge of Orchy), Ph 01855 851259, S£30, D£50 ◆ Glencoe Hotel, Glencoe, Ph 01855 811245, £36pp ◆ Alexandra Hotel, The Parade, Ft William, Ph 01397 702241, D£100 ◆ Others; Ballachulish, Ft William

i;
TIC, Albert Rd, Ballachulish, Ph 01855 811296 ◆ TIC, Cameron Sq, Ft William, Ph 01397 703781

Bike Shop;
Off Beat Cycles, 117 High St, Ft William, Ph 01397 704008

725mi Just after Crianlarich

750mi Entering Glencoe

1945 VE day, May 8, is the end of WWII in Europe

117

18 FORT WILLIAM TO LEWISTON

Fort William to;

Spean Bridge	10.5mi	c, b&b, hotel, i	*222600 781800*
Invergarry	25.9mi	c, b&b, hotel	*230900 801200*
Fort Augustus	34.0mi	h, hotel, i	*237900 809500*
Invermoriston	40.4mi	c, b&b, hotel	*241800 817100*
Lewiston	50.0mi	c, h, b&b, hotel, bike shop	*251000 829200*

Continuing north on the A82 from Fort William to Loch Ness, the route enters the Great Glen, a northeast-southwest trending perforation across Scotland resulting from movement on the Great Glen Fault about 350 million years ago. This fault, and other parallel ones, has left many of the lochs, islands, coastlines (and subsequently roads) across the Highlands with a distinctive northeast linear orientation.

The A82 between Fort William and Invergarry closely follows one of General Wade's military roads, built in the early 1720's to help open up the Highlands to government control and suppress the Highlanders following the 1715 Jacobite uprising (although Bonnie Prince Charlie himself used the road in 1746, during his escape from the Duke of Cumberland). [The Great Glen Cycle Route offers an off-road cycle route between Fort William and Inverness, however it mainly follows forest tracks and is not recommended for road bikes. The Fort William Tourist Information Centre has details].

At Spean Bridge the road crosses a bridge built by Thomas Telford in 1819, and heads up the only hill of consequence on the stage, a short, tough, climb to a memorial marking the efforts of British Commandos who trained in the area during WWII. From here the road drops through plantation forest to the shores of the charmingly named Loch Lochy (Lake of the Dark Goddess). The road next to the loch is flat with a wide shoulder agreeable for cycling and the loch is flanked by the grassy slopes of the Glen which steepen upward to rocky crags with dramatic effect.

At the northeast tip of Loch Lochy the road passes Laggan Locks and makes a short skip to Loch Oich. At the southern end of Loch Oich the road crosses the Caledonian Canal at Laggan Swing Bridge and heads up the western shoreline to Invergarry [the Loch Lochy YHA youth hostel is located in Laggan].

Half a mile past the swing bridge is the Well of the Seven Heads, where a plaque tells the gruesome 17th century story of Ian Lom, who murdered seven brothers as payback for two MacDonnell killings and washed their heads here before presenting them to the clan chief at Glengarry.

Just before Invergarry, a short detour to the right takes you to the ruins of Invergarry Castle, burned by the Duke of Cumberland in 1746 following the Battle of Culloden. Invergarry has a hotel and several bed & breakfasts, and is a popular base for salmon fishing on the Garry River.

At the northern end of Loch Oich is the Bridge of Oich, a suspension bridge built in 1854 after severe flooding 5 years earlier swept the old bridge away and badly damaged the Caledonian Canal. From here you can stay on the A82 to Fort Augustus, or take a 5-mile stretch of the Great Glen Cycle Route, next to the canal. The cycleway is flat, beautiful, and avoids the traffic of the A82, however, the track has large gravel in places, making it a rough ride for road bikes. The A82 is quicker, but busier. If you want a break off the bike there are some good forest walks to the west of River Oich between the bridge and Fort Augustus, through forests of birch, ash and oak.

Fort Augustus is a pretty village with a stairway of 4 locks that drop the Caledonian Canal 40ft into Scotland's most famous Loch, Loch Ness. Government troops set up

1947 India, lead by Mahatma Gandhi, gains independence and splits into India and Pakistan

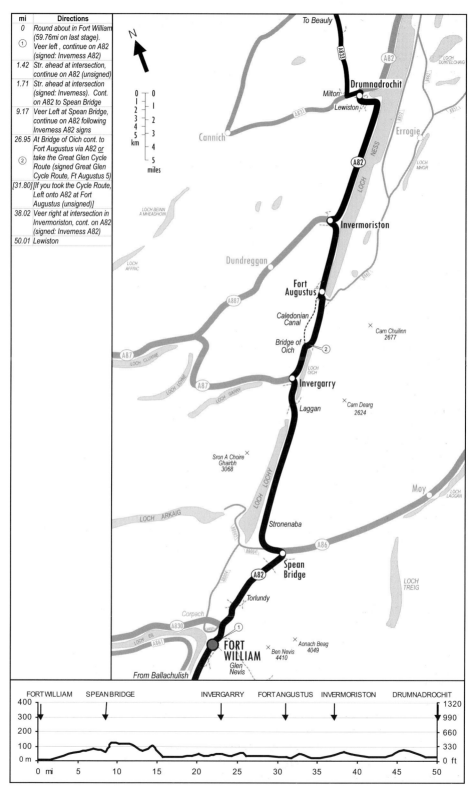

mi	Directions
0 ①	Round about in Fort William (59.76mi on last stage). Veer left , continue on A82 (signed: Inverness A82)
1.42	Str. ahead at intersection, continue on A82 (unsigned)
1.71	Str. ahead at intersection (signed: Inverness). Cont. on A82 to Spean Bridge
9.17	Veer Left at Spean Bridge, continue on A82 following Inverness A82 signs
26.95 ②	At Bridge of Oich cont. to Fort Augustus via A82 or take the Great Glen Cycle Route (signed Great Glen Cycle Route, Ft Augustus 5)
[31.80]	[If you took the Cycle Route, Left onto A82 at Fort Augustus (unsigned)]
38.02	Veer right at intersection in Invermoriston, cont. on A82 (signed: Inverness A82)
50.01	Lewiston

To Beauly

A833   A82   LOCH DUNTELCHAIG

Drumnadrochit
Milton
Lewiston   A831
A831   Erogie

Cannich   LOCH NESS   LOCH MHOR

A82

Invermoriston

LOCH BEINN A MHEADHOIN

Dundreggan

Fort Augustus   Carn Chuilinn 2677

Caledonian Canal

A887

Bridge of Oich   ②

A87 LOCH CLUANIE   LOCH OICH

A87   LOCH GARRY   Invergarry   Carn Dearg 2624

Laggan

Sron A Choire Ghairbh 3068

Moy   LOCH LAGGAN

LOCH ARKAIG   LOCH LOCHY

Stronenaba   A86   LOCH TREIG

Spean Bridge

A82

Torlundy

Corpach   A830

FORT WILLIAM   ①   Aonach Beag 4049
Ben Nevis 4410
A861   Glen Nevis

From Ballachulish

	FORT WILLIAM	SPEAN BRIDGE		INVERGARRY	FORT ANGUSTUS	INVERMORISTON	DRUMNADROCHIT	

400 300 200 100 0 m

1320 990 660 330 0 ft

0 mi   5   10   15   20   25   30   35   40   45   50

1947 The table soccer game Subbuteo is released

119

camp at this location after the 1715 clan uprisings, and in 1729 General Wade built a fort, naming it, prophetically, after George II's youngest son William Augustus, Duke of Cumberland. Jacobites laid siege to the fort in 1746, on their way to the Battle of Culloden, and it fell after 2 days. 43 days later, after his victory at Culloden, Cumberland regained the fort. In 1876 it became a monastery for Benedictine monks, then a few years later a full Abbey, which operated until 1998. A local businessmen recently bought the Abbey with plans to open a visitor centre.

The final 18 miles to Lewiston hug the shores of Loch Ness and the road is often thick with tourist traffic. Just past Fort Augustus there is Cherry Island, the remains of a tiny and ancient artificial lake dwelling. Invermoriston is a small village with plaques marking the deaths of Roderick Mackenzie and John Cobb. Mackenzie was one of Prince Charlie's bodyguards who posed as the Prince when Cumberland was in hot pursuit. He was killed, but the decoy allowed the real Prince to escape. Cobb was killed 200 years later trying to take his jet-powered boat past 200mph on the loch. He held the world land speed record (394mph) at the time and was attempting to break the water-speed record when his boat hit a wave, flipped, and disintegrated.

Just before Lewiston are the impressive ruins of Urquhart Castle. The castle dates from the 13th century (some think even Pictish times) and was repeatedly fought over, partially destroyed, and rebuilt before finally being blown up in 1692 to prevent its use by the Jacobites. A storm blew more of the south wall down in 1715 but the remains are still impressive. Probably the most familiar photo of the castle is, ironically, a shot of two long lumps disturbing the surface of the Loch just north of the castle, taken in 1955 by Peter McNab and now thought by many to be a hoax.

Lewiston and Drumnadrochit sit in Urquhart Bay. There is hotel, hostel and campground accommodation in the Bay.

Thomas Telford and The Caledonian Canal

Born in 1757, the son of a shepherd, in a remote Scottish valley northeast of Langholm, Thomas Telford rose to become one of the Britain's pre-eminent engineers and was buried in the nave Westminster Abbey. He designed roads, bridges, and ports in Britain and beyond but his most dramatic engineering achievement in his homeland was the Caledonian Canal - linking the Irish sea with the North Sea, and giving seafarers an alternative to the trip around Cape Wrath at the tip of Scotland.

After starting out as a stonemason, Telford's career took off when he was made surveyor of public works for Shropshire on the recommendation of a patron. His first big project was the Ellesmere Canal (1793-1805) and other commissions soon followed.

In 1801 he start surveying the Caledonian Canal, with construction starting at either end (Loch Linnhe, and the Moray Firth at Inverness) in 1803. Telford's plan was for 22 miles of canal with locks linking the natural waterways along the Great Glen Fault, to give a navigable waterway over 60 miles long. At a time when the Highland Clearances where underway, the project provided much needed jobs. The Caledonian took 19 years to build, effectively by hand, and opened for through traffic in 1822.

Unlike most canals, which have to be topped up by reservoirs, the Caledonian makes use of the lochs themselves to replenish the system. Loch Oich is the high point along the route, about 105ft above sea level. From Loch Oich water flows down staircases of locks to both to the Irish and North Seas. The greatest single drop is Neptune's Staircase, near Corpach at the northeast end of Loch Linnhe, where 8 locks lift and lower vessels 65 feet to the canal that joins Loch Lochy.

Unfortunately the Caledonian Canal, like many others, was superseded after just 25 years by the advent of rail and large steam ships, and the last Fort William to Inverness passenger service on the canal ran in 1930.

1951 Britain's population is about 50 million

The canal locks were mechanised in the 1970's, but each set of lochs still has a resident lock-keeper to assist with navigation. These days the majority of canal users are on holiday cruisers, although fishing boats, blue-water yachts, and navy ships still use the system. The average through trip takes 3 days. Tourists can hire motor-cruisers or yachts at Laggan Locks or Inverness, and after a few hours training make the trip along the Caledonian unaccompanied.

Camping;
Stronaba Caravan Site, Spean Bridge, (2½mi N of Spean Bridge on A82), Ph 01397 712259, T£7 ◆ Faichem Park Caravan & Camping Park, Faichem, Invergarry, Ph 01809 501226, T£8 ◆ Lock Ness Caravan & Camping Park, Easter Port Clair, Invermoriston, Ph 01320 351207, T£8 ◆ Borlum Farm Caravan & Camping, Drumnadrochit, Ph 01456 450220, T£8 ◆ Others; Gairlochy (4mi NW of Spean Bridge on B8004), Invergarry, Lewiston

Hostel;
YHA Loch Lochy, Laggan, Ph 01809 501239, Dorm£10 ◆ YHA Loch Ness, Glenmoriston (4mi NE of Invermoriston on A82), Ph 01320 351274, Dorm£9 ◆ Lock Ness Backpackers, East Lewiston *(also limited camping)*, Ph 01456 450807, Dorm£10 ◆ Others; Roy Bridge (3mi E of Spean Bridge), Ft Augustus

B&B;
Inverour Guest House, Spean Bridge, Ph 01397 712218, S£18, D£36 ◆ Glengarry Castle Hotel, Invergarry, Ph 01809 501254, S£55, D£90 ◆

Bracarina House, Invermoriston, Ph 01320 351279, S£22, D£36 ◆ Glen Rowan House, West Lewiston, Drumnadrochit, Ph 01456 450235, S£35, D£45 ◆ Others; Ft Augustus, Spean Bridge, Invergarry, Lewiston, Drumnadrochit

Hotel;
Drumnadrochit Hotel, Drumnadrochit, Ph 01456 450218, £25pp ◆ Caledonian Hotel, Ft Augustus, Ph 01320 366256, £20pp ◆ Spean Bridge Hotel, Spean Bridge, Ph 01397 712250, S£37, D£49 ◆ Others; Spean Bridge, Drumnadrochit

i;
Scotland Tourist Board, Spean Bridge, Ph 01397 712567 ◆ Tourist Information, car park on A82, Ft Augustus, Ph 01320 366367

Bike Shop;
Wilderness Cycles, The Cottage, Drumnadrochit, Ph 01456 450233 ◆ Others; Ft William, Inverness

775mi Fort William

800mi On the A82 between Invergarry and Bridge of Oich

1952 A fog, worsened by chimney smoke and so dense people cannot see their feet, envelops London for 5 days during December, killing 4,000

19 LEWISTON TO TAIN

Lewiston to;

Beauly	13.0mi	c, b&b, hotel	*252600 846400*
Evanton	28.2mi	c, h, b&b, hotel	*260700 866100*
Invergordon	35.8mi	b&b, hotel	*270800 868400*
Tain	46.7mi	c, b&b, hotel, i	*277900 882100*

At Drumnadrochit, just north of Lewiston, the tour leaves the A82 and heads west on the A831 briefly, before turning north on the A833 towards Beauly. The first 3 miles of the A833 are a tough climb. After this there is a great 9-mile sweep downhill to Beauly. The road passes wheat fields and paddocks dotted with Highland cattle, fearsome looking beasts with woolly coats and huge horns. They are the oldest surviving European cattle breed, dating from the 12th century, and are hardy enough to stay out over winter and survive on the slim pickings of Highland shrubs and gorse.

Flowerpots line the bridge into Beauly and the town proudly displays its "Britain in Bloom" winning plaque. Mary Queen of Scots stayed in the Beauly Priory (now a ruin) and also liked the area - ordering local tartan outfits for herself and her entourage.

1½ miles after Beauly B9169 splits off and climbs a ridge to a monument honouring a local soldier, Hector McDonald. After the monument the road follows the ridgeline, overlooking Dingwall and Cromarty Firth.

The route temporarily joins the A9, crossing the Firth via Cromarty Bridge, which was built in 1982, before taking B817 through Evanton and Alness. During WWII these towns had busy flight training schools, Evanton for bombers and Alness for Sunderland flying boats. Alness expanded in the 1970's to accommodate workers for developing industries at nearby Invergordon, including an aluminium smelter and support services for North Sea oil production. The town suffered a tough blow when the smelter closed suddenly in the 1980's, but bounced back recently with the opening of a high-tech business park - a sort of Scottish Silicon Valley - at the old flying boat base.

After Alness the route follows the Firth coastline for several miles to Invergordon, an excellent deep-water anchorage. A harbour was first built in 1828 and since the 1970's it has earned a steady income from the construction and repair of North Sea oil rigs. More recently the port has become a stopping point for cruise liners circling Britain or visiting from Europe, including the QEII which visited recently.

The A82 from Kildary is the quickest way to Tain. A quieter route, fractionally shorter but hillier, is shown on the map opposite. This road climbs through woods before emerging to good views over the Firth and a sweeping downhill into Tain.

Tain became a place for medieval pilgrimages after St Duthac (also known as Duffus) was born there in 1000. James IV is thought to have made at least 18 visits, and his son, James V, made his pilgrimage barefoot.

Oil and Whisky

Oil and whisky are two of Scotland's biggest export earners. Invergordon, on the shores of Cromarty Firth, is a centre for oil rig and drill ship servicing, and Tain, up the road on the shores of Dornoch Firth, is home to the Glenmorangie Distillery, makers of Scotland's most popular whisky.

Invergordon grew considerably after British Petroleum (BP) discovered large natural gas reserves in the North Sea in 1965, followed by the Montrose oil field in 1969. The gas and oil originate from algae and plankton which died 200 million years ago and were deposited on an ancient seafloor. Burial and breakdown of these

1954 Roger Bannister becomes the first person to run a mile in under 4 minutes

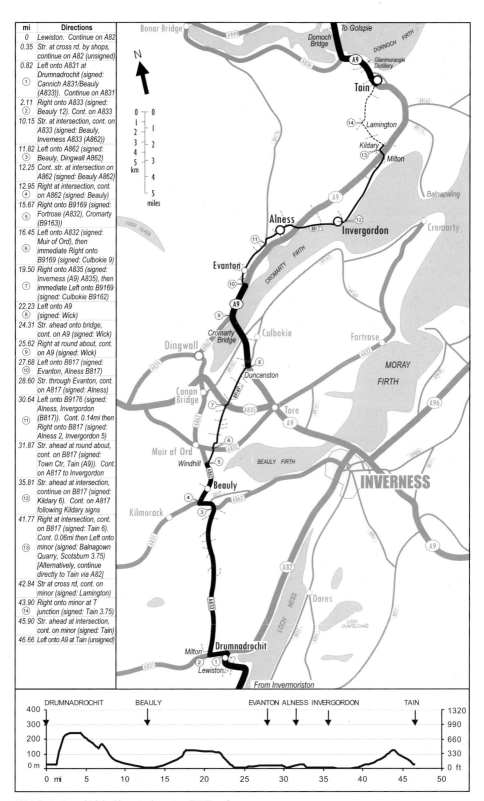

mi	Directions
0	Lewiston. Continue on A82
0.35	Str. at cross rd. by shops, continue on A82 (unsigned)
0.82 ①	Left onto A831 at Drumnadrochit (signed: Cannich A831/Beauly (A833)). Continue on A831
2.11 ②	Right onto A833 (signed: Beauly 12). Cont. on A833
10.15	Str. at intersection, cont. on A833 (signed: Beauly, Inverness A833 (A862))
11.82 ③	Left onto A862 (signed: Beauly, Dingwall A862)
12.25	Cont. str. at intersection on A862 (signed: Beauly A862)
12.95 ④	Right at intersection, cont. on A862 (signed: Beauly)
15.67 ⑤	Right onto B9169 (signed: Fortrose (A832), Cromarty (B9163))
16.45 ⑥	Left onto A832 (signed: Muir of Ord), then immediate Right onto B9169 (signed: Culbokie 9)
19.50 ⑦	Right onto A835 (signed: Inverness (A9) A835), then immediate Left onto B9169 (signed: Culbokie B9162)
22.23 ⑧	Left onto A9 (signed: Wick)
24.31	Str. ahead onto bridge, cont. on A9 (signed: Wick)
25.62 ⑨	Right at round about, cont. on A9 (signed: Wick)
27.68 ⑩	Left onto B817 (signed: Evanton, Alness B817)
28.60	Str. through Evanton, cont. on A817 (signed: Alness)
30.64 ⑪	Left onto B9176 (signed: Alness, Invergordon (B817)). Cont. 0.14mi then Right onto B817 (signed: Alness 2, Invergordon 5)
31.87	Str. ahead at round about, cont. on B817 (signed: Town Ctr, Tain (A9)). Cont. on A817 to Invergordon
35.81 ⑫	Str. ahead at intersection, continue on B817 (signed: Kildary 6). Cont. on A817 following Kildary signs
41.77 ⑬	Right at intersection, cont. on B817 (signed: Tain 6). Cont. 0.06mi then Left onto minor (signed: Balnagown Quarry, Scotsburn 3.75) [Alternatively, continue directly to Tain via A82]
42.84	Str at cross rd, cont. on minor (signed: Lamington)
43.90 ⑭	Right onto minor at T junction (signed: Tain 3.75)
45.90	Str. ahead at intersection, cont. on minor (signed: Tain)
46.66	Left onto A9 at Tain (unsigned)

organisms resulted in fine-grained sedimentary formations containing fossil fuels. Favourable folding and faulting of the seafloor then concentrated these hydrocarbons in porous sandstone reservoirs. To date, geologists have found over 100 commercially viable fields between Britain and Norway. North Sea oil, known as Brent crude, is a "sweet" oil; rich in the low molecular weight hydrocarbons that make up gasoline, and low in sulphur (as opposed to Saudi crude which has heavier hydrocarbons, more sulphur, and requires more refining).

The deep-water of Cromarty Firth provides an ideal location for servicing oil platforms and you are likely to see several huge rigs parked in the channel at Invergordon, waiting for a refit or an improvement in market conditions. The town also produces submarine pipes, used to transport oil and gas from the seafloor to onshore terminals, such as the one at nearby Nigg.

Oil has resulted in jobs and capital for Scotland, but there have been problems. In 1988, Piper Alpha, a rig belonging to the American company Occidental Petroleum, exploded after a pump being repaired was accidentally turned on. The initial gas explosion and fire were relatively contained at first, however, nearby rigs did not immediately shut down their submarine pipelines which also fed gas and oil to Piper Alpha, and a huge fireball eventually engulfed the rig. At the time of the accident the rig had been producing up to 10% of Britain's North Sea production, and had 225 men on board. Most of the 58 men who survived jumped over 100ft into the sea.

This tragedy was followed in the 1990's by a controversy over the Brent Spar oil storage platform. Shell had been planning to sink this structure at sea until Greenpeace protesters boarded it in June 1995, claiming it had 5,000 gallons of oil and toxic waste aboard. Following a public outcry, which included a costly boycott of Shell's service stations in Europe, the company backed down and decided to dismantle the platform on land (despite many scientists' opinion that, environmentally, this might be worse). Later that year Greenpeace publicly apologised to Shell for overestimating the amount of oil on the platform, and an independent assessment estimated there were only about 150 gallons on the platform. In 1999 Shell had the platform broken down in Norway and sections were used to build a vehicular ferry terminal. Despite these setbacks oil and gas continue to provide a huge contribution to Scotland's economy.

The other, more traditionally, significant liquid for the Scots is whisky (or "whiskey" if you're American). From the Gaelic for "water of life", whisky has been distilled in Scotland since at least the 15th century, and Tain's "Glenmorangie" is currently the number 3 premium malt brand in the world.

Glenmorangie has been in production since 1849, when William Matheson converted an existing brewery at Morangie Farm into a distillery, apart from enforced breaks during WWI, The Depression, and WWII. Things have changed a bit since the early days. Back then the cycle of whisky production followed the seasons, with local farmers providing the first sacks of barley at the end of the summer harvest. Distilling would take place from the end of autumn, through winter and into the start of summer, then a "silent season" would follow.

When barley arrived it was taken by "maltmen", soaked, and laid out on the floor of a maltbarn for at least a week to germinate. The grain was constantly turned with wooden shovels to control the germination process. Once the seed's starches had turned to malt sugars the germination was stopped by drying the grain over peat fired kilns. The peat came from the moors to the north and was also used to fire the stills [southbound trains from Wick and Thurso cross these barren moors before Helmsdale]. The malt was then mixed with water from Tarlogie Spring (located in the hills behind the distillery) and yeast to initiate fermentation. The resulting "wash" was vaporised and caught in coils that condensed the spirit. Finally the liquid was transferred to Spanish oak barrels to age,

1959 The Mini, designed by Alec Issigonis, is released and becomes fashionable in swinging London after the Queen test-drives one

with the wood letting a portion of the whisky evaporate - the "angels share".

By the end of the 20th century the age-old distilling cycles at Tain had changed significantly. The peat used to fire the stills gave way to coal, then oil. Spanish oak was replaced by Ozark oak from Missouri, and by the 1980's malting was being done elsewhere. In 2000, Brown-Forman, the Louisville owners of Jack Daniel's and Southern Comfort, bought 10% of Glenmorangie. Despite these changes, the fundamentals of making Glenmorangie remain the same, the water still coming from Tarlogie and the grain is still peat dried to give the smoky malt taste characteristic of Scotch whisky. If you plan on stopping at the distillery mid-ride for a tour and taste-test remember the whisky is upwards of 43% alcohol by volume (75 proof).

Camping;
Lovat Bridge Caravan Park, <u>Beauly</u>, Ph 01463 782374, T£8 ◆ Druimorrin Caravan & Camping Park, Orrin Bridge, <u>Urray</u> (2mi NW of Muir of Ord), Ph 019997 433252, T£9 ◆ Camping & Caravanning Club Site, Jubilee Park, <u>Dingwall</u>, Ph 01349 862236, T£9 ◆ Black Rock Caravan & Camping Park, <u>Evanton</u>, Ph 01349 830917, T£10 ◆ Meikle Ferry Caravan Park, Meikle Ferry, <u>Tain</u>, Ph 01862 892292, T£7 ◆ Others; <u>Beauly</u>, <u>Dingwall</u>

Hostel;
<u>Evanton</u> (bunkroom at Black Rock Park - *see Camping*)

B&B;
Heathmount Guest House, Station Rd, <u>Beauly</u>, Ph 01463 782411, S£20, D£40 ◆ Kiltearn House, <u>Evanton</u>, Ph 01349 830617, £25pp ◆ Mrs Docherty, 10 Ross Crs, <u>Invergordon</u>, Ph 01862 842380, S£18 D£36 ◆ Carringtons B&B, Morangie Rd, <u>Tain</u>, Ph 01862 892635, £18pp ◆ Golf View House, 13 Knockbreck Rd, <u>Tain</u>, Ph 01862 892856, £25pp ◆ Others; <u>Beauly</u>, <u>Evanton</u>, <u>Invergordon</u>, <u>Tain</u>

Hotel;
Lovat Arms Hotel, High St, <u>Beauly</u>, Ph 01463 782313, D£90 ◆ The Novar Arms Hotel, Balgonie St, <u>Evanton</u>, Ph 01349 830210, S£40, D£50 ◆ Marine Hotel, 19 High St, <u>Invergordon</u>, Ph 01349 852419, S£45, D£65 ◆ The Royal Hotel, High St, <u>Tain</u>, Ph 01862 892013, £40pp ◆ Mansfield House Hotel, Scotsburn Rd, <u>Tain</u>, Ph 01862 892052, £50pp ◆ Others; <u>Beauly</u>, <u>Invergordon</u>, <u>Tain</u>

i;
Tain Through Time Visitor Centre, Tower St, <u>Tain</u>, Ph 01862 894089

Bike Shops;
Nearest; <u>Dingwall</u>, <u>Inverness</u>

825mi Drumnadrochit

850mi Cromarty Firth Bridge

1963 The War Minister, John Profumo, resigns after lying about an affair with Christine Keeler, a woman involved with a Soviet naval attaché

125

Tain to;

Golspie	18.5mi	b&b, hotel	*283100 899900*
Brora	24.0mi	b&b, hotel	*290600 904100*
Helmsdale	35.2mi	h, b&b, hotel, i	*302700 915300*
Berriedale	44.4mi	b&b	*312000 922900*

Leaving Tain, the A9 passes Glenmorangie Distillery, with stacks of oak barrels ageing outside (quite a sight considering each barrel contains about 275 bottles at £20+ a bottle).

2½ miles past Tain the A9 crosses the golden sands and purple heather lining Dornoch Firth, at Meikle Ferry. In the early 18th century a ferry running across the Firth sank, with over 100 lives lost. Later, a bridge was built by Thomas Telford at Bonar Bridge, 9 miles to the west, during road improvements for the 1st Duke of Sutherland (the present A9 bridge, built in the 1980's, saves travellers this detour).

The tour continues north on the A9, past the turn off to Dornoch (which suffered a media blitz in 2000 when Guy Ritchie and Madonna wed at the ultra exclusive Skibo Castle - built in 1898 for Scottish-born American Andrew Carnegie).

At the western end of Loch Fleet the road crosses a half-mile causeway with tidal gates, known as "The Mound" - another Telford construction. Before The Mound was finished in 1816, travellers had to make another ferry crossing here. Loch Fleet is a 1,150-acre estuarine nature reserve, popular with birdwatchers.

Golpsie is a small town just before Dunrobin Castle with a supermarket, a pleasant promenade by the sea, and a restored water-powered mill where you can buy oatmeal porridge - the traditional Scot's breakfast.

Dunrobin Castle is the ancestral home of the Earls and Dukes of Sutherland, and is one of the biggest houses in the Highlands. A structure is thought to have stood on this cliff-top site since the 13th century, although the oldest parts of the current house date from the 16th. Sir Charles Barry, architect of the Houses of Parliament, undertook an extensive remodel of the castle and gardens in the 1850's, resulting in a baronial mansion that looks like a French chateau. Unfortunately a fire in 1915 gutted much of the interior, which was then redesigned by another famous architect, Sir Robert Lorimer.

The house is open from April to October and is well worth a stop to see how the Dukes lived relative to their tenants. There are falconry displays and the family museum, in the Summer House, has an excellent collection of artefacts including Pict stones, military memorabilia, and geological and natural history specimens - even a bone reputedly from Mr Jan de Groot himself, found under his original house at John O' Groats. The 5th Duke lived when safaris were fashionable, and there are numerous glassy-eyed trophies, or photos of dead quarry, from his expeditions around the world.

Continuing north, it is a beautiful ride through stone-walled fields separating the coast from the road. About a mile past Dunrobin Castle is Carn Liath broch, an Iron-Age circular fort, easily accessible from the road.

Brora is a small town on the River Brora, popular for the salmon fishing.

Helmsdale is the last town with more than a few shops before Wick, 35 miles further on. The ruins of Helmsdale Castle stood beside the river here, before being demolished in 1971 to make way for the new A9 bridge into town. In 1567 the 11th Earl and Countess of Sutherland were given poisoned wine in the castle by a rival aunt. The plan came badly unstuck when the aunt's son accidentally drank the wine too, and the Earl's son was late back from hunting and missed dinner (Shakespeare's *Hamlet* is said to be loosely based on this plot). The information centre at Helmsdale has details

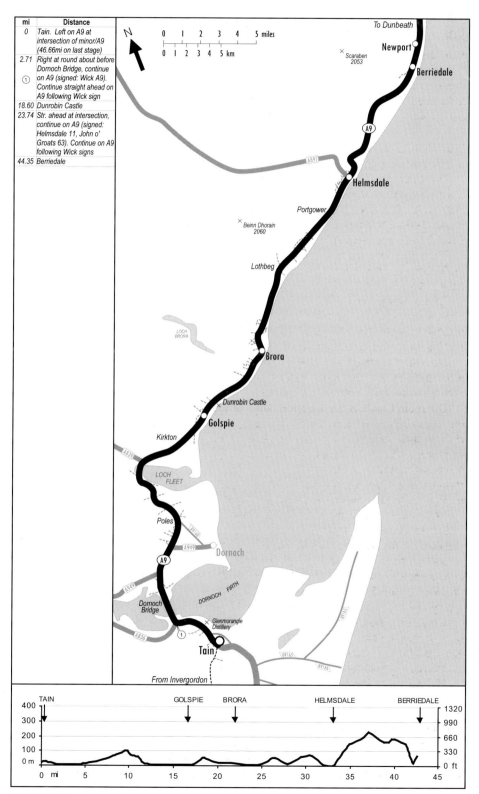

mi	Distance
0	Tain. Left on A9 at intersection of minor/A9 (46.66mi on last stage)
2.71	Right at round about before Dornoch Bridge, continue on A9 (signed: Wick A9). Continue straight ahead on A9 following Wick sign
18.60	Dunrobin Castle
23.74	Str. ahead at intersection, continue on A9 (signed: Helmsdale 11, John o' Groats 63). Continue on A9 following Wick signs
44.35	Berriedale

0   1   2   3   4   5 miles
0 1 2 3 4 5 km

To Dunbeath

Newport

× Scaraben 2053

Berriedale

A9

A897

Helmsdale

Portgower

× Beinn Dhorain 2060

Lothbeg

LOCH BRORA

Brora

Dunrobin Castle

Golspie

Kirkton

A839

LOCH FLEET

Poles

B9168

A949

Dornoch

A9

A949

Dornoch Bridge

DORNOCH FIRTH

Glenmorangie Distillery

A836

B9165

B9166

Tain

From Invergordon

TAIN   GOLSPIE   BRORA   HELMSDALE   BERRIEDALE
400   1320
300   990
200   660
100   330
0 m   0 ft
0 mi   5   10   15   20   25   30   35   40   45

1966 Bobby Charlton, part of the World Cup winning team, is voted Footballer of the Year

on accommodation available along the coastline between here and Wick.

There is a tough 4½-mile climb after Helmsdale, away from the coast and into the surrounding hills. This is followed by a gradual descent, then a very steep drop, back to the coast at Berriedale, which sits at the confluence of the Langwell and Berriedale River valleys. There is a B&B on the left on the steep climb out of the village.

The Dukes of Sutherland

Golpsie is looked down on by a larger than life statue of George Granville-Leveson Gower - the 1st Duke of Sutherland - perched on Beinn a' Bhragaidh hill, 1,200ft above town. There was talk recently of removing the statue, due to the Duke's activities during the Highland Clearances, but a compromise was reached and the Duke gets to stay - with plaques added to give a more balanced assessment of his contribution to the area.

The origins of the Sutherland clan go back to the 12th century, when a Flemish ally of David I, named Freskin, was given the Highland areas known as Sutherland (from the Norse for Southern Land). His family continued to support the Scottish kings and in the 13th century King William I made Freskin's grandson, William, the 1st Earl of Sutherland.

There have been 24 generations of Earls and Countesses of Sutherland since then, including tumultuous periods of family feuding involving poisonings, and beheadings. The 16th and 17th Earls supported the government during the 1715 and 1745 Jacobite Rebellions, raising local armies to assist George I and II, respectively. When the 18th Earl died his baby daughter Elizabeth became Countess, despite legal challenges from male relatives that had to be settled by the House of Lords. In 1785 the Countess married another member of the peerage - Viscount Trentham - the aforementioned George Granville-Leveson Gower.

Gower, who later became the Marquis of Stafford, was rich in his own right, receiving a large annual benefit from his uncle's canal business (his uncle being the Duke of Bridgewater). The new lord used his wealth to initiate a wide ranging, and controversial, improvement programme on the estate, which by that time was the largest private landholding in Europe. The two key components to the plan were infrastructure improvements and changes to traditional farming practices.

At the time, almost no roads or bridges existed. The Marquis, subsidised by the government, built hundreds of bridges and miles of roads during the first two decades of the 19th century, enabling a stage coach service to start from Tain to Wick.

His land-use reforms were more controversial. Until then land was rented out as crofts - small farms that barely produced enough to live off. With only 2% of Sutherland land arable, and the crofters only able to graze small numbers of cattle, the Marquis decided large-scale sheep farming would be more economic. Thousands of crofters were evicted off his land, often forcibly, and some by the burning of their cottages, to make way for the sheep. This depopulation of the straths (valleys) became known as the Highland Clearances. Many of the evicted headed to the coast to try to survive by fishing or in related industries, some moved to the growing slums of Glasgow, and some emigrated to New Zealand, Australia, or the Americas.

In 1833 Gower was made a Duke for his political activities (he had a hand in the Reform Bill and did a stint in France as British Ambassador). But before the year was out the 75-year-old Duke had died at Dunrobin Castle and was buried at Dornoch Cathedral. His eldest son, also George, became the 2nd Duke (another son became Earl of Ellesmere and inherited the Duke of Bridgewater's estates after a cousin died heir-less).

Another George followed as the 3rd Duke, marrying a daughter of the Earl of

1966 *A sketch of a bike, complete with chain drive & reportedly dating from the 1490's, is found among the works of Leonardo da Vinci's students. British scholars are sceptical*

Cromartie and expanding the family estate even further. A son named Cromartie became the 4th Duke (after his elder brother died as a youngster) and hosted Queen Victoria at Dunrobin in 1874. Cromartie's first son (George) became the 5th Duke in 1913. When he died without an heir in 1963, his niece, Elizabeth, assumed the title Countess of Sutherland, although the Dukedom, which was stipulated for males only, passed to a relative - John Sutherland Egerton, the 5th Earl of Ellesmere. The Countess is the head of the Sutherland clan and still lives in the area. The 6th Duke of Sutherland died recently and the title passed to his son, Francis Egerton.

There is a good chronology of the family history hanging as portraits in the dining and drawing rooms of Dunrobin Castle.

Camping;
Nearest; Dornoch (9mi N of Tain)

Hostel;
YHA Helmsdale, Helmsdale, Ph 01431 821577, Dorm£9

B&B;
Granite Villa Guest House, Fountain Rd, Golspie, Ph 01408 633146, S£30, D£50 ◆ Clynelish Farm, Brora, Ph 01408 621265, S£25, D£40 ◆ Lynwood, Golf Rd, Brora, Ph 01408 621226, S£28, D£35 ◆ The Old Manse, Stittenham Rd, Helmsdale, Ph 01431 821597, S£20, D£30 ◆ Broomhill House, Helmsdale, Ph 01431 821259, £20pp ◆ Kingspark Llama Farm, Berridale, Ph 01593 751202, £14pp ◆ The Factors House, Berriedale, Ph 01593 751280, D£35 ◆ Others; Dornoch (9mi N of Tain), Golpsie, Brora, Portgower, Helmsdale

Hotel;
Sutherland Arms Hotel, Old Bank Rd, Golspie, Ph 01408 633234, S£25, D£40 ◆ The Links & Royal Marine Hotels, Golf Rd, Brora, Ph 01408 621252, S£65, D£100 ◆ Sutherland Arms Hotel, Fountain Sq, Brora, Ph 01408 633234, S£39, D£49 ◆ Navidale House Hotel, Helmsdale, Ph 01431 821258, S£30, D£50 ◆ Others; Dornoch (9mi N of Tain), Golpsie

i;
TIC, Coupar Park, Helmsdale, Ph 01431 821640 ◆ Others; Dornoch (9mi N of Tain)

Bike Shops;
Nearest; Dingwall, Wick

875mi Dornoch Bridge

900mi On the A9 between Brora and Helmsdale

1969 The British, in conjunction with the French, unveil the
supersonic airliner Concorde

Berriedale to;

Dunbeath	6.8mi	b&b, hotel, i	*316200 929800*
Lybster	13.9mi	b&b, hotel, i	*324800 936100*
Wick	25.6mi	c, b&b, hotel, i, bike shop	*336300 951000*
John O'Groats	42.5mi	c, h, b&b, hotel, i	*338000 973400*

The final stage. A steep hill leads out of Berriedale, via a tight hairpin that has seen numerous traffic accidents. The climb levels off after a mile, with views out to the North Sea dotted with oil rigs, and eventually the road starts dropping, to another river valley village - Dunbeath.

A dramatic 17th century castle sits on the cliff-edge here overlooking the fishing fleet in the harbour. The Marquis of Montrose captured this castle briefly, in 1650, in an attempt to restore Charles I, who had been exiled in the wake of the Civil War. The Marquis had been the King's defender in Scotland but his support dwindled after Cromwell's victory and he fled to Europe. His 1650 return was a fairly futile effort, and with only 1,200 men he was defeated in a battle at the head of Dornoch Firth. He escaped but was captured deep in the Highlands when the head of the MacLeod clan betrayed him. He was hung in Edinburgh's town square a few weeks later (although his son was rewarded with the return of lands following the Restoration).

Dunbeath has a heritage centre, hotel, and several B&B's.

After Dunbeath the A9 gradually climbs again for about 2 miles, to the Laidhay Croft Museum. This little museum has interesting displays on the life of the crofters, including details on the Clearances, housed in a traditional 18th century long-house (also known as a byre-dwelling). A couple of miles further on, just before Latheron, the road passes an interesting farm fence, framed by whale ribs and topped with a huge vertebra.

At Latheron the A99 to Wick and John O' Groats splits off the A9 - a pretty flowerbed pointing the direction. There is a 15ft standing stone near the intersection, and this whole area is rich in prehistoric constructions. About a mile up the first minor road on the left past Latheron is Wag of Forse, an Iron Age village excavated in the 1930's and 40's with a circular wall and numerous long-houses.

The tour continues northeast on the A99, skirting the village of Lybster. About 4 miles further on, near Mid Clyth, a short detour to the left leads to another ancient site; Hill O' Many Stanes - with hundreds of small stones arranged geometrically. Ulbster, about 3 miles up the road from Mid Clyth, is another interesting location - to the right a precipitous set of 365 stairs leads down to a small natural harbour with fishing boats, at Whaligoe Bay, and to the left a minor road, then a walking track, lead to Cairn O' Get - an ancient chambered tomb.

Wick is a sizable town of about 8,000 with most services, including a bicycle shop (p.134 has a town map and description). If you plan to return south by train consider booking a place now, if you haven't done so already, as spaces for bicycles are limited.

Take the A99 out of Wick for the last 16½ miles to John O' Groats. The road doglegs at Reiss and passes the long sandy curve of Sinclair's Bay. The ruins of Keiss Castle, once home to the Earls of Caithness, are at the northern end of the bay and there is a Viking heritage centre just north of Nybster, which details how the Norsemen arrived, and eventually blended into the area.

The last uphill of the tour gently climbs the side of Wrath Hill, cresting to look out over John O' Groats, the island of Stroma, and the Orkney Islands in the distance. The last 2½ miles to John O' Groats are pleasantly downhill.

1970's A network of oil rigs, pipelines, and terminals is established to tap North Sea oil. 1 in 10 of the deep-sea divers assisting with construction are killed

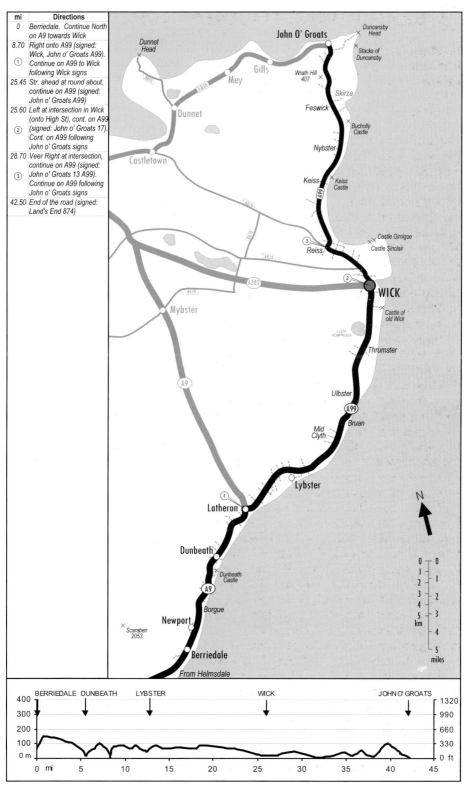

mi	Directions
0	Berriedale. Continue North on A9 towards Wick
8.70 ①	Right onto A99 (signed: Wick, John o' Groats A99). Continue on A99 to Wick following Wick signs
25.45	Str. ahead at round about, continue on A99 (signed: John o' Groats A99)
25.60 ②	Left at intersection in Wick (onto High St), cont. on A99 (signed: John o' Groats 17). Cont. on A99 following John o' Groats signs
28.70 ③	Veer Right at intersection, continue on A99 (signed: John o' Groats 13 A99). Continue on A99 following John o' Groats signs
42.50	End of the road (signed: Land's End 874)

1970 The Beatles break up

The A99 ends in a loop next to a small harbour, a stones throw from the famous John O' Groats hotel, which is traditionally the finish line for End to End trips. There is a campground just to the east of the road end, right on the beachfront, and several hostels, B&B's, and hotels back up the road. A small information centre, open April to October, has details on transport back to Wick or on to the Orkney Islands.

One last spot worth riding to is Duncansby Head, 2 miles to the east. During breeding season (centred around June) colonies of puffins, guillemots, and razor bills nest in these cliffs and the nearby Stacks of Duncansby (impressive rock pillars rising out of the sea). Seals from the colony on Stroma are also seen here sometimes.

Puffins

If you arrive at John O' Groats between late April and early July it's worth riding out to Duncansby Head to try and spot a puffin. This is one of the few places on the British mainland that Altantic puffins *(Fratercula arctica)* can be seen, as they mostly breed on offshore islands free from mammalian predators such as rats and foxes. Good places to look for them are at Sclaites Geo, an notch eroded into the sandstone cliffs just north of the carpark, and on the cliffs and sea stacks along the coastal walkway south of the parking lot.

These curious black and white birds, with their distinctive blue, red, and yellow striped bills, belong to the Auk family - a northern hemisphere group of diving seabirds that use their wings to swim and feet to steer underwater. Atlantic puffins spend most of the year at sea feeding in the North Atlantic and range as far north as the edge of the Arctic pack ice. During this time they lose their colourful beak markings and have a rather drab winter plumage, with dark feathers around their faces (in fact they look so different that they were once thought to be a different species).

Puffins arrive back on land around April, to nest in colonies in Iceland, Norway, North America, and Britain. Puffins usually mate for life (they live to be about 20) and often return to the same burrow from year to year. Courtship is marked by a constant and curious nibbling of bills as they shake their heads from side to side. Females lay a single egg, usually in a burrow dug into a grassy slope or a crevice in a protected cliff, lined with twigs and feathers. Male and female puffins take turns warming the egg under a wing.

After about 40 days a down covered chick hatches, too small for the first week or so to keep itself warm, so its parents continue to keep it under their wing. Once the chick can maintain its own body temperature the parents leave it to go on feeding forays and bring back food. When the baby puffin is about 40 days old it is ready to leave the nest. The parents stop feeding it and under the cover of darkness the hungry young puffin emerges and heads to sea, where it spends the next two years before returning to land. Leaving the nest is a dangerous journey - Black-backed Gulls will gobble a young puffin whole, and some young birds mistake nearby lights for the moon and head inland (in Iceland children collect these chicks and return them to the sea the next day).

Puffins are not great fliers, having to flap their stubby wings at 300 beats a minute to stay airborne, and they often crash into bushes or other birds on landing. It is underwater that these wings become effective propellers, enabling puffins to dive to 80ft in search of small fish and crustaceans. Puffin's distinctive beaks have special back-pointing projections designed to hold fish, and puffins have been seen with a beakfulls of over 60 small fish.

The biggest threats to puffins are predation by black-backed gulls and human influences (human influences being degradation of their habitat by over-fishing, oil pollution, and harvesting for food in some parts of the world).

1973 Britain joins the European Common Market

Camping;
John O' Groats Caravan Site, <u>John O' Groats</u>, Ph 01955 611329, T£8 ◆ Stroma View Camping Site, <u>Huna</u> (1½mi W of John O' Groats), Ph 01955 611313, T£9 ◆ Others; <u>Wick</u> *(see p.136)*, <u>Thurso</u>

Hostel;
YHA John O' Groats, 2mi W of <u>John O' Groats</u>, Ph 01955 611424, Dorm£9 ◆ Others; <u>Thurso</u>

B&B;
Tormore Farm, <u>Dunbeath</u>, Ph 01593 731240, £18pp ◆ Bolton House, Greys Pl, <u>Lybster</u>, Ph 01593 721282, £18pp ◆ The Farmhouse, <u>Freswick</u>, Ph 01955 611254, £20pp ◆ Mill House, <u>John O' Groats</u>, Ph 01955 611239, £18pp ◆ Stroma View, <u>Huna</u>, Ph 01955 611313, £15pp ◆ Others; <u>Dunbeath</u>, <u>Latheron</u>, <u>Wick</u> *(see p.136)*, <u>Keiss</u>, <u>John O' Groats</u>

Hotel;
Dunbeath Hotel, <u>Dunbeath</u>, Ph 01593 731208, S£40, D£65 ◆ Portland Arms Hotel, Main St, <u>Lybster</u>, Ph 01593 721721, S£45, D£68 ◆ Seaview Hotel, <u>John O' Groats</u>, Ph 01955 611200, £20pp ◆ Caber Feidh Guest House, <u>John O' Groats</u>, Ph 01955 611219, £17pp ◆ Others; <u>Wick</u> *(see p.136)*, <u>Keiss</u>, <u>John O' Groats</u>

i;
Dunbeath Heritage Centre, <u>Dunbeath</u>, Ph 01593 731233 ◆ Clan Gunn Heritage Centre, <u>Latheron</u>, Ph 01593 741700 ◆ Lybster Heritage Trust, <u>Lybster</u>, Ph 01593 721520 ◆ TIC, Country Rd, <u>John O' Groats</u>, Ph 01955 611373 ◆ Others; <u>Wick</u>

Bike Shops;
<u>Wick</u> *(see p.136)* ◆ Others; <u>Thurso</u>

925mi The start of the A99, 0.5mi after Latheron

950mi Just past Kiess

958mi John O' Groats

1975 Faulty Towers airs on TV

133

WICK

Wick started out as a Viking settlement ("Vic' means bay in Norse), and grew dramatically in the 19th century when the town became a centre for herring fishing. Thomas Telford built a large harbour for the fishing fleet and designed a new suburb on the north side of the river called **Pultneytown**. By the early 20th century over-fishing had nearly wiped out the herring and the town started shrinking.

The A99 into town runs through Old Wick, across the river and into the centre of town. Bridge St and High St are the two main thoroughfares. The **Tourist Information Centre** is on Whitechapel Rd, just off High St. Details on accommodation options in Wick are on p.136.

Wick has an excellent **Heritage Centre** on Bank Row. The Heritage Centre houses the **Johnston Photographic Collection** (photos of the town taken over a 100-year period by members of a local family) and has a good history of the fishing industry. The **Harbour** and old **Fish Market** are just down the road.

About a mile south of the harbour, along a cliff-top walkway, is the **Castle of Old Wick**, a 12th century keep, now in ruins. The track continues south, past **sea stacks**, to a small harbour at **Sarclet** known as **The Haven,** 5 miles from Wick. There is a **heated pool** on Matha Tce on the way back to Wick.

Other sites include the **Caithness Glass Factory**, which has demonstrations of glassblowing, and a **coastal walkway** heading northeast which leads to the side-by-side cliff-top ruins of **Castles Girnigoe** and **Sinclair** (Sinclair being the smaller one). The 4th Earl of Caithness suspected his son of treachery and imprisoned him at Grinigoe for 7 years, before starving him to death.

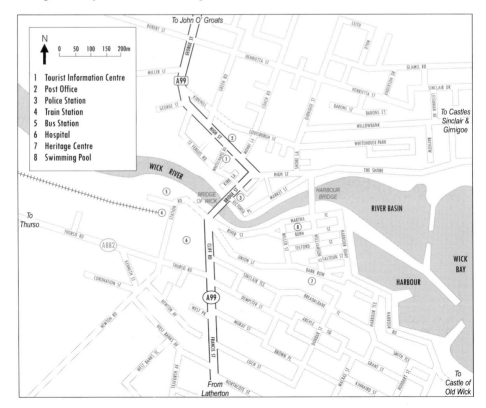

1975 A major reorganisation of local government changes county boundaries, with many towns ending up in different counties

THURSO

Thurso is equidistant, about 20 miles, from Wick and John O' Groats and is the most northerly town on mainland Britain. End to End cyclists often end up here after visiting **Dunnet Head**, the northerly tip of Britain, which is between Thurso and John O' Groats.

The town was mainly a fishing village and seaport until 1954, when the **Dounreay Experimental Nuclear Power Station** was built 9 miles to the west and the population doubled (a visitor centre is open in summer but, at nearly 50, the station's future is unsure). Locally, sport **fishing** is popular, with salmon and trout being fished in River Thurso.

The **Tourist Information Centre** is on Riverside Rd and there is a **Heritage Museum** on High St with Pictish, Norse, and other artifacts.   Many of Thurso's buildings were constructed from local stone in the 1700's, although **St Peter's Church** dates from the 16th century and the ruins of **Old St Peter's Kirk**, near the river mouth, can be traced back to a 13th century church established by the Bishop of Caithness. Also near the river mouth are the ruins of **Thurso Castle** (private), the ancestral home of the Sinclair's - a prominent local family (Sir John Sinclair was a leading light in improving Scottish agriculture at the end of the 18th century).   Another famous local was Sir William Alexander Smith, founder of the Christian boys' organization; The Boys' Brigade. He was born at **Pennyland House** in 1854.

Thurso has a long sandy beach flanked by rocks. The reef on the east side of the bay, known as Castle Reef, is one of the best **surfing** breaks in Britain. 2 miles west of town is **Scrabster**, the ferry terminal for the Orkneys and the Shetlands. North of here there is a clifftop walkway to **Holborn Head**, at the entrance to Thurso Bay.

Some of the accommodation options available in Thurso are listed on p.136.

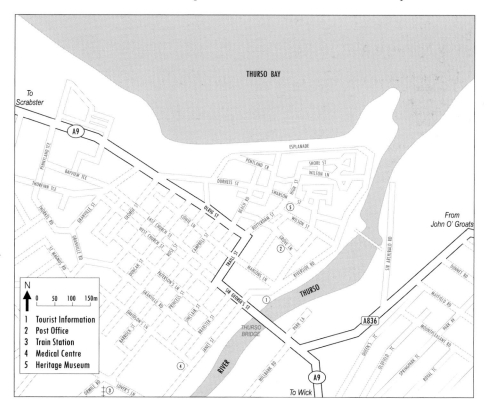

1 Tourist Information
2 Post Office
3 Train Station
4 Medical Centre
5 Heritage Museum

WICK ACCOMMODATION

Camping;
Riverside Caravan Club, Riverside Drive, Wick, Ph 01955 605420, T£5

Hostel;
Nearest; John O' Groats

B&B;
Hebron, South Rd, Wick, Ph 01955 603515, £20pp ◆ Brae End, Scalesburn, Wick, Ph 01955 602735, £20pp ◆ The Clachan, South Rd, Wick, Ph 01955 605384, £28pp ◆ Others; Wick

Hotel;
MacKay's Hotel, Union St, Wick, Ph 01955 602323, £37pp ◆ Norseman Hotel, Riverside, Wick, Ph 01955 603344, £25pp ◆ Nethercliff Hotel, Louisburgh St, Wick, Ph 01955 602044, £25pp ◆ Others; Wick

i;
TIC, Whitechapel Rd, Wick, Ph 01955 602596

Bike Shops;
Wheels Cycle Shop, Glamis Rd, Wick, Ph 01955 603636 ◆ The Spot, Francis St, Wick, Ph 01955 602698

◆　◆　◆　◆　◆

THURSO ACCOMMODATION

Camping;
Thurso Caravan Park, Scrabster Rd, Thurso, Ph 01847 805503, T£5

Hostel;
Thurso Hostel, Ormlie Lodge, Ormlie Rd, Thurso, Ph 01847 896851, Dorm£8 ◆ Sandra's Backpackers Hostel, 24 Princes St, Thurso, Ph 01847 894575, Dorm£9 ◆ Others; Thurso

B&B;
Annandale, 2 Rendel Govan Rd, Thurso, Ph 01847 893942, S£25, D£36 ◆ Achnabat, 54 Queens Tce, Thurso, Ph 01847 893784, £20pp ◆ Others; Thurso

Hotel;
Pentland Hotel, Princes St, Thurso, Ph 01847 893202, S£30, D£50 ◆ Royal Hotel, Traill St, Thurso, Ph 01847 893191, S£45, D£65 ◆ The Park Hotel, Thurso, Ph 01847 893251, S£35, D£70 ◆ Others; Thurso

i;
TIC Thurso, Riverside, Thurso, Ph 01847 892371 (seasonal)

Bike Shops;
Wheels Cycle Shop, 35 High St, Thurso, Ph 01847 896124 ◆ Leisure Activities, 11a Princes St, Thurso, Ph 01847 895385

1976 Britain, in an economic crisis, seeks assistance from the IMF

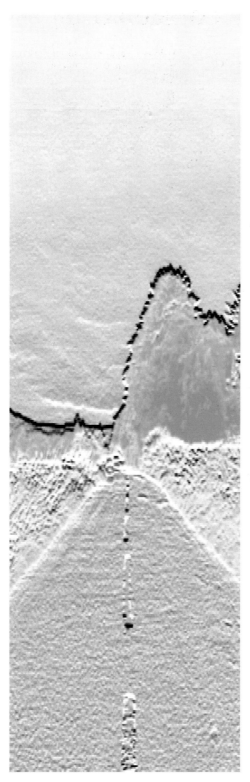

APPENDICIES

*1977 Marc Bolan, lead singer of T-Rex, is killed when his
Mini crashes on a London bridge*

APPENDIX A: ISLES OF SCILLY

The 150 or so islands of the Isles of Scilly, about 30 miles from Land's End, form the southwestern tip of the British Isles. The Scilly's are easy to get to from Penzance and are fun to explore for a day by bike. The ferry from Penzance to Hugh Town on the main island of St Mary's takes about 2 hours, and sails daily during the summer season. Day fares are £35 (£32 low season), and period returns are £74 (£65 low season). Bikes are a few £ extra, but you can easily hire a bike on the island and with a loop of St. Mary's only a couple of miles, this may be a good option. You can also fly to St Mary's from Land's End, Bristol, and Exeter. The climate is mild and balmy in summer, but during winter these low islands get windswept by gales off the Atlantic.

St Mary's is the largest of the five inhabited islands and has been settled since at least the Bronze Age (the islands have many pre-historic sites). The current population is around 1,500, with most people living in Hugh Town - a town with shops, banks, churches, hotels, a campground, and a Post Office. Hugh Town is separated from the rest of the island by a sandbar. Crossing the sandbar, a circular tour of the island passes woods, heather, marshes and dunes. With generally quiet roads and the highest point only about 150ft above sea level, St Mary's, on a nice day, is a very pleasant ride. There are several castles, or remnants of castles. Star Castle overlooking Hugh Town was built by Frances Godolphin in 1593 and is the best preserved. There are also the remains of a prehistoric fort ("Giant's Castle"), Ennor (a 13th century castle), and a structure built by Henry VIII. The Scilly's were also the final Royalist stronghold during the Civil War - St Mary's being a stopping point for young Prince Charles before he fled for France. Other attractions include; a museum (with items salvaged from the many wrecks on the islands), local arts and crafts, and from late April to early August boat trips to see nesting puffins.

Ferries depart Hugh Town for other islands in the group. Tresco, the second largest, is one of the most interesting. The Dorrien Smith's, who have leased the island from the Duchy of Cornwall for the last 167 years, run the island. In the 12th century, Henry I gave Tresco, and the other islands, to Tavistock Abbey (in Devon), which owned them until the Dissolution. The Godolphin family leased the islands from 1571 to 1830, before they passed to the Duke of Cornwall. At that time the Scilly's primary industries were smuggling, looting shipwrecks, and harvesting seaweed (for iodine), and the islanders were barely surviving. Several years later the Duke leased the Scilly's to Augustus Smith, a Hertfordshire banker, who built himself a mansion on Tresco. In effort to stimulate the local economy Smith re-introduced law and order, reformed land ownership, and made education compulsory. Smith's nephew, Thomas Dorrien Smith, started the trade in exporting early-season flowers to London; a business that, along with tourism, remains a mainstay of the island's economy. Tresco is one of the few islands in the group with any significant cliffs, and the scenery is particularly diverse and interesting. The island has a rich history of monks and pirates, and several Civil War castles that were used during the Battle of Tresco (1651). Augustus Smith's Mansion, Tresco Abbey, is open to the public and has an extensive sub-tropical garden including a collection of figureheads from lost ships.

The other inhabited islands have only limited roads for exploring by bike. St Martin's has a hotel and campground (the island's Daymark, a conical tower built in 1683 to guide ships, is one of the first Scilly sights you see as the ferry nears). St Agnes has guesthouses and campsites. Bryher is the smallest inhabited island but still has some roads, a hotel, B&B's, and a campground.

1977 A cycling group, which eventually becomes Sustrans, is formed to promote cycle networks. Their first route is a disused Bath to Bristol rail line

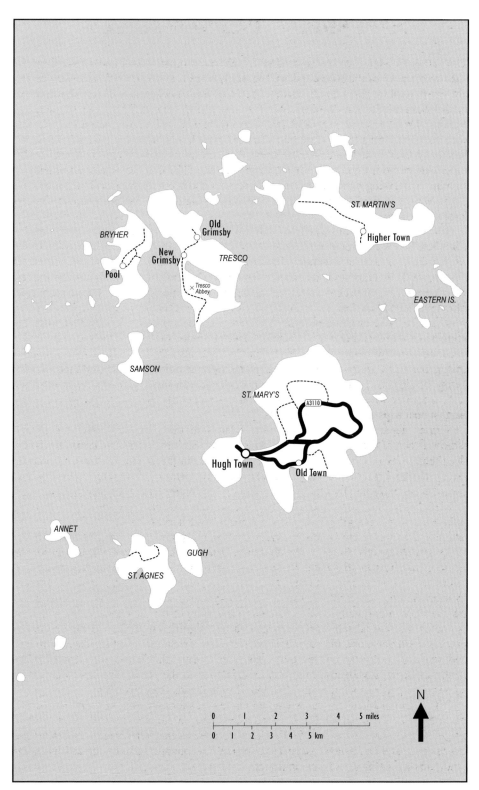

BRYHER

Pool

Old Grimsby

New Grimsby

TRESCO

× Tresco Abbey

ST. MARTIN'S

Higher Town

EASTERN IS.

SAMSON

ST. MARY'S

A3110

Hugh Town

Old Town

ANNET

GUGH

ST. AGNES

N

0 1 2 3 4 5 miles

0 1 2 3 4 5 km

1978 Georgi Markov, a dissident Bulgarian broadcaster, is killed in London by a poison pellet fired from an umbrella

APPENDIX B: ORKNEY ISLANDS

The ancient isles of Orkney are a great place to visit once you've reached John O' Groats and the end of the mainland. If you still feel like cycling, the Orkney's are mostly low lying, have dramatic panoramas, and are full of historic sites - although the weather, especially the wind, can be harsh.

The passenger ferry from John O' Groats wharf runs everyday from May through September and takes 45 minutes to make the 8 mile crossing to Burwick, on South Ronaldsay (£15 one-way, bikes £3 extra). The ferry also connects with a good-value bus tour that takes in many of the Orkney's attractions (£31 for day trip ferry and tour).

The 70 or so islands of the Orkney's are at a strategic location on the doorstep of Britain, and much of the their history involves invaders and warring. The islands have been home to Stone Age inhabitants, Picts, Celts, Vikings, and Europeans. Today the population, supported mainly by agriculture, fishing, and tourism, is around 20,000.

A cycling tour of the Orkney's could involve heading north from Burwick to Kirkwall (21 miles), then doing a loop around "Mainland" (about 55 miles). There are numerous offshore islands, linked by ferries and off the beaten track, which can be explored too. Heading north from Burwick the A961 crosses the Churchill Barriers linking South Ronaldsay and 3 other islands with Mainland. These 4 seawalls were constructed by Italian POW's during WWII to protect the inner waters from U-Boats, after the Royal Oak was torpedoed in 1939 with the loss of over 800 men. On the last little island is the Italian Chapel, two Nissan huts ornately decorated by the prisoners with the materials they had at hand. Continuing north the road looks over the massive protected anchorage of Scarpa Flow. After WWI the surrendered German Fleet (over 70 ships) was bought into Scarpa Flow, unfortunately the German sailors, on a prearranged signal on 21 June 1919, scuttled their own boats, although many were subsequently raised. Across Scarpa Flow the flare from Flotta oil terminal is visible.

Kirkwall is the capital. St Magnus Cathedral, founded by the Viking Earl Rognvald in the 12th century, is in the centre of town, surrounded by tourist shops that cater to the increasing number of cruise liners that stop here. Ferries and flights leave Kirkwall for outer islands in the group.

Heading northwest out of Kirkwall, then anticlockwise around Mainland, the road passes through Finstown village, then Tingwall where ferries depart for the less visited islands of Wyre, Rousay, Eglisay. A few miles north of Tingwall, on the coast, is Broch of Gurness, a well-preserved prehistoric site. Around the top of the island the road runs between lochs and a wild coastline that includes the Marwick Head Nature Reserve.

Skara Brae on the northwest coast is an impressive 4,500-year-old Neolithic settlement, discovered in 1850 after a storm during high tide uncovered one of the houses. Built of sandstone slabs and linked by passages, the dwellings have been preserved complete with stone cupboards, beds, and fireplaces. Other Neolithic monuments are located inland in the central lochs area, including the Ring of Brogar, the Standing Stones of Stenness, and Maeshowe (a megalithic burial chamber some consider the finest prehistoric tomb in Britain).

Stromness is the other large town in the Orkneys, a pretty port with cobble streets and several art studios. Ferries from Aberdeen and Scrabster arrive here and depart for Lerwick in the Shetland Islands.

The south coast road leading back to Kirkwall passes near Orphir where there are the remains of Scotland's last medieval circular church, dating from the 12th century.

There is a tourist information centre and bike shop in Kirkwall that can provide more details on rides and places to visit in the Orkneys.

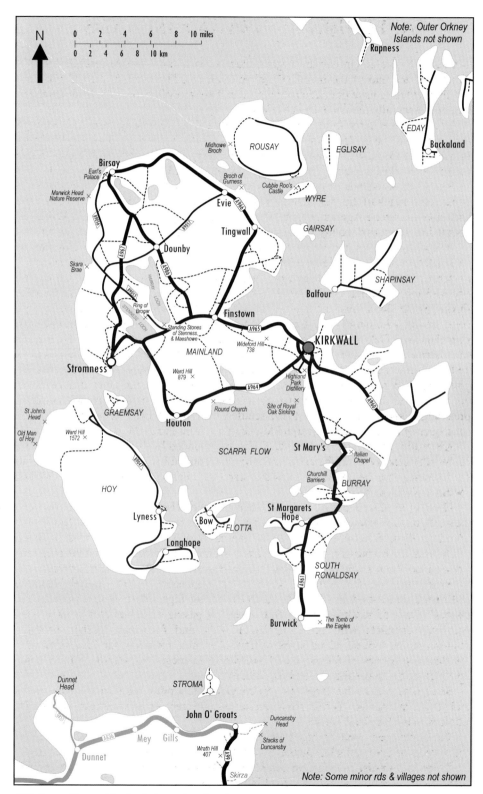

N

0   2   4   6   8   10 miles

0 2 4 6 8 10 km

Rapness

EDAY

Backaland

Midhowe
Broch

ROUSAY

EGLISAY

Birsay

Earl's
Palace

Broch of
Gurness

Cubbie Roo's
Castle

WYRE

Marwick Head
Nature Reserve

Evie

A966

Tingwall

GAIRSAY

Dounby

A967

A986

Skara
Brae

HARRAY LOCH

A965

SHAPINSAY

Balfour

Ring of
Brogar

STENNESS LOCH

Finstown

Standing Stones
of Stenness
& Maeshowe

A965

KIRKWALL

Stromness

MAINLAND

Wideford Hill
738

A960

Ward Hill
879 ×

A964

Highland
Park
Distillery

St John's
Head

GRAEMSAY

Round Church

Site of Royal
Oak Sinking

Old Man
of Hoy

Ward Hill
1572 ×

Houton

SCARPA FLOW

St Mary's

Italian
Chapel

A961

Churchill
Barriers

BURRAY

HOY

Lyness

Bow

FLOTTA

St Margarets
Hope

Longhope

SOUTH
RONALDSAY

A961

Burwick

The Tomb of
the Eagles

Dunnet
Head

STROMA

John O' Groats

Duncansby
Head

A836

Mey

Gills

Stacks of
Duncansby

Dunnet

Wrath Hill
407

A9

Skirza

*1979 Bryan Allen pedals the kevlar and mylar plane
"Gossamer Albatross" across the English Channel*

APPENDIX C: SHETLAND ISLANDS

The Shetland Islands are about half way between Britain and Norway. So far north in fact they share the same latitude as parts of Greenland, and are only 400 miles south of the Arctic Circle (the locals see the Northern Lights occasionally). Despite the location, the climate in these 100 plus islands is not too bad, thanks to an offshoot of the Gulf Stream that sweeps warmer water north from the Gulf of Mexico. Still, be prepared for cold, wet and changeable weather, and wind - which is almost always present. The population of about 23,000 live on 15 inhabited islands, the largest of which is Mainland.

Ferries to Lerwick, the Shetland's capital, leave Aberdeen five times a week with fares starting at £110 (return) depending on the season. Bicycles are an extra £10 return. Standard return fares from Scrabster (near Thurso) to Stromness (in the Orkney Islands) and from Stromness to Lerwick are around £33 and £81, respectively. Flights are also available from the Orkney's and larger Scottish cities. With over 1000 miles of roads the Shetland Islands offer some great cycling and Shetland Islands Tourism have produced a brochure with 20 suggested rides (see *www.visitshetland.com*).

With surface transport arranged from Lerwick, or a flight to Sumburgh, a cycling route from south to north could start at Sumburgh Head on Mainland and end at Skaw, near the northern tip of Unst, two ferry crossings and about 85 miles distant.

Sumburgh Head, at the end of a minor road about a mile south of Sumburgh, has impressive cliffs with abundant birdlife. Near Sumburgh is a major archeological site known as Jarlshof, which was occupied by Bronze Age, Iron Age, Norse, and medieval inhabitants before shifting sands finally covered the settlement. A storm in the late 1800's unearthed it again.

The A970 is the main road north. The route north passes fishing villages and crofts dotted with Shetland sheep, a breed that gives the fine wool used to knit Fair Isle and Shetland sweaters. The Shetland Crofthouse Museum near Boddam, north of Sumburgh, is a typical 19th century Shetland homestead, with thick stone walls and a thatched roof weighted down with stones.

Lerwick and Scalloway, on opposite sides of the island about half way up Mainland, are the two biggest towns. Scalloway is a fishing port with the remains of a castle built by an unpopular (he was eventually executed) Earl of Orkney in 1600. Lerwick, 25 miles from Sumburgh, has a population of 7,500. It also has a tourist information centre and is home to the Shetland Museum.

North of Lerwick the A970, then the A968 passes lochs and voes (fjords) strung out along the north-south trending faults that give the islands their distinctive outline. A ferry from Toft (28 miles from Lerwick) takes you to Ulsta on Yell, where you can head up the west side of the island (10 miles) or the east side (a 13 mile B road) to Mid Yell Voe. From here it is another 8 miles to Gutcher and the ferry to Belmont on Unst (both ferries make daily runs).

From Belmont it's about 13 miles to Skaw - a tiny crofting village that has the most northerly house in Britain. Unst is a great place to view Shetland's wildlife, in particular the birdlife, and the Herma Ness National Nature Reserve is well worth a visit. Muckle Flugga, a rock capped with a lighthouse, is just north of the Reserve and is considered the northern tip of Britain.

The top of Unst is the end of the road in Britain, but you can continue touring by taking a ferry from Lerwick to Bergen (summer only), in Norway, and finding your way onto the 3,750-mile North Sea Cycle Route which passes through the coastal areas of 7 European countries (see www.northsea-cycle.com).

1980 Britain's population is about 56 million

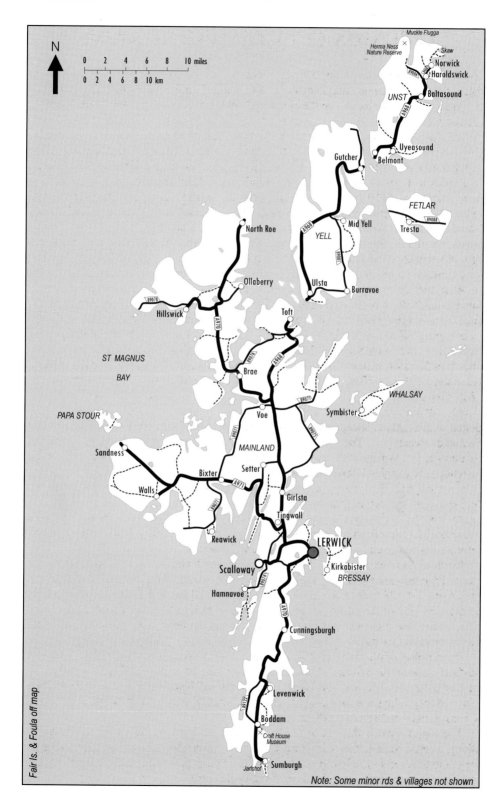

N

0 2 4 6 8 10 miles
0 2 4 6 8 10 km

Muckle Flugga
Herma Ness
Nature Reserve
Skaw
Norwick
Haroldswick
Baltasound
UNST
Uyeasound
Belmont
Gutcher

FETLAR
Tresta
B9088

North Roe
Mid Yell
YELL
B9081
Ollaberry
Ulsta
Burravoe
B9078
A970
Hillswick
Toft
WHALSAY
Symbister
ST MAGNUS
BAY
Brae
B907T
PAPA STOUR
Voe
B9075
MAINLAND
Sandness
Setter
Bixter
A971
Girlsta
Walls
Tingwall
Reawick
LERWICK
Kirkabister
BRESSAY
Scalloway
A970
Hamnavoe
Cunningsburgh
Levenwick
A972
Boddam
Croft House
Museum
Jarlshof
Sumburgh

Fair Is. & Foula off map

Note: Some minor rds & villages not shown

APPENDIX D: TEMPERATURE AND RAINFALL

Plymouth

Month	Jan	Feb	Mar	Apr	May	June	July	Aug	Sept	Oct	Nov	Dec
Av. Low (°C)	4	4	5	6	9	12	13	13	12	9	7	5
Av. High (°C)	8	8	10	12	14	17	19	19	17	14	11	10
Av. Rain (mm)	107	84	79	56	63	56	64	74	76	94	107	114

Gloucester

Month	Jan	Feb	Mar	Apr	May	June	July	Aug	Sept	Oct	Nov	Dec
Av. Low (°C)	1	1	2	4	7	10	12	12	10	6	3	2
Av. High (°C)	6	7	10	13	17	20	21	21	18	13	10	7
Av. Rain (mm)	65	49	43	50	53	46	61	60	58	68	71	64

Manchester

Month	Jan	Feb	Mar	Apr	May	June	July	Aug	Sept	Oct	Nov	Dec
Av. Low (°C)	1	1	2	4	7	10	12	12	10	7	4	2
Av. High (°C)	6	6	8	11	15	17	19	19	16	13	8	7
Av. Rain (mm)	71	58	58	52	62	71	87	93	82	93	85	87

Dumfries

Month	Jan	Feb	Mar	Apr	May	June	July	Aug	Sept	Oct	Nov	Dec
Av. Low (°C)	1	1	2	3	6	9	11	10	9	6	3	1
Av. High (°C)	6	6	8	11	14	17	19	18	16	13	8	7
Av. Rain (mm)	110	77	81	53	72	63	71	93	104	117	100	107

Glasgow

Month	Jan	Feb	Mar	Apr	May	June	July	Aug	Sept	Oct	Nov	Dec
Av. Low (°C)	1	1	2	3	6	8	11	10	8	5	2	1
Av. High (°C)	6	6	8	11	14	17	18	18	15	12	8	6
Av. Rain (mm)	109	77	69	58	61	70	95	104	102	112	103	114

Fort William

Month	Jan	Feb	Mar	Apr	May	June	July	Aug	Sept	Oct	Nov	Dec
Av. Low (°C)	2	2	3	5	7	10	12	11	10	7	4	3
Av. High (°C)	6	6	7	10	13	15	17	16	13	11	8	6
Av. Rain (mm)	209	124	178	91	108	109	116	129	197	233	229	228

Inverness

Month	Jan	Feb	Mar	Apr	May	June	July	Aug	Sept	Oct	Nov	Dec
Av. Low (°C)	1	1	2	3	6	9	11	11	8	6	3	2
Av. High (°C)	5	6	8	10	13	15	17	17	14	11	7	6
Av. Rain (mm)	50	40	38	38	45	48	66	71	58	66	60	52

Kirkwall

Month	Jan	Feb	Mar	Apr	May	June	July	Aug	Sept	Oct	Nov	Dec
Av. Low (°C)	2	1	2	3	5	8	9	10	8	7	3	2
Av. High (°C)	6	6	7	9	11	14	15	15	14	11	8	7
Av. Rain (mm)	107	73	84	56	51	52	56	78	102	116	123	113

London

Month	Jan	Feb	Mar	Apr	May	June	July	Aug	Sept	Oct	Nov	Dec
Av. Low (°C)	1	1	2	3	7	10	12	11	12	7	3	5
Av. High (°C)	7	7	9	12	16	19	22	22	18	15	10	8
Av. Rain (mm)	79	51	61	53	63	56	46	56	69	74	79	79

Note: These data are approximate averages for selected cities. Conditions are likely to vary outside these averages, and it's always possible you could strike a significantly hotter, colder, or wetter month

1982 Britain goes to war with Argentina over the Falkland Islands

APPENDIX E: ADDITIONAL INFORMATION

Interesting Reading;

A History of Briatin Vol 1: At the Edge of the World? 3000BC-AD1603. Simon Schama. BBC Consumer Publishing 2000.

The English. Jeremy Paxman. Penguin Books 1999.

The Oxford Companion to Scottish History. Michael Lynch (Ed). Oxford University Press 2001.

Complete British Wildlife. Paul Sterry. Collins 1997.

The Hidden Landscape. Richard Fortey. Pimlico 1994.

Weatherwise. Philip Eden. Pan 1995.

The Bicycle Touring Manual. Rob van der Plas. Bicycle Books Inc. 1998.

Britain Under Thatcher. Anthony Seldon, Daniel Collings. Longman 1999.

The Collected Poems of Robert Burns. Wordsworth Editions Ltd 1994.

Internet Sites;

www.visitbritain.com The British Tourist Authority (BTA) official site

www.bbc.co.uk The BBC's site is "the UK's number one digital destination"

www.royal.gov.uk The Queen's web-site

www.roads.detr.gov.uk The British Highway Code

www.met-office.gov.uk The weather in Britain

www.rail.co.uk Info on UK rail services

www.cycleweb.co.uk British cycling links

www.hostels.com Hostels in Britain and elsewhere

www.travelengland.org.uk Accommodation in England

www.visitscotland.com Accommodation and tourist information for Scotland

APPENDIX F: ENGLISH KINGS & QUEENS

Anglo-Saxon					
827-836	Egbert	1307-1327	Edward II	**Hanoverians**	
837-858	Ethelwulf	1327-1377	Edward III	1714-1724	George I
866-871	Ethelred I	1377-1399	Richard II	1727-1760	George II
871-899	Alfred the Great	**Lancastrians**		1760-1820	George III
899-925	Edward the Elder	1399-1413	Henry IV	1810-1820	No Monarch
925-940	Athelstan	1413-1422	Henry V		(Regency)
959-975	Edgar	1422-1461	Henry VI	1820-1830	George IV
978-1016	Ethelred II	**Yorkists**		1830-1837	William IV
1016	Edmund Ironside	1461-1483	Edward IV	1837-1901	Victoria
1016-1035	Canute The Dane	1483	Edward V	**Saxe-Coburg**	
1035-1040	Harold I	1483-1485	Richard III	1901-1910	Edward VII
1041-1042	Hardicanute	**Tudors**		**Windsor**	
1042-1066	Edward The	1485-1509	Henry VII	1910-1936	George V
	Confessor	1509-1547	Henry VIII	1936	Edward VIII
1066	Harold II	1547-1553	Edward VI	1936-1952	George VI
Norman		1553-1558	Mary I	1952-	Elizabeth II
1066-1087	William The	1558-1603	Elizabeth I		
	Conqueror	**Stuarts**			
1087-1100	William II	1603-1625	James I		
1100-1135	Henry I	1625-1649	Charles I		
1135-1154	Stephen	1649-1660	No Monarch		
Plantagenets			(Commonwealth)		
1154-1189	Henry II	1660-1685	Charles II		
1189-1199	Richard I	1685-1688	James II		
1199-1216	John	1688-1694	William III and		
1216-1272	Henry III		Mary II		
1272-1307	Edward I	1694-1702	William III		
		1702-1714	Anne		

APPENDIX G: METRIC CONVERSIONS

TEMPERATURE

To convert °C to °F multiply by 1.8 and add 32
To convert °F to °C subtract 32 and multiply by 0.555

°C	=	°F		°F	=	°C
50		122		120		49
45		113		110		43
40		104		100		38
35		95		90		32
30		86		80		27
25		77		70		21
20		68		60		16
15		59		50		10
10		50		40		4
5		41		30		-1
0		32		20		-7
-5		23		10		-12
-10		14		0		-18
-15		5		-10		-23

DISTANCE

To convert kilometres to miles multiply by 0.621
To convert miles to kilometres multiply by 1.61

km	=	miles		miles	=	km
1		0.621		1		1.61
2		1.2		2		3.2
3		1.9		3		4.8
4		2.5		4		6.4
5		3.1		5		8.1
6		3.7		6		9.7
7		4.4		7		11.3
8		5.0		8		12.9
9		5.6		9		14.5
10		6.2		10		16.1

To convert metres to feet multiply by 3.28
To convert feet to meters multiply by 0.305

m	=	ft		ft	=	m
1		3.28		1		0.305
2		6.6		2		0.6
3		9.8		3		0.9
4		13.1		4		1.2
5		16.4		5		1.5
6		19.7		6		1.8
7		23.0		7		2.1
8		26.2		8		2.4
9		29.5		9		2.8
10		32.8		10		3.1

(To convert metres to yards multiply by 0.91)
(To convert yards to metres multiply by 1.09)
(To convert square km into square miles multiply by 0.39)
(To convert square miles into square km multiply by 2.59)

1989 An unpopular poll tax is introduced

WEIGHT

To convert kilograms to pounds multiply by 2.20
To convert pounds to kilograms multiply by 0.455

kg	=	lbs		lbs	=	kg
1		2.20		1		0.455
2		4.4		2		0.9
3		6.6		3		1.4
4		8.8		4		1.8
5		11.0		5		2.3
6		13.2		6		2.7
7		15.4		7		3.2
8		17.6		8		3.6
9		19.8		9		4.1
10		22.0		10		4.6

To convert grams to ounces multiply by 0.35
To convert ounces to grams multiply by 28.4

g	=	oz		oz	=	g
1		0.35		1		28.4
2		0.7		2		57
3		1.1		3		85
4		1.4		4		114
5		1.8		5		142
6		2.1		6		170
7		2.5		7		199
8		2.8		8		227
9		3.2		9		256
10		3.5		10		284

1 British ton = 1019kg (2240lbs)
1 US ton = 910kg (2000lbs)
(To convert British tons to US tons multiply by 0.893)

VOLUME

To convert litres to US gallons multiply by 0.264
To convert US gallons to litres multiply by 3.79

litre	=	US gal		US gal	=	litre
1		0.264		1		3.79
2		0.5		2		7.6
3		0.8		3		11.4
4		1.1		4		15.1
5		1.3		5		19.0
6		1.6		6		22.7
7		1.8		7		26.5
8		2.1		8		30.3
9		2.4		9		34.1
10		2.6		10		37.9

(1 litre is 1.5 US pints, and 1.8 UK pints)
(1 imperial gallon = 4.55 liters (1.18 US gallons))
(To convert US gallons to imperial gallons multiply by 0.845)
(1 cubic meter = 35.3 cubic feet, 1 cubic foot = 0.0283 cubic meters)
(1 Acre = 0.4047 hectares, 1 hectare = 2.47 acres)

1990 On August 3, the highest temperature ever recorded in
Britain, 37.1°C, is reported in Gloucestershire

INDEX

Pages with photos in **bold**

1990 The Labour Party, lead by Tony Blair, gains power

1991 The "Birmingham 6" are released after an Appeals Court finds their 1974 convictions, for pub bombings, unsatisfactory

149

1996 Charles and Diana divorce

2000 Britain's population is about 60 million (England 50M, Scotland 5M, Wales 3M, and N. Ireland 1.7M). The projected population for 2025 is 65 million

153

2001 Britain's worst ever Foot and Mouth Disease outbreak occurs, resulting in the slaughter of millions of farm animals

NOTES:

About the Author

Born and raised in New Zealand, Paul developed a passion for cycle touring while studying geology at Auckland University. He has cycled extensively in a number of countries, including a tip to tip tour of New Zealand and across Australia. He cycled Land's End to John O' Groats with his wife Eileen. Paul currently works as a geologist in California.

www.epicguides.co.nz

QUESTIONNAIRE

We hope this guide had the information you needed for an epic End to End tour. If we've missed something, or things mentioned in the guide have changed drastically since publication - we'd like to hear.

We'd also like to hear how you liked the route and any comments you have about accommodation and services along the way. We value your feedback.

How did you hear about this guide?

Bookshop (which one?)................☐ Friends................☐
Bike Shop (which one?)................☐ Internet................☐
Other..

Where did you get "Bike Britian"?

Bookshop (which one?)................☐ Gift....................☐
Bike Shop (which one?)................☐ Internet................☐
Other..

Which parts of this guide did you find most useful?................................
....

What would you like to see changed or included in the next edition?..............
....

What other countries would you like to see an Epic Cycling Guide for?...........
....

Comments..
....
....

An Epic Guide for Australia is available, and a guide for New Zealand is due out soon. Would like further information on these guides?

Bike Australia, Cycling Australia   Bike New Zealand, Cycling NZ
From Perth to Sydney..............☐   From Cape Reinga to Bluff.......☐

Name:............................... Address:................................
.... E-mail:................................

Post to: Epic Guides, P.O. Box 31053, Milford, New Zealand